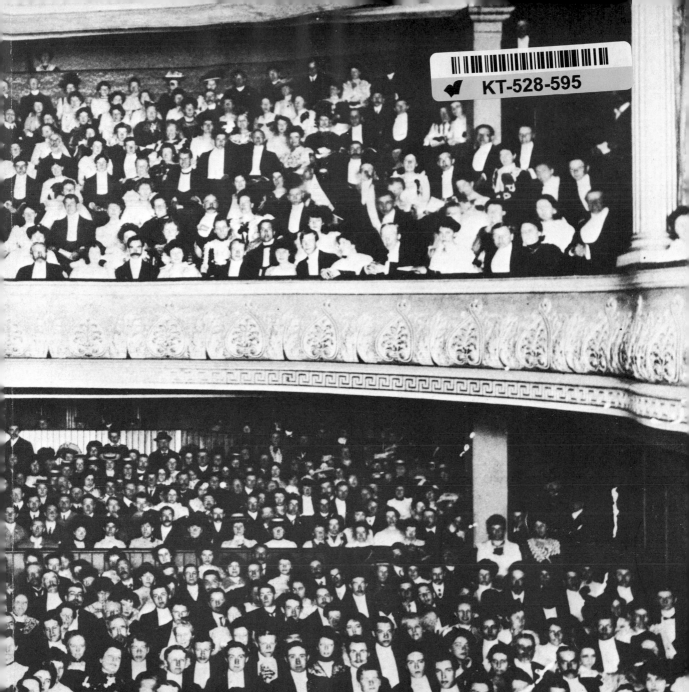

Footlights!

ARS EST CELARE ARTEM

FOOTLIGHTS!

A Hundred Years of Cambridge Comedy

ROBERT HEWISON

With a preface by
ERIC IDLE

METHUEN LONDON

for Alexandra

First published in Great Britain 1983
by Methuen London Ltd
11 New Fetter Lane, London EC4P 4EE

ISBN 0 413 51150 2

Made and printed in Great Britain
by Butler & Tanner Ltd
Frome and London

Contents

Preface

Comedy is a very odd activity. To stand on stage in front of hundreds of other people and make them laugh is a very strange thing to do. For some bizarre anthropological reason, since earliest times a few people have found it necessary to be amusing. Why should this be so? Clearly when someone goes to such lengths to attract the admiration of strangers we can observe that they must feel desperately unloved, but this does not explain why we, the audience, should tolerate and actively encourage them in their odd behaviour. Nor why comedy should prove to be so popular or so universal.

It seems no coincidence that England, a land rich in absurdities, should be so rich in comedians. Writing about comedy is difficult, but it is not half so difficult as writing comedy. For example, I am writing this in the room to which I have come every morning for the past few weeks, but today is different. Today I have only to write *about* comedy, I don't actually have to write the bloody stuff itself. If I'm wrong when I'm writing about comedy then some minor critic in Penge will abuse me over his saltimbocca, but if I'm wrong when I'm writing comedy then – horror of horrors – nobody laughs: there is nothing but the sound of one hand clapping. It is this difference that gives comedy its edge. It is a bit like tightrope walking. You really have to do it to know it, and indeed that is also the only way to learn how to do it.

If it were nothing more than gilded youths dressing up as women then you could hardly be blamed for thinking of the Cambridge Footlights as an effete collection of privileged wankers. It has from time to time been just that, but collectively it is far more than that. In fact it has proved to be a durable training ground for people who have gone on to become excellent in their own right. This is Footlights' triumph and its justification. It is also pre-eminently a self-inventing form. No University Official stepped forward and said 'Let there be Footlights.' In fact they have flourished so healthily without direct encouragement that this might be seen as yet another triumph for Cambridge subversion.

Comedy is a shared experience. Without an audience it is nothing. Far more so than tragedy, comedy is intimately connected with the audience's response. We weep alone, but we all laugh together. It is this shared communality that makes it so powerful and so popular. It is constantly reminding us of our own absurdity in this vast universe. It is frequently to do with scale, cutting us down to size, laughing at our human weaknesses. For a few moments it removes us from the prison of our own personalities, the trap of our own self-created selves, and unites us in a warm shared response by making us laugh at the trivia in which we continually enmesh ourselves. It is an uplifting experience. We are taken out of ourselves, and made to laugh at ourselves. This is both slightly painful (laughing does hurt) and healthy (because it is done communally). It is instant group therapy.

It achieves this effect by demonstration rather than persuasion. We do not decide to laugh, we find ourselves laughing. In the dark amidst hundreds of strangers we suddenly find ourselves united in a tribal explosion of noise, which begins in a shout of recognition and ends in the sound of a gurgling drain or a goose being strangled. For a few seconds we are all barking mad together.

To be on the other side of a laugh, causing it, triggering it off and feeling the great wave of human noise come back at you is one of the most powerful and addictive sensations that there is. It is a great welcoming sound that wraps round the performer, enmeshing him in approval. He can learn to play with it, to play with the audience's expectations, to tickle the laugh, to surf along it, hold it back and then finally release it, but he can learn this only by doing it. To be sure, such ability is partly instinctive – some people *are* just funny – but it can also be learned, or at least honed and improved by experience. This is why a structure like the Footlights is so useful. It is both a training ground, and a safety net, which prevents hundreds of people who are drawn to it but are otherwise unsuitable, from pursuing it too far.

This is the history of a comedy club. A loose association of extraordinary people with almost nothing in common except that they all belonged to it. Nothing dates faster than comedy. Today's topical witticism is tomorrow's puzzled yawn. From the many extracts in this book it is easy to chuckle at the sketches near our own time, but at the distant end of the century the humour is elusive and we can only stare blankly at the lines and wonder 'Did they really laugh at this?' I think the reason for this is quite simple. Comedy consists of two elements: the content and the manner. The content is the contemporary trivia of day-to-day shared experience from which the comedian draws his material. The manner is the secret that belongs to the performer. An odd mixture of 'timing' and a strange persuasive power which reassures the audience and lulls them into a state of confidence in which they can accept that virtually anything he says is funny. Looking at old scripts we are left only with what they said, not how they said it, and that is to miss perhaps sixty per cent of the comedy. A good comedian can make you laugh at almost anything.

The value of the Footlights for me was that, while learning about content, how to write, rewrite and cut sketch material, you were nevertheless obliged to go out and learn performing in front of quite difficult audiences. In my short time there I experienced directly almost every kind of audience. We performed cabaret professionally at least twice a week. We played in theatres, we played at Edinburgh Festivals, before factory audiences, before dinner-jacketed hoorays and ball-gowned debs, in Butlin's holiday camp, before drunks, before dinner, before Round Table businessmen, and ultimately in radio and television studios. Had one sat down to plan a crash course in showbusiness one could hardly have bettered this as a learning experience. A University which permits such activity is clearly doing its job, by doing absolutely nothing.

Despite repeated complaints about the Footlights – that it is somehow too professional (but then who wants amateur comedy?); that it is elitist (though nobody laughs because they are impressed by the social rank of those on stage); that it is privileged (nobody laughs out of kindness either); and that it is undergraduate (they *are*, after all, undergraduates) – it has nevertheless self-created its own tradition. A tradition which seeks after excellence, and then seeks to hide that excellence. *(Ars est celare artem.)* The measure of the Footlights is that it is continually reinventing itself. It is impressive that with no encouragement from the University, no financial support, no grants nor University premises, and with hardly any real continuity except for a few dedicated officers (take a bow Harry Porter), it should survive for a hundred years.

We should be grateful to Robert Hewison, a man who has suffered the advantages of an Oxford education, for so excellently researching and writing this history of Cambridge humour.

Eric Idle
Sydney 1982

Aladdin 1883: the first Footlights cast photograph

Introduction

The idea of teaching people to be funny is in itself comic — and yet the University of Cambridge is as famous for its funnymen as for its physicists. That is why the hundredth anniversary of the foundation of the Footlights is worth taking seriously.

The Footlights Dramatic Club is one of those student institutions which create the opportunities for invention and performance, for trial and error, essential for the development of talent. The club's formation was spontaneous and its continuance is voluntary, sustained by the vitality of its tradition and the efficiency of the methods it has evolved. It is a justification of the amateur tradition in British culture: it has become so by always being professional.

One of the themes of this book is the relationship between the Footlights performances and the professional stage. Each illuminates the other, and ultimately they blend, for so many members of the Footlights have become professional performers, writers or producers. The focus here is on their amateur experience at Cambridge; no attempt has been made to follow their subsequent careers in detail, once the often gradual transition in status has been achieved. Nor, of course, has every Footlights member turned comedian and, although most of those with the most professional aptitudes have taken that route, we must not forget the contribution made by those who did equally well in other professions. Finally, because the Footlights have a specific role, as jesters to the University of Cambridge, it has been important to say something about the specific concerns of undergraduate life as they have changed over the past hundred years.

This is the biography of a club, rather than of its individual members (though its officers and leading contributors are listed in the Appendix). Something like a collective character emerges and it is clear that there is an ambitious as well as a genial side to that personality. But without ambition there is no drive, and without drive there is no success, which, for the amateur just as much as the professional, is what counts.

It would have been impossible to write this book without the help of the Footlights themselves. I would like to thank first of all the present and immediately past Presidents of the club, Neil Mullarkey and Tony Slattery, for agreeing that the project should go ahead. I have been greatly assisted, in interviews and correspondence, by past and present members of the club and its friends: I would like to thank in particular Richard Baker, Humphrey Barclay, Eleanor Bron, Barry Brown, Robert Buckman, Graham Chapman, Russell Davies, Patric Dickinson, Jimmy Edwards, Gavin Ewart, David Hatch, Ronald Hill, Sir Robert Helpmann, Eric Idle, Simon Jones, Lord Killanin, Daniel Massey, Jonathan Miller, Richard Murdoch, Jimmy Mulville, D'Arcy Orders, John Pardoe, Simon Phipps Bishop of Lincoln, Jan Ravens, Griff Rhys Jones, Peter Tranchell, Richard Turner, Julian Slade and Geoffrey Strachan. (To Geoffrey Strachan I owe especial thanks, as editor and publisher, as well as witness.)

My greatest thanks, however, go to Dr Harry Porter, who has served the Footlights first as Senior Treasurer, and now as Archivist, since 1962. Another theme of this book is the importance of the continuity (and on occasion wise protection) provided by the club's senior members; none has worked so hard for the club as Dr Porter. As Archivist, he has given me complete access to the records of the club and allowed me to plunder his own research, while giving me absolute freedom to come to my own conclusions.

Finally, I should like to thank those who helped me in the preparation of this book; in Cambridge, Carol Hutton (for her research) and Heather Procter (for her hospitality); in London, Briar Silich and Caroline Lucas.

'For many years Cambridge had been well-known among the members of the professional stage as the town that provides the worst audiences in England. Jokes are made about the people of Wigan; but the people of Cambridge are beyond a joke.'

Granta

'. . . Everyone was theatre mad. The tiny ADC stage was busy every night of the term with rehearsals, nurseries, club performances. Enthusiastic amateur groups queued to use halls and lecture rooms. . . . Supervisors would forbid their pupils any further acting before Tripos only to find them a week later appearing behind pseudonyms and false beards in French Club productions of Racine. . . .'

Ronald Bryden

'I think it is degrading and fantastically backward
looking that women should not have the same
opportunities at University as men, and it is rather sad
that the Footlights lag even behind the Union in this.'

Footlights President

'It's hard to forget the plays, the Balls,
The walks by the river in Spring,
The dons we placated, the lectures we missed,
But soon they won't mean a thing.
    So if I let nostalgia blind me,
    And my resolution is slack,
    I'll remind you to remind me
    We said we wouldn't look back.'

Julian Slade Salad Days

May Week pleasures

CHAPTER I

'Banjos and Beer'

'With plenty of material, a good start, an evident intention of doing things in first-rate style, and the experience that time alone can give, the "Footlights" ought to take a high place among our permanent institutions.'
Cambridge Review 13 June 1883

Summer in Cambridge is a sudden reward for enduring the bitterness of a Fenland winter. With the beginning of summer comes the end of the University year, and for a third of the undergraduates, the end of their brief lives as students. But between the dense hours of examinations and the wide open spaces of the long vacation there are seven days dedicated to pleasure. These are the days of races on the River Cam, of cricket at Fenners, of open air plays in College courts, of garden parties, College Balls and clichés about English life. In accordance with the logic of the University's calendar, this week, May Week, always takes place in June.

The traditions of May Week were well established by 1883, when on Saturday 9 June a newly formed student dramatic society put on its first production: a popular burlesque of heroic tragedy, *Bombastes Furioso*. The audience laughed, and May Week audiences have been returning to laugh ever since, for *Bombastes Furioso* laid the foundations of another enduring Cambridge summer tradition: the Footlights May Week Revue.

According to the Footlights' own traditions, the club began not with a play, but with a cricket match at Fulbourn lunatic asylum. This must have been in 1882, for in February 1883 members of the same team returned to Fulbourn, this time as part of an undergraduate concert party that was putting on entertainments in the villages around Cambridge. The group was sufficiently well known for a local newspaper reporter to cover the event:'. . . the assistant medical officer took the lead in the arrangements, and the pieces were very well rendered, and afforded infinite amusement to all those present, who loudly expressed their applause.' The success of these shows so encouraged one of

M. H. Cotton as Widow Twankey

H. A. Hickin

their number, Morten Henry Cotton, that he decided to put them on a more permanent basis. According to one of his co-founders, Henry Arthur Hickin, Cotton '. . . had a brilliant idea – "Let us call ourselves the Footlights! The Footlights Dramatic Club!"'

Neither Cotton nor Hickin nor any of the enthusiastic amateur entertainers of 1883 had any idea of the effect the Footlights were to have on the profession of comedy over the next hundred years. Nor were they particularly aware of the changes taking place in English theatre which meant that the Footlights would be recognised as the training ground for several generations of comic writers and performers. They were not even aware of the Footlights' contribution to the development of revue, for as a genre revue did not exist.

Cambridge in the 1880s was itself changing. The University – with an academic population of about three thousand – was very much a male dominated society, but from 1881 College Fellows had been allowed to marry, and, although there was almost no mingling of the sexes other than at the door to the lecture room and women were not members of the University, girl students from Newnham and Girton were allowed to sit the University's Tripos examination, even though they could not claim a degree. The Vice-Chancellor still exercised considerable powers over Cambridge Town, through the University police, the Proctors. The University regulated markets and tradesmen, and even maintained a private prison, the Spinning House, for the detention of prostitutes and other offenders.

The Vice-Chancellor's powers extended to control of the theatre. The history of the theatre is also the history of censorship; the regulation and deregulation of the theatre charts the attitude of authority as it responds to changes in public needs and taste. In Cambridge, (as at Oxford) the Vice-Chancellor retained the right to ban all theatrical per-formances within the borough. This power went back to 1592, but had been reconfirmed in Section 10 of the Theatres Act of 1843, the latest of a series of measures to ensure government control of the stage. Though the powers were older than that, an Act of 1737 had formally placed the censorship of plays in the hands of an official of the Royal household, the Lord Chamberlain. In London he also controlled the use of theatre buildings, though elsewhere the licensing of theatres was carried out by local magistrates – except in special circumstances such as Oxford and Cambridge. The Act of 1843 consolidated these powers, but created a fundamental division between the 'legitimate' and the 'musical' theatre, by excluding from censorship per-formances that consisted mainly of music, singing, dancing and short sketches, the sort of entertainments put on in public houses. In the 1850s these entertainments began to develop into music hall, which remained outside the Lord Chamberlain's jurisdiction until 1911, when all theatre shows came under his control. Theatre censorship remained in force until 1968.

Cambridge had had a public theatre since the 1730s, though it was only permitted to operate for a few weeks outside the University term, from mid-September to early October, the period of the Stourbridge Fair. By Cambridge standards the theatre was well away from the centre, in the Barnwell area on the east side of the city. At the beginning of the nineteenth century the theatre was burnt down, but in 1815 a new 'Theatre Royal' opened in Barnwell, on the Newmarket Road. The architect was William Wilkins, himself from a theatre-owning family. He was designer of the National Gallery in London and of Downing College in Cambridge; he also built the Theatre Royal, Bury St Edmunds, which formed part of the same East Anglian touring circuit with Cambridge. (Both buildings still stand, but the Barnwell's theatrical function has been reduced to serving as a scenery workshop and costume store.)

Mid-Victorian Vice-Chancellors continued to restrict the use of the Barnwell theatre, although a further Act of 1856, which expressly limited Cambridge performances to the vacations, meant that the season was no longer confined to the period of the Stourbridge Fair, and performances might be permitted at Christmas and Easter. This Act also modified the Vice-Chancellor's powers, for now the Mayor of Cambridge shared his right to license performances.

These restrictions were not merely the result of academic disdain for the coarse acting of the stock companies and the riotous behaviour of a largely proletarian audience. By the 1850s Barnwell had become one of Cambridge's most notorious slums. There were thirty-seven drink shops within two hundred yards of the theatre, and the area was rife with prostitution. When the theatre's season was allowed to extend in October into the first week of the University's Michaelmas Term the undergraduates took full advantage of the Barnwell's reputation by doing their best to break up the performances.

But while the Theatre Royal Barnwell — and the old popular barnstorming acting associated with it — went into decline, in Cambridge, as elsewhere, a new attitude to the theatre was developing among the middle classes. Amateur dramatics were becoming increasingly popular, precisely because they were not associated with the working-class tastes and doubtful morality of the professional theatre. In 1855 an undergraduate at Trinity, F. C. Burnand, who was to prove a prolific author of farce and burlesque, founded the Amateur Dramatic Club. Other clubs had preceded the ADC at Cambridge, among them the Garrick Club from

1834 to 1843, but Burnand caught the turn of the tide. He began with private performances in a room at the back of the Hoop Hotel in Jesus Lane, and managed to attract the support of the younger dons. In 1860 the club moved into larger rooms and in 1861 the then Prince of Wales, himself an undergraduate, became an honorary member, and later President.

In spite of this patronage, progress was not entirely smooth. College Tutors combined to attempt to suppress the club in 1864, and again in 1870. In October 1871 the authorities imposed new rules which limited performances to the Michaelmas Term and banned the production of burlesques. Would-be actors at Oxford suffered worse harassment in the same period. In 1869 Oxford's Vice-Chancellor banned all theatrical performances of any kind in the city, with the exception of plays in Greek, and only the Victoria Theatre continued in Oxford as a music hall.

By the 1880s, however, the climate was perceptibly changing. In 1879 the novelist Henry James commented: 'Plays and actors are perpetually talked about, private theatricals are incessant, and members of the dramatic profession are "received" without restriction. They appear in society, and the people of society appear on the stage; it is as if the great gate which formerly divided the theatre from the world has been lifted off its hinges.' The bars were lifted also at the Universities. In 1881 the Oxford Philothespians were formally permitted a single performance. In 1882 the Cambridge ADC, having established a private theatre in Park Street, bought their premises for £3,475, and in the same year the Cambridge ban on burlesque was relaxed. It is not so surprising that in 1883 a group of comedy-minded undergraduates who had been performing until then outside the borough of Cambridge should choose to form themselves into a new dramatic society.

The entire history of Cambridge theatre might have been very different, had it not been for the contribution of one man, William Beales Redfern. Redfern was born in Cambridge in 1840, and went to Glasgow to train as a painter. He studied with William Glover, the celebrated scenic artist of the theatre in Dunlop Street. Redfern returned to Cambridge in 1871 with a passion for the stage. In 1875 he founded the Bijou Amateur Dramatic Club, a town society that put on performances at premises in Peas Hill. His big opportunity came in 1878 when the Theatre Royal Barnwell came up for sale. But at the auction Redfern found his bids were consistently topped by the London Evangelisation Society, which intended to turn the theatre into a mission hall. Beaten by £25 he dropped out at £1,875. Redfern then turned his attentions to the old Cambridge Corn Exchange, but was frustrated both by the University

William Redfern

and the same Evangelical group, who, in Redfern's words, rejoiced that the Barnwell 'had been wrenched from the services of the Devil to those of God.' Clearly not all sections of Victorian society yet approved of the theatre. The Barnwell became Bennett's Mission Hall, and remained so until the 1920s. A temperance slogan can still be seen on the auditorium walls.

The Barnwell as Mission Hall

Redfern had more luck with St Andrew's Hall, in St Andrew's Street, near Emmanuel College. The property, belonging to the Conservative Club, had been used both as a roller skating rink and for amateur theatricals. Between 1878 and 1881 St Andrew's Hall housed Saturday night concerts known as 'Penny Pops', in which various College concert parties put on entertainments for the townspeople, following the same philanthrophic urge that sent the proto-Footlights into the surrounding villages. In 1882 Redfern leased the Hall and converted it into a theatre, though the new seats, gas stage lighting and raised gallery scarcely disguised its previous existence as a skating rink. On 20 November the 'New Theatre Royal, St Andrew's Hall' opened with a performance of *The School for Scandal* by a professional company. Redfern's was in fact the second 'Theatre Royal' to open in Cambridge in 1882, for in May the newly built Sturton Town Hall had also been licensed

A Footlights Beauty: C.B. Scott as Emily Bellingham in *The New Dean*, 1900

for dramatic performance by the Vice-Chancellor and Mayor. But the Sturton Hall was even further from the centre than Barnwell, whereas Redfern's premises were within the University precincts.

Redfern proceeded cautiously at first, limiting the number of term-time performances, and referring to his theatre as a 'Hall' in advertisements, in order to gain as much respectability as possible from the non-theatrical associations of the word, just as saloons licensed for singing and dancing had adopted the term 'music hall'. It was an astute move to stage in the second week of his first season *Ajax*, by Sophocles, in the original Greek. The production earned scholarly approval, and established the tradition of the Cambridge Greek Play. Redfern also had to overcome the traditions of the undergraduates, who brought with them the bad habits of the Barnwell. He wrote later:

> At the very outset, in fact almost on the opening night, a party of undergraduates commenced to create a disturbance. Seating myself in their midst I gave them to understand that I would not tolerate rowdyism, and that I was trying to establish a proper theatre to be open in term time, and that any disturbance at the outset would fatally prejudice the University authorities against anything of the kind. These young fellows, being gentlemen, took the rebuke in good heart, and one of them very soon afterwards became the founder of the present flourishing Footlights Club.

In 1883 there were rumours that the Vice-Chancellor was indeed about to suppress Cambridge's suddenly thriving theatres, but a petition from the townspeople and the generally 'elevating tendency' of the plays ensured their survival. In November 1883 Redfern was himself elected Mayor of Cambridge, and until 1887 he enjoyed the privilege of giving himself permission to put on plays at his own theatre. Technically, Redfern had no right to call his converted roller skating rink a 'Theatre Royal', for he had no royal warrant, but when Prince Albert Victor, eldest son of the Prince of Wales and, like his father before him, an undergraduate at Trinity, came to see F. R. Benson's company in *Hamlet* in October 1883, the Prince turned a blind eye to the coat of arms above the proscenium arch.

The first Footlights show was billed as a 'private performance for one night only.' *Bombastes Furioso* was preceded by a farcical curtain raiser, *The Lottery Ticket*. Neither was a new script. Samuel Beazley's one-acter was first performed in 1826, and William Barnes Rhodes's *Bombastes* dated back to 1810. (The ADC had also chosen

THE CAMBRIDGE BOATING SONG

Recitative

Oh! glorious Cam, England's aquatic school,
E'en now, methinks, I scent sweet (?) Barnwell Pool.
I hear the cox'n's shout, the ringing smack of oars,
The coach maligning Seven's back, begging to Bow
To row with much more zest,
And telling Four to pull in to his chest.
I was a great oar once, in forty races,
I pulled my boat – down – one and forty places.

Oh when I was a Fresher and an addle-headed cub,
(O, poor young fellow)
I found myself in no time on the river, in a tub,
(O, poor young fellow)
On the sweetly scented (?) waters, I made a fearful dab,
(O, poor young fellow)
But soon I found I'd caught what boating people call a crab.
(O, poor young fellow)

Chorus

And the man who steered the boat,
Bellow'd through his lusty throat –
Bow, you're hurrying, Bow, you're late,
Bow, you're bucketing, Bow, sit straight,
Bow, your back's out ever so far,
What a very consummated muff you are.

When I'd been up about a year, I got into a four,
(O, poor young fellow)
And the man behind me bruised my back all over with his oar,
(O, poor young fellow)
The torture was tremendous, worse than little ease or rack,
(O, poor young fellow)
For the man who rowed before me hit my knuckles with his
    back.
(O, poor young fellow)

As rowing was a failure, well, I turned into a coach,
(O, poor young fellow)
And found, although it is a subject delicate to broach,
(O, poor young fellow)
It's easier to teach the art of rowing than to learn,
(O, poor young fellow)
For there's nothing very difficult in sitting in the stern.
(O, poor young fellow)

Encore

If towards the river any afternoon you turn your eyes
(O, poor young fellow)
You'll see me making strenuous essays to minimise
(O, poor young fellow)
Convexity of spinal cord, concavity of chest,
(O, poor young fellow)
A task of most absorbing int'rest it must be confessed
(O, poor young fellow)

Chorus

At some wretched, panting fellows,
I shout and sreeech and bellow –
Bow, you're hurrying, Two, you're late,
Three, your bucketing, Nine, sit straight,
Six, your back's out ever so far,
What a set of consummated muffs you are.

Bombastes Furioso for their opening programme in 1855, and it was performed by Oxford undergraduates at Henley Regatta in the 1840s.) But burlesques provided plenty of opportunities for the introduction of local jokes and topical songs. The *Cambridge Review* – a 'journal of university life and thought' which began its sober life in 1879 and has continued ever since – reported: 'The house was crowded with a large and enthusiastic audience, who testified their enjoyment by no stinted applause.' M. H. Cotton founded the Footlights tradition of theatrical parody with an imitation of England's leading actor-manager, Henry Irving. (Irving was offered a knighthood by Gladstone in 1883, the first professional actor to be so honoured.) But the hit of the show was written and performed by a freshman from Christ's, Lance Outram. This was 'The Cambridge Boating Song', to music by H. A. Hickin.

The Footlights have always recognised good material when they see it; the song was published and became Outram's signature tune. It next appeared in *Aladdin*, the club's second production at St Andrew's Hall, on 10 November 1883. *Aladdin* has become a familiar vehicle for pantomime, but this was H.J. Byron's burlesque of 1861. In the 1880s pantomime and burlesque were distinct genres, burlesque being essentially witty parody of other plays and theatrical styles, without having any of the seasonal connotations of pantomime. Widow Twankey (played by M. H. Cotton in the Footlights' production) is now a traditional panto figure, but she began as a specific H. J. Byron creation. Burlesque has obvious popular appeal with its opportunities for local jokes, but it also sanctioned what was necessary for Cambridge actors: the playing of female parts by men. Whereas in Oxford in 1884 the newly formed Oxford University Dramatic Society was expressly for-

St Andrew's Hall

bidden to perform *en travestie*, in Cambridge the Footlights and the ADC had no choice. Moral prejudice against actresses coincided happily with an undercurrent of British humour that finds men dressed as women irresistably funny, whether it is pantomime or *Monty Python*.

Lance Outram was the Footlights' first star. After playing 'Abanazar' in *Aladdin*, in June 1884 he played Mathias in Henry Irving's staple melodrama *The Bells*, by Leopold Lewis. In 1884 he 'stage-managed' – that is to say directed – Boucicault's *The Corsican Brothers*, and played the twins. And in June 1885 he consolidated the Footlights' growing reputation by writing and probably directing the club's first original production, a comic operetta in one act, *Uncle Joe at Oxbridge*.

Uncle Joe at Oxbridge is worth looking at in some detail, for it contains just about every joke made about Cambridge life, and features all its stock figures of fun. The music has been lost, but the script, hand-written in a quarto exercise book, survives in the British Library, just as it was when it was submitted to the Lord Chamberlain for his reader's

Lance Outram, as Abanazar

The Lord Chamberlain's copy of *Uncle Joe at Oxbridge*, 1885

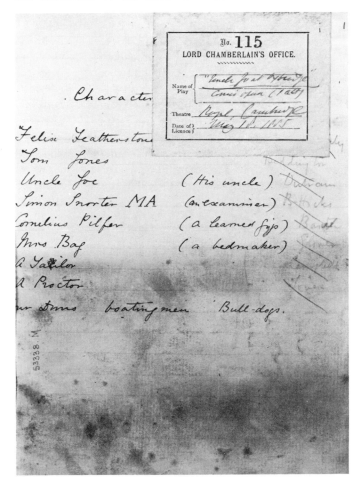

approval. The music, we can imagine, was derived from Gilbert and Sullivan; the plot is pinched from Anstey's novel and play, *Vice-Versa*.

It is, needless to say, a morning in May Week. The action takes place in the rooms of Tom Jones, an idle undergraduate of drunken habits. The scene is set by two caricature college servants, Cornelius Pilfer, Jones's gyp★, and Mrs Bags his bedmaker. As Pilfer's name implies, it was a standing joke that college servants stole the undergraduates' tea and whisky, and he and Mrs Bags are no exception. They conduct a sub-Dickensian dialogue which establishes that Tom's Uncle Joe is paying him a visit, and that the previous night he was as drunk as his nephew.

The servants are interrupted by the entrance of Felix Featherstone, a keen but laughably fat rowing type. Featherstone wants Tom Jones to stroke his college eight that day, as a trial for a place in the University boat. But Jones is due to sit his 'general' – the term for examinations for a BA degree – besides having a terrible hangover. Confronted by this dilemma Tom sings an early student protest song:

To the mighty British nation, I present a protestation,
Protesting most persistently that really 'tis too bad
To sing in lively measures of Cambridge joys and pleasures
For there's naught but woe and misery for the wretched
     undergrad.

Now when you've had your dinner and the dean an awful
     sinner
Hauls you up next day, and up you go as meek as any worm.
In the agony of coppers, you tell him lots of whoppers
And get gated for your trouble the remainder of the term.

★ For a glossary of Cambridge terms see page 187.

Bulldogs, Proctor, undergraduate

CAUGHT IN THE ACT—"WHAT IS YOUR NAME, AND COLLEGE, SIR?"

Or when you've toiled in patience for vile examinations
In pulleys problematical and all that horrid stuff,
A wretched thing to tell on, they chuck you like a felon,
With half a dozen answers written neatly on your cuff.

There's the tyranny of gate pence, the fine of six and
    eightpence
For discarding academicals, (enough to break a chap)
And one's anger you may fancy, when one hears a nasty
    man say
'Are you aware sir of the bad condition of your cap?'

There's the proctor – (I'm not joking) – says 'Sir I saw you
    smoking'
Your crammers contradictory the cleverest can't conceive
You tell a reg'lar cracker, say you never tasted bacca
With a Larinaga burning up like blazes in your sleeve.

When you've forgot to make fast your oak and are at
    breakfast
With Aunty Prue and Cousin Sue, it really isn't fun
To feel yourself turn yellow, as a very nasty fellow
Pops in and shows the face of an uncompromising dun.

What with the duns and dons and doctors, professors,
    porters, Proctors,
Subscriptions, bulldogs, algebra and all such horrid stuff
Sure we deserve your pity but not I'll end my ditty
I think that you'll agree with me that I have sung enough.

The solution to Tom Jones's dilemma, whether to pass up the chance of a place in the University boat or be sent down for not sitting his exams, is supplied by Uncle Joe (played by Outram). Uncle Joe will sit to be examined in his nephew's place. (A feigned illness allows the examination to be held in Jones's rooms.) There follows a series of scenes from University life, as Uncle Joe is visited by a fawning tailor, four duns, and finally his examiner. All this provides plenty of local jokes and what in a later age might have passed for satire.

> 'Couldn't you dynamite the Senate House?'
> 'I should be very glad to, only I haven't got any
> dynamite. They only make it in Ireland.'

Uncle Joe's farcical attempts to answer the Examiner's questions are interrupted by the arrival of the Proctor and his bulldogs, and are brought to an end only with the return of Tom Jones and the College eight. They sing 'The

Cambridge Boating Song', and in chorus all are reconciled.

Although the *Cambridge Review* carped at the way the Footlights went 'on the lines of the provincial "star" system, one performer being extremely good, the rest for the most part poor', the finale of *Uncle Joe at Oxbridge* was Outram's moment of triumph. It was also his last appearance in Cambridge. He took his degree that summer, and went into the Church, spending two years as a curate in New Zealand. He died in 1895, at the age of thirty.

Uncle Joe . . . was the first original script, and the club's growing confidence was marked by the decision to present it (along with a curtain raiser, H. T. Craven's *The Chimney Corner*) as a public performance for a run of three nights. The *Cambridge Chronicle* had already written of their production of *The Corsican Brothers* in December 1884: 'Comparisons are always odious, but we warn the ADC of the necessity to produce first-rate pieces and well-studied performances if they wish to keep in advance of this juvenile of only two years' standing.' According to a writer in *Granta*, the new humorous undergraduate magazine, launched in 1889, at this time 'the only persons apparently eligible for election to the ADC consisted of old members of the Eton and Harrow cricket elevens.' The natural consequence was the birth of the Footlights Club, 'as a means by which these Irvings of 5 stone 7lbs might find some outlet for their hidden genius.'

Like many of his successors, the *Granta* writer was poking fun, but he had a point, for although the Footlights had a clear taste for comedy, their policy was by no means set. In the year following Outram's departure a 5 stone 7lb Irving emerged in the shape of J. J. Withers, an Old Etonian at King's. Withers persuaded the club to mount Lord Bulwer-Lytton's historical drama in blank verse, *Richelieu*, as their Michaelmas 1885 production, with himself in the title role. Withers proved to be no Irving, Macready or Phelps and the production was a disaster. He redeemed himself somewhat by writing and directing a short clerical farce *Disestablishment* for the May Week programme of 1886, but the production earned the club the first the-Footlights-are-not-so-good-as-they-used-to-be notice. The *Cambridge Review* commented,

> The performances of the Footlights company during the race weeks have become a regular feature of our June programme, and usually afford a great deal of amusement in a pleasant way. . . . The performance this year was of a very uneven character in many ways. . . . Vulgarity is the bane of English fun, and where are we to look for something better unless to those who know what refinement is?

Programme cover, 1886

Richelieu, 1885.
J. J. Withers is
second from the
left, second row.

The disaster of *Richelieu* did at least force some policy decisions on the club. There are no minute-books surviving from the early days, but we can assume that it quickly evolved the usual organisational structure of President, Secretary, Treasurer and Committee. This arrangement is listed for the first time in the May Week programme of 1886 (see Appendix). The club chose as its insignia an arm holding up the mask, not of comedy, but of tragedy, and the motto, 'Ars est celare artem' – 'the trick is to hide the art'. Most importantly, the club rented its own rooms, at number 62 on the west side of Sidney Street, on the site now occupied by Boots.

The possession (or otherwise) of a private room has proved an important factor in the club's life. The club room is a focus for activities throughout the year; it is the meeting place for undergraduates otherwise separated by their colleges; it ensures continuity, and above all it supplies a powerful reason for undergraduates to join the club in the first place. The Footlights did not run to a private theatre, like the ADC, but it did have room enough to entertain itself and its guests. In January 1889 *Granta* chose the Footlights

Disestablishment, 1886

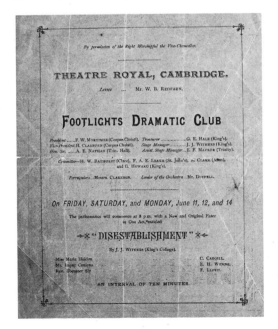

for the first of a series of profiles of leading Cambridge institutions. The club, *Granta* reports, '. . . has now by its energy established itself on a firm footing among the permanent clubs at Cambridge. The club itself consists of about fifty or sixty members, mostly from the smaller colleges. It is distinctly Bohemian, but Bohemian with a clean shirt . . .' The club rooms 'if not sumptious are sufficiently commodious'; the newspapers are taken, and the club supplies writing paper. It also evidently supplies beer, for a feature of the club's programme is 'the fortnightly "socials"'.

It is curious that the *Granta* writer does not use the usual word for these events, and call them 'smokers'. 'Smoking concerts' were an established part of University life, as they were of Victorian male society. The admission of smoking implied the exclusion of women, so 'smokers' were understood to be relaxed, somewhat drunken and usually coarse-minded affairs. The early Footlights smokers seem to have been no exception:

> Banjos and beer, Boheeism and Bohemianism, are the leading features of these entertainments, which consist of a sort of penny reading, without the parson: any members who care to do so attend and form themselves into a mutual admiration society, and in turn loudly applaud the histrionic, musical or dramatic efforts of their friends, or themselves perform for their friends delectation. Members may take guests, and we can only say these socials are often well worth a visit.

And for the Footlights, of course, they served as a proving ground for the material and performances that went into the May Week shows.

One of the decisions taken after *Richelieu* was to double subscriptions. It is not certain to what, but by the 1890s membership cost £5 a year – well over £100 in current terms – which must have kept membership fairly small. (In fact, it has rarely risen above a hundred.) J. J. Withers's career within the club was unimpeded, for in his final year, 1886-1887, he became club President. (He became a solicitor, was knighted in 1929 and was MP for the University from 1926 until his death in 1939.) However, after *Richelieu*, the club decided never to attempt straight drama again.

Instead, they relied on stock scripts, mostly farces presented two or three at a time. May Week was the main focus of attention, but performances were also put on in the Theatre Royal in the Michaelmas and Lent Terms. Between November 1887 and June 1892 they performed twenty-three different one-acters and full length comedies, including three by W. S. Gilbert and three by F. C. Burnand, the founder of the ADC. Some, if not all, received the Footlights treatment. *Braganzio the Brigand*, performed both in March and June 1890, was a thorough reworking of a burlesque by Frank Marshall, brought 'up to date' by R. W. H. M. Palk, who also played the part of Bettina. Palk's duet with Braganzio (played by the director, H. J. Chart) brought in proposed changes in the 'General' exams and the University Boat Race, as well as the suggestion that the honour of 'Blues' should be awarded for Hockey and Chess – 'to which skittles and loo were playfully added, to the great delight of the audience.' In December 1890 Palk put on *Ion Revised*, a send-up of Euripides's *Ion*, in which he had himself acted in the previous week. The humour extended beyond the Cambridge Greek Play, however, with jokes about the campaign for women's rights, and a pastiche of the dancing in Gilbert and Sullivan's hit of 1889, *The Gondoliers*.

In 1892 the Footlights settled on their unbroken tradition of presenting an original show for May Week. Both words and music of *Alma Mater* were written by members of Trinity College, A. P. Shaw (the club's Vice-President) and the musical director, E. A. Philpots. As the title suggests, this was another very localised production, and indeed it ran into local censorship when the Vice-Chancellor objected to the inclusion of 'two humorous proctors', who were instantly cut. Billed as a 'comedy burlesque', this was the club's most ambitious production yet. Although the title is not listed in the Lord Chamberlain's records, the libretto and lyrics are in the club's archives.

The moral I will now pronounce in verse
I promise that it shall be short and terse.
You first year men if you for fame would seek,
Don't think it's yours because you are unique
And sport a strange attire, and grow the hair,
And cause your fellow-undergrads to stare:
For in the present state of society,
You're sure to gain – not fame, but notoriety.
Your second year don't run up any little bills,
They end in duns and other kindred ills.
Your third year beware this dread May Week
To your friend's sister think before you speak.
Last, but not least, for parents I've a word
For their behaviour sometimes is absurd.
Whene'er your hearts by sad small bills are wrung
Remember what you did yourselves when young.
Or if a College course you did not take
See the temptations and allowance make.
To you, whose good words tonight we cater,
We bid adieu. Three cheers for Alma Mater!

Closing recitation *Alma Mater* 1892

Alma Mater, 1892

Herbert Pollitt, 1898

Alma Mater saw the rise of a new Footlights star, Herbert Pollitt, who was by then in his third year at Trinity. Pollitt played the 'Première Beddeuse', a tribute to his skills as a dancer as well as a female impersonator. Pollitt's 'Serpentine Dance', a version of the 'skirt dance' made famous by Loie Fuller, became as celebrated in Cambridge as Outram's 'Boating Song'. It reappeared in Shaw's next script, *The Mixture*, in 1893, and the following year, in *The Mixture Remixed*. Without knowing it, the club was working towards revue, for, as 'Pittite' reported in *The Cam*, '. . . it matters little about the plot, as the performance really consists of a series of "Variety Entertainments" strung together with delightful inconsequence.' Dancing was an integral part of what was becoming known as Variety, and in *The Mixture Remixed* Pollitt, as 'Diane de Rougy', wowed them first in white silk, and then in black and silver, 'in a manner which would make many women green with envy', Pittite enthused. 'And when he finally subsided into his throne he reminded me forcibly of one of Rossetti's women brought to life.'

The sight of undergraduates as a beefy *corps de ballet* remained one of the Footlights' enduring sources of popular appeal. While the ADC kept to its private premises in Park Street, from the beginning the Footlights were appreciated by Town as well as Gown. In 1887 the *Cambridge Express* reviewed their performances of *A Regular Fix* and *To Parents and Guardians*:

> The Footlights Dramatic Club stands alone as the only amateur company, at present, who appeal to the suffrages of the general public at Cambridge, and it is probable this factor has made their performances so acceptable amongst the many different classes of which life at Cambridge is made up. Be the cause what it may, the Footlights are never called upon the meet a 'beggarly array of empty benches'; smiling faces and good-sized audiences little disposed to be hypercritical are generally revealed at the rise of the curtain. The Footlights Dramatic Club is undoubtedly a popular institution.

It was entirely appropriate that this popular club should acquire a popular senior member of the University as President: Oscar Browning of King's. Browning (1837-1923) made an enormous contribution to the gaiety of University life. His biographer H. E. Wortham remembered him as 'a joyous epicurean don who had nothing in common with the remote, if not repellent, order to which he belonged.' But his eccentricities were not without their drawbacks.

Browning took up the Fellowship of King's to which his former schooling at Eton entitled him in 1876, having been forced to resign his housemastership at Eton after fifteen years as a teacher there. He had fought a long battle with the Master of Eton over reforming the school; the battle had not been free of the innuendo that this bachelor had paid too much attention to certain boys.

At Cambridge, Browning became a 'social' rather than teaching don. He had a wide acquaintance outside the University, including John Ruskin, Walter Pater and Oscar Wilde. He was a founder of the *Cambridge Review*, and it is said that *Granta* was founded to annoy him. An earlier paper, *The Gadfly* had been suppressed for satirising Browning too vividly; when *The Gadfly's* editors heard that Browning was about to launch a serious magazine under the 'Granta' title they stepped in to pre-empt him with a new humorous magazine of their own. He rode a tricycle, and was President of the University Bicycle Club. 'O.B.' was also an officer of the Swimming Club, Hockey Club, Musical Club and Liberal Club. So public a figure was a constant target for undergraduate humour.

> O.B., Oh be obedient
> To Nature's stern decrees
> For though you be but one O.B.
> You may be too obese.

Browning became President and Honorary Treasurer of the Footlights in 1887. Unfortunately – as the Cambridge Union discovered during his Treasurership from 1881 to 1901 – finance was not his strong point, for he had the habit of keeping the monies of the various clubs for which he was responsible in his own bank account. It is said that the Cambridge Union only succeeded in getting rid of him by presenting him with a portrait on the occasion of a retirement which had not until then been considered. Finance also seems to have been at the bottom of his enforced withdrawal from the Principalship of his great achievement, the Day Training College for elementary school teachers.

The details are obscure, but Oscar Browning's Treasurership contributed to the near collapse of the Footlights in 1895. Ironically, the crisis was brought about by William Redfern's success. Having established the theatre as a regular and accepted part of Cambridge life, especially among undergraduates, Redfern used his position as Mayor to lobby for the removal of the Vice-Chancellor's right to interfere with the Town's theatre. (The University's control over ordinary citizens of Cambridge was becoming irksome, a situation highlighted by the proctors' arrest of two suspected prostitutes in 1891.) In 1894 section 11 of the

Oscar Browning

Cambridge University and Corporation Act transferred the licensing of theatres to the County Council. Freed of all University control, Redfern proceeded to pull down the old 'New Theatre Royal, St Andrew's Hall' in order to rebuild to an up-to-date design. On 29 May 1895 a performance of *Patience* brought down the curtain on St Andrew's Hall for the last time.

The date is important, for it meant that there could be no Footlights May Week performance that year. The lack of a theatre coincided with a cash crisis in the club, and both membership and funds declined. By now the club had moved from its original premises to rooms at 68 Bridge Street, the only building to house the Footlights that is still standing. Number 68 is a seventeenth-century building and at one time was a pub, 'The Bell', although the Footlights leased their premises from Henry Cox, the managing clerk of Whitmore wine merchants, who had a branch office at number 67. Now, as then, number 66 is occupied by Gallyon, the Gunsmith. It was on the door of the club rooms at 68 Bridge Street, therefore, that in October 1895 at the beginning of the Michaelmas Term Oscar Browning pinned a notice declaring the closure of the club.

In the best traditions of the Hollywood musical, however, 'three enthusiastic members' tore down the notice and went off to find rooms elsewhere. The story is told by Harry Rottenburg, who had just come up to King's in the autumn

Harry Rottenburg, 1898

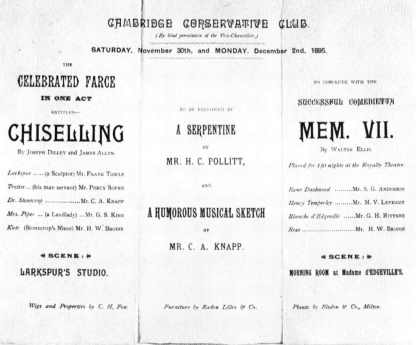

Footlights at the Conversative
Club, December 1895

of 1895, and who was to remain associated with the club until after the Second World War. It is unlikely that as a freshman Rottenburg was one of the enthusiastic trio, but it is quite likely that Pollitt was. (Pollitt took his BA in 1892, but stayed on and took an MA in 1896. He did not leave Cambridge until 1897.) In what looks very much like a *coup d'état*, Pollitt took over the Presidency from Oscar Browning in January 1896, and called a general meeting at which it was agreed that from thenceforth the Treasurer would be elected annually, though Browning's face was saved when he was re-elected Treasurer until October 1896. Pollitt's 'Serpentine' danced on, for it formed the centrepiece of a Footlights programme at the Conservative Club in Market Passage on 30 November and 2 December, 1895. The *Cambridge Review* reported: 'As for Mr Pollitt, the wonders of his dancing have been photographed everywhere, and sung in French poetry, so that eulogy is unnecessary.'

The Footlights had flickered, but they had not gone out.

Footlights Committee, Lent Term 1896.
From left to right, back row: J. S. A. Cock; J. W. Towle; S. G. Anderson; H. J. Graham. Seated: H. H. Rittner; Oscar Browning; H. C. Pollitt; F. P. P. Soper; M. V. Leveaux. Foreground: H. W. Brodie

A Footlights audience at the New Theatre, 1896

CHAPTER II

'Cheer-Oh Cambridge!'

'I really must point out, Hulbert', the glasses were now polished and back in position, 'this is a University, not a drama school.'

Redfern's 'New Theatre, Cambridge' opened on 20 January 1896 with speeches, recitations and a gala matinée of *Hamlet*, performed by Herbert Beerbohm Tree's company from the Theatre Royal, Haymarket. (Tree had laid the foundation stone in June 1895.) The new building in St Andrew's Street was an altogether more splendid and professional one than its predecessor. The architect was Ernest Runtz, designer and co-designer for a dozen theatres of which the New Theatre Cardiff is the most prominent of the four that survive. Built at a cost of £15,500, the theatre held 1,400 people, as opposed to St Andrew's Hall's 800. There was electric lighting, a plush foyer and bars.

The photograph of a Footlights audience of the 1890s shows the social as well as physical arrangement of the auditorium. In the front stalls and dress circle (5/– and 4/–) full evening dress is worn, but behind a wooden barrier in the pit stalls (2/–) and up in the gallery (6d.) the townspeople are in ordinary clothes. (The pit, which once had occupied all the ground floor of an auditorium, as at the Barnwell, was gradually going out of fashion, replaced by the more expensive orchestra stalls.)

The smartly dressed mixed audience reflects the rising popularity of the theatre as an entertainment. It was estimated in 1892 that there were 1,300 places of entertainment in the nation's 530 towns: 200 theatres, 950 concert halls, and 160 musical halls. In London there were fifty theatres. As a businessman Redfern benefitted from the boom. Although Oxford's Vice-Chancellor did not relinquish the powers that Cambridge's had held, Redfern helped Arthur Bourchier (a founder member of the Oxford University Dramatic Society turned professional actor-manager) to establish the New Theatre at Oxford, and arranged joint bookings for the two towns. At one time Redfern had four separate companies under his

The New Theatre

Bar at the New Theatre

management, and employed over a hundred people.

Both the style and business of the theatre was changing, and with it the actor's profession. Provincial stock companies were supplanted by new touring companies that used the railways as a rapid means of bringing London successes to the provinces. (After their gala matinée on 20 January 1896, Tree's company returned to London to play *Trilby* that night.) As many as 200 companies could be on tour at one time. Their programmes ran from Shakespeare at one end of the scale to melodrama at the other, but with the emergence of the 'problem play' – for instance Arthur Wing Pinero's *The Second Mrs Tanqueray* of 1893 – and sophisticated comedies by Oscar Wilde and others – quintessentially *The Importance of Being Earnest* in 1895 – there was an increasing demand for a more gentlemanly kind of actor, in fact, one who was himself a gentleman. Acting was recognised as a 'profession' for the first time in the census of 1861; from then on the rapidly increasing number of performers (7,321 by 1891) were recruited almost entirely from the middle-class. As Michael Baker points out in his excellent study, *The Rise of the Victorian Actor*, 'Ironically, as professional standards rose and the stock system declined, the amateur theatre became one of the chief recruiting grounds for the Victorian stage.' The *Cambridge Express* made the same point in March 1888 when it reviewed the Footlights production of *Vice-Versa*:

> Now that play acting is so fashionable a pursuit, and withal so remunerative that actors and actresses seek a University education before finally treading the boards as a profession, the existence of means for affording a technical schooling during academic days is not only desirable, but a necessity. These means exist at Cambridge in the Footlights, and their elder brothers, the ADC.

Under the Presidency of H. C. Pollitt the revived Footlights of 1896 took a more professional attitude to their own affairs. A new minute-book (possibly their first) was begun, with 'Footlights Club Minute Book' embossed on the front in gilt. On the first page there is an instruction from Pollitt that '. . . if ever the Footlights Club be broken up, this book is to be given to the University Library by the Secretary in office.' In March 1896 the club took a nineteen-year lease on rooms above Catling's Sale-Rooms at 8, Corn Exchange Street. The building later housed the printers Fabb & Tyler, who produced souvenir booklets of lyrics for the club; it was demolished in 1972 as part of the Lion Yard redevelopment. The rooms were officially launched with an 'At Home' on 7 March. Entries in the minute book show that the room was furnished with writing desks and at least a dozen cane chairs; there was a small stage and evidently a bar, for two whisky bottles were 'tampered with' during the Easter vacation of 1897. There was a clock presented by R. H. Adie of Trinity, who replaced Browning as Treasurer in 1896. (Adie became a Lecturer in Chemistry at St John's, and remained Treasurer until 1907, when he became an Honorary Vice-President.) A cigarette machine appeared in 1898. The club took *Pearson's Magazine*, *The Sporting Life*, *Black and White*, the *Illustrated Sporting and Dramatic News*, and the popular theatre paper *The Era*.

The club also employed staff, for in November it was decided that 'Beale' should be given 3/6d for his help at smokers (later raised to 5/–) and 'the woman who washed up' 2/–. In 1897 the club decided to buy 'the page boy' a new pair of trousers. In 1910 a man simply referred to as 'Suttle' began more than twenty years service as Club Steward.

On 6 March 1897 the Club held a first anniversary smoker, for which two hundred invitations were issued. The *Cambridge Review* was there:

R. H. Adie in *The New Dean*, 1897

> The entertainment, which was very successful, consisted of songs by members of the club and others, and sketches by G. Anthony. The latter's imitations of various musical instruments were extremely clever, and his scientific lecture much appreciated. Mr Rottenburg sang of football, and Mr Burgess of the sea. Mr Burgess has a large fund of dry humour. Mr Jack Marshall and his banjo contributed to the programme, and Messrs Severn and Brodie also sang. Mr Cock opened the proceedings with a pianoforte solo.

John Cock was the club's Musical Director that year, Rottenburg appeared in the May Week show, as did Hew Severn and Hugh Brodie. Samuel Burgess made the cast the following year, but G. Anthony (who was already performing two staple items in Footlights cabarets) does not appear to have been a member. The total cost of the evening was £5 6s 10d, and the club made a profit of 11/2d. At the club's annual general meeting in October 1897 the Footlights were declared to be free of debt, with £19 in hand. The meeting agreed a new set of rules establishing a committee of eight: President, Vice-President, Honorary Secretary, Honorary Treasurer, Stage Manager, Musical Director, Assistant Treasurer and Assistant Stage Manager.

The expansion of both professional and amateur theatre in Cambridge worried the University authorities, particularly after the Vice-Chancellor lost his powers under the Corporation Act of 1894. The following year the Council of the Senate produced a special 'Report on Entertainments'. 'The attention of the Council has been called to the increase in the number of dramatic and musical societies consisting chiefly of members of the University *in statu pupillari. . . .*' Until then the only formal control over student entertainments had been a regulation of 1878 introduced to cover dinners and suppers in public places. This laid down that Proctorial permission had to be obtained if five or more persons were involved. (Only once did the Footlights transgress, when they held a supper at the Maypole, Portugal Place, in March 1891 without permission. Oscar Browning, however, was able to set things straight with the Proctors.) As it happened, the ADC was in the habit of voluntarily submitting its rules to the Vice-Chancellor, but there were no formal regulations applying to dramatic clubs. Following the Council's investigation, a Grace of the Senate of 6 June 1895 ruled that every University and College Society that gave musical or dramatic entertainments in public must submit their constitution to the Vice-Chancellor for approval, and that every entertainment had to be sanctioned by the Proctors.

The Clubs were thus brought under control, but the Senate went a step further. There was concern that some of the entertainments in the town '. . . may possibly be such that in the judgment of the Vice-Chancellor persons *in statu pupillari* should be forbidden to attend them.' A measure of control over the Town's theatre was introduced by the back door, by assuming the right to place such entertainments out of bounds. However the New Theatre, which had J. W. Clark, Fellow of Trinity and Senior Treasurer of the ADC on its board, was not the main target. It is more likely that the authorities were concerned about the Arcadia Music Hall, in Downing Street, which opened its doors in 1894 and closed them again three years later.

It is worth noting that the regularisation of Cambridge's dramatic clubs paralleled the split between 'legitimate' and musical theatre created by the Theatres Act of 1843. In 1894 the ADC had adopted new rules which included a commitment to perform 'works of literary excellence and acknowledged merit', while the Footlights were the accepted entertainers. Since they performed in a licensed theatre they were subject to the control of the Lord Chamberlain, but until well after the Second World War they were also subject to the censorship of the Vice-Chancellor. The club minutes for 22 November 1896 note that the outline for the following year's 'burlesque' had to go to the Vice-Chancellor for his approval.

The term burlesque was however going out of fashion.

The new genre was musical comedy, as developed by George Edwardes at the Gaiety Theatre. As readers of the *Era*, and regular London theatre-goers, members of the Footlights would have noticed that from *The Shop Girl* in 1894 onwards Edwardes had transformed the idea of burlesque into an altogether more sophisticated production, full of spectacle, colour, dance, extravagant costumes and, of course, the elegant chorus line, Edwardes's Gaiety Girls. The transition from burlesque to musical comedy matched the move from barn-stormers to domestic comedies in the legitimate theatre and the Footlights followed suit. For their first appearance in the New Theatre, in June 1896 they presented a full scale musical comedy, *The Sham Duke*, with

The Sham Duke, 1896

My friends, if your reception isn't quite what you expect
It's all the agricultural depression,
The rents of my estates are getting hopeless to collect
Of course it's agricultural depression.
Why is it that our breakfasts seem to cost us all so dear?
Why is it that we fail to win the boat race every year?
You only have to think awhile, the cause is very clear
It's all the agricultural depression.

Why is it that the ladies want to have BA degrees?
It's all the agricultural depression.
Why should we probably consent if offered double fees?
Because of agricultural depression.
Why do some college boats get bumped successive days?
And why do I indulge in rather lamentable lays?
It's all the agricultural depression.

H. T Whitaker and H. Lennard *The Sham Duke* 1896

the book by a professional writer, Horace Lennard, who specialised in pantomime. (The title is probably a play on Gilbert and Sullivan's *The Grand Duke* of the same year.)

Unfortunately the script of *The Sham Duke* has not survived, although the lyrics have been preserved in the booklet sold for sixpence at the theatre. (The programmes that year were free.) The production was evidently a success, for, after a revival at the Conservative Club from 27 to 30 November, *The Sham Duke* was given as a charity performance at the Court Theatre in London. Now known as the Royal Court, the scene of the Footlights London début was to see two brilliant moments in English theatre

Waiting for the vote, 1897

The vote declared, 1897

history, the Vedrenne-Granville Barker seasons of 1904-1907 and George Devine's launching of the English Stage Company in 1956. An obscure Court production of 1893, *Under the Clock*, was one of the earliest London revues. (*Airs on a Shoestring*, one of the most successful revues of the early nineteen-fifties was also a Court production.)

As the title suggests, *The Sham Duke* lay somewhere between comic opera and musical comedy proper. The same is true of the 1897 production, *The New Dean*, but here the Footlights, albeit with the gentlest of touches, were dabbling in controversial waters. *The New Dean* represents Footlights parochialism at its best, for it is a comment on an issue that had been temporarily resolved less than a month before the production opened.

In 1896 the pioneers of higher education for women made a second attempt (the first had been in 1887) to extend the rights of women in the University. In particular they wanted women to be allowed to use the actual titles of the degrees – BAs and then MAs – they had earned by sitting the Tripos Examinations, but which they were not granted. Following a year's debate, a committee recommended that women should be awarded a diploma saying they had the title of the degree they had earned, but made it clear that this would not make them members of the University. (The point being that they were still refused any say in University government.) Even this concession was too much and senior members of the University were unscrupulous in stirring up undergraduate opinion against the girls of Newnham and Girton. Of a total undergraduate population of about 3,000, 2,137 signed a motion against any concession to women, 298 voted in favour. A debate in the Cambridge Union voted 1,083 to 138 against women. The issue was formally decided by a poll of MAs on 21 May. As MAs and undergraduates gathered outside the Senate House to await the result of the vote a near riot developed. The effigy of a woman in bloomers was strung, riding a bicycle, from a window above the crowd. Fireworks were thrown at the MAs in front of the Senate House, and a bonfire was lit in Market Square. Unable to quell the rising disorder, the Proctor and two bulldogs had to be rescued by the Town Police. The result of the vote was 661 in favour of the concession to women, 1,707 against.

The New Dean, which opened at the New Theatre on 10 June, took an oblique view of these events by pretending to take place in Cambridge in AD2000. To save the University from bankruptcy an American magnate, Colonel John Z. Hopkins (a play on the American University foundation), has taken the place over and installed 'a woman's government'. At the College of St Marbles the undergraduates and gyps (who were formerly the Fellows) are gathered to celebrate the erection of a statue to Hopkins,

The New Dean, as revised 1900

who is much favoured by the Vice-Chancellor, the Honourable Mrs Croydon-Gresham MA. Hopkins and Croydon-Gresham agree to marry. Meanwhile the disposessed dons provoke the intervention of 'Captain Forsythe, RN' and his chorus of sent-up sailors, who arrive with a gun boat on the Cam. Forsythe, however, is not what he seems. He is in fact one Rugginshaw, the long lost husband of Mrs Rugginshaw, a leader of that long-standing Cambridge joke, the Bedmakers' Union.

Love interest is supplied by the affair between Frank, an undergraduate of St Marbles, who has secretly married the Dean, Emily Bellingham, MA, LLD, contrary to the rules. Meanwhile the Bedmakers' Union goes on strike, the gyps revolt and Mrs Rugginshaw is made the new Dean, while Emily becomes her parlourmaid. The fun-loving Mrs Rugginshaw institutes a régime of college smokers and the dons remain gyps. In the end Forsythe/Rugginshaw is reunited with his wife, and the situation is resolved by all the women officials of the University falling in love and resigning their posts in order to be able to marry. As the MAs' vote of 21 May ensured, order is restored when the rule of men is confirmed.

> Now feminine rule is ended, once more to men we bow
> For guidance and light: and acknowledge their right
> To rule us as they know how.

Harold Ellis

The New Dean was a highly professional production — but then the Footlights had a great deal of professional help. The librettist was Harold Ellis, an Oxford trained lawyer and minor musical comedy writer. (One script, *The Blue Moon*, was published in 1905.) The director was Lawrence Grossmith, the actor son of the entertainer George Grossmith, a well-known performer in Gilbert and Sullivan, and brother of George Grossmith junior, an actor and revue-writer in the First World War and after. The musical director was John Ivimey, a graduate of the Guildhall School of Music, who later gained a Doctorate in Music at Oxford. In the 1890s he taught music at Harrow School and was hired in London '. . . to write the music for the burlesque and conduct on the three nights of the performance for £26 6/–, he keeping the copyright.' (The minutes also record that twelve club members put up a guarantee of 17 guineas to pay for the music.) A professional 'stage manager' – which in the terminology of the time we may understand to mean Lawrence Grossmith – was paid £10 for the week, plus expenses.

Lawrence Grossmith

John Ivimey

Grossmith, Ellis and Ivimey formed a long standing connection with the Footlights. Grossmith directed five shows for them between 1897 and 1911. (Ernest Lambart, of the Lyric Theatre, London, directed in 1900 and 1908.) Harold Ellis wrote the script for *A Classical Trip* in 1898 and *The Freshman* in 1899, the latter for £60 plus 10% of the gross receipts. *The New Dean* was revived in 1900 and 1904, *The Freshman* in 1902 and *A Classical Trip* in 1906. But the longest connection was formed by Ivimey, who wrote and/or conducted the music for fourteen shows between 1897 and 1919. His main occupation remained music teaching in various public schools (he retired as Director of Music at Marlborough in 1933 and died in 1961) but in the 1890s he also taught music part-time at Cambridge, which is how his association with the Footlights must have begun.

Some of the amateurs, meanwhile, were turning professional. More obscure members of the club may have taken the path outlined by the *Cambridge Express* in 1888

Montagu Leveaux

Harry Rottenburg and H. E. Monro
in *The New Dean*, 1900

Davy Burnaby in *The Oriental Trip*, 1901

before him, but the earliest member of the Footlights known to have entered the world of entertainment professionally was Montagu Leveaux, of St. John's. He joined the Footlights committee during Oscar Browning's Presidency of 1884/5, became Secretary, and finally President in 1897/8. He did not perform very much with the club, but his offices prepared him for the life of a theatre administrator. He was on the staff of Charles Wyndham's new theatre in the Charing Cross Road in 1900 and became Assistant Acting Manager at the Garrick, under Arthur Bourchier, in 1901. In 1912 he went into partnership with the great revue producer André Charlot at the refurbished Alhambra in Leicester Square. Their opening production was a Charlot-George Grossmith (brother of Lawrence) revue, *Kill That Fly!*

The club was also producing writers. (Henry Clabburn, a founder member, had become a prolific novelist under the pseudonym 'James Blyth'.) In 1896 the part of a policeman in *The Sham Duke* was played by John Hay Beith, who, as Ian Hay, was to be one of the mainstays of the light stage between the wars, with adaptations of his own and other novels and his collaborations with writers like P. G. Wodehouse. The poet Harold Monro, founder of the *Poetry Review* and the Poetry Bookshop, was club secretary in 1900, and played in *The Freshman* and the revival of *The New Dean*.

The actor Leslie Faber, who created the part of the undergraduate Bulger in *The New Dean*, evidently turned professional without bothering to complete his university course. In October 1898 the club committee decided '. . . that Mr Faber be asked to take part in the Invitation Smoker on 12 November at 3 guineas and expenses paid.' Faber joined Frank Benson's company (Benson had begun his career at Oxford) and appeared in Charles Wyndham managed plays at the New Theatre and Wyndhams, where he may have known Leveaux. He married the daughter of the playwright H. A. Jones. He won the MC during the First World War and was captured. He returned to the stage as a character actor, but never became a star; he died at the age of fifty in 1929.

Reginald White also had a minor theatrical career after playing with the Footlights from 1899 to 1901. And in 1901 the Footlights launched its first true star, Davy Burnaby, though the connection was brief, for Burnaby only spent one year at Pembroke before joining Lily Langtry's company and then a concert party, 'The March Hares'. In 1921 he revived the pre-war 'end of the pier show' and created an all-star Pierrot troupe, the Co-Optimists. Stanley Holloway, Elsa Macfarlane and Gilbert Childs were in the same company. The Co-Optimists struck a rich vein of nostalgia

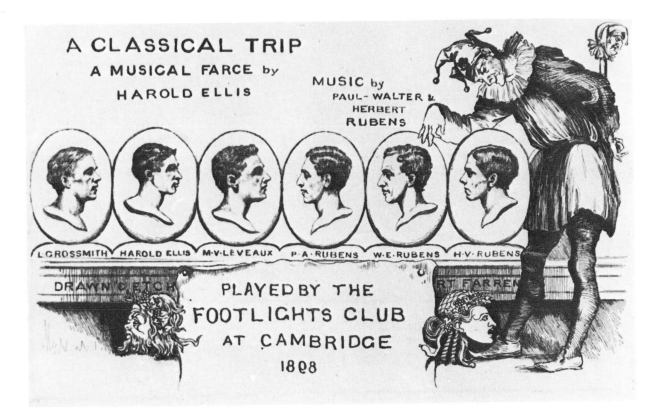

Souvenir of *A Classical Trip*, 1898

and ran in London until 1927, with subsequent revivals until 1935. Burnaby kept a fatherly eye on the club in the 1920s; he died in 1949.

Early experience with the Footlights was the foundation of the all too brief musical career of Paul Rubens. Rubens was one of three musical brothers; he himself had been at New College, Oxford, where he conducted an amateur orchestra. In 1897 he and his brother Walter (who worked on the Stock Exchange) contributed numbers to *The New Dean*. The following year the third brother, Herbert, came up to King's and together all three wrote most of the music for *A Classical Trip*. On 15 June 1898 the club voted to give £10 to Paul, Walter and Herbert Rubens 'in recognition of their valuable services', and their portraits are honourably placed in the souvenir of the show.

Paul Rubens continued to contribute to May Week shows until 1907. By the time *Paying the Piper* was revived in 1911, he had written the music for several long-running West End musical comedies, including *Lady Madcap* in 1904 and *Miss Hook of Holland* in 1907. He kept up with changing fashion, and wrote the music for a 'revusical comedy', *After the Girl*, at the Gaiety in 1914. His blossoming career was cut short by his death in 1917.

'Chrysis', from the Souvenir of *A Classical Trip*, 1898

The New Dean set a fashion for May Week shows that presented Cambridge to itself in a number of flimsy disguises. *A Classical Trip* (1898, 1906) moved the university back to ancient times – and set another fashion with its pun on the Tripos exams. *The Oriental Trip* (1901) went east, *The Agricultural Trip* (1903) took to the land.

Lyric Book, 1901   1903   1905   1908

Paying the Piper (1905, 1911) went back to medieval Cambridge and *The Varsity BC* (1908) back even further. The author of *The Varsity BC*, Harry Rottenburg, has left this account of the production:

> It was the first play in which the Club indulged in stage properties of a mechanical nature. These included a prehistoric flying machine which entered from above. . . . The *pièce de resistance*, however, was a prehistoric animal, referred to in the programmes as a 'brontosaurus'. Only its head and neck appeared, but they were sufficient to reach from the 'flies' to the stage where the animal picked up and devoured one of the characters. All went well on the first night, and the man was duly gobbled up. After the animal appeared, however, the second time, the rope got caught in the pulley, with the result that on its way up the whole load,

including the men inside, broke loose and fell with a crash to the stage. An excited stage hand cried 'They're killed,' and rang down the curtain, for which he was unsympathetically fined. Luckily no one was hurt, and though cut out for the next evening, 'Brontie' duly appeared again on the third night.

Songs and situations celebrated Cambridge life and the Footlights' taste for theatre. The two themes come together in the plot of *The Freshman* (1899), where the villain

1899

Baynes is both Master of Peterbroke Hall College and in fantasy an actor. Undergraduate behaviour in the New Theatre was often bad and Redfern regularly included in the theatre programmes an admonitory paragraph from the *Cambridge Review*, under the heading A DEEP-ROOTED EVIL. 'It is surely unnecessary as it is ungentlemanly for . . .

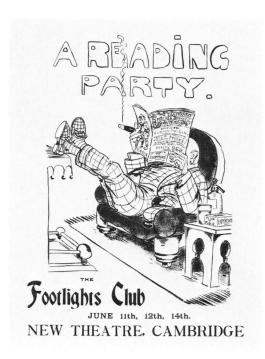

THE
Footlights Club
JUNE 11th, 12th, 14th.
NEW THEATRE, CAMBRIDGE

Poster, 1909

theatre-goers to express in an audible undertone their criticism of each scene during its performance. . . .' In *The Freshman* the hero, young Tom Marshall organises a riot at the theatre in order to extract the pretty actress Clarice, member of the Saucy Girl Touring Company, from Baynes's clutches. Baynes' song 'When I Went On the Stage' records his reception.

> For the end of a brick
> Is Unsympathetic
> When you're trying to imitate Irving!

In November 1899 there was an actual riot at the theatre, when drunken undergraduates threw money on the stage during a touring company's performance of *The Runaway Girl*.

The Freshman also shows the Footlights responsiveness to the whims of theatrical fashion — and adds to the long line of Footlights Shakespeare jokes:

> Now dis nigger craze am in all de plays
> In Shakespeare soon you'll hear de coon
> And *Hamlet* will a nigger ditty boast!
>   Den among de sugar cane
>   Dere de Melancholy Dane
> Will sing it to his fader's ghost!
> Wid a —
>   Bogie! Bogie! I'se a jolly darkey!
> Don't stay on the ramparts, 'cos de night am getting parky!

The scripts sparkle with topical references. *A Reading Party* of 1909 is a genial celebration of that now almost defunct institution, but the Naval Race with Germany and Guy du Maurier's contemporary propaganda play *An Englishman's Castle* are also noted:

> In the press you notice daily
>   Learned people do debate
> On the Navy situation
>   Dreadnoughts six or Dreadnoughts eight
> Everyone calls out for Dreadnoughts
>   Lest the wily Teuton may
> Suddenly invade our islands
>   On a dark and foggy day.
> Men are being now recruited
>   By Du Maurier's noted play.

The writers also took in the sittings of the 1909 Parliamentary Committee on censorship:

Oh it's going just a bit too far
When our Censor's lack of humour is a bar
To our drama being potted
And what's rotten being rotted.

The Footlights flourished with the rest of Edwardian theatre. They continued a regular series of smokers, mounted farces in the Michaelmas terms, gave Footlights Balls in the Masonic Hall in Corn Exchange Street, and held regular dinners in London and Cambridge. In 1896 the Footlights and the Oxford University Dramatic Society exchanged mutual courtesies by making each other honorary members of their respective clubs. The mainstay of the club was Harry Rottenburg. The freshman of 1895 had become a celebrated rugger blue; in 1898 he took the Mechanical Science Tripos, and the following year got a First in Engineering. (That year he played rugger for the University and Scotland and 'Amelia' for the Footlights.) He moved to Pittsburg for two years, but returned to Cambridge and became an Assistant Demonstrator in the Engineering Department. He settled in Cambridge for good in 1911.

As might be expected, he became affectionately known as 'the Rotter'. (The word has somewhat changed its meaning; in those days 'to rot' was to joke.) Rottenburg became President in 1905/6, and, as a senior member of the University, held the post of Treasurer from October 1906 until June 1922. Rottenburg spared the Footlights the need to hire a professional scriptwriter, for, starting with *The Honorary Degree* in 1907, he wrote eight Footlights shows. The *Cambridge Review* was full of praise for *The Honorary Degree*: '. . . for really good May fooling, we doubt they have often given us anything equal.' It also noted what was to become a feature of Rottenburg's performances. 'As a stage device, his trick of transforming himself into a pillar box was alone worth going to see. . . .'

Rottenburg was a prolific inventor as well as writer; some of his inventions had commercial applications, but not all were equally successful. The brontosaurus in *Varsity BC* was almost certainly a Rottenburg device. The story is told that he devised an early form of stage-mist, and managed to persuade the director of a West End production of *A Midsummer Night's Dream* to use it during the dance of the fairies. The mist was produced by a mixture of ammonia and sulphuric acid, and under Rottenburg's supervision at the dress rehearsal the stage hands managed to produce a lovely effect. Rottenburg was not allowed backstage on the opening night, however, and the crew got their proportions wrong. As a result Bottom's fairies blundered about blinded, while the audience found itself involuntarily in tears.

1907

LYRIC BOOK

THE HONORARY DEGREE.

Written by H. Rottenburg.

Composed by J. W. Ivimey.
Extra Numbers by Paul Rubens, Herbert Haines, Kenneth Duffield.

The world has many a pleasant spot
Which thousands flock to see.
Their famed attractions move me not:
There's but one place for me.
It's where the Cam with lazy stream
By Grassy Corner flows
For it's there upon a summer afternoon
My Peggy always goes.

And she's my Grassy Corner Girl,
Shy and sweet.
And my heart is in a whirl
When we meet.
Just we two in my canoe
With none to come between.
But we're never quite alone
We've cupid as our chaperone,
My own little Grassy Corner Queen.

P. G. Wodehouse *The Honorary Degree* 1907

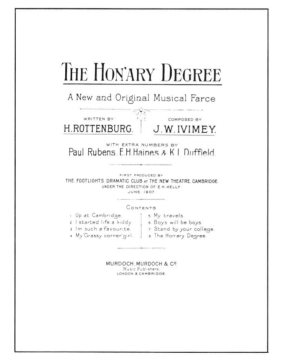

Sheet music, 1907

Besides launching Rottenburg's writing career, *The Honorary Degree* also contained a contribution from a young comic writer making his way in London. As published by Murdoch Murdoch & Co the lyrics of 'My "Grassy Corner" Girl', to music by Kenneth Duffield, of Trinity, are credited to 'G. P. Wodehouse' – a misprint for 'P. G.' Duffield became a professional composer and producer. He toured his native Australia with a repertory revue company in the 1920s, and established Watford Repertory Company in the 1930s.

The steady rhythm of Footlights May Week shows was interrupted in 1910, when official mourning for the death of Edward VII caused their June production to be postponed to November. *The Socialist* was Rottenburg's fourth script in a row, and was described as 'a musical satire' rather than musical comedy. *The Gownsman* noticed 'a distinct Gilbert and Sullivan flavour ... without any suspicion of unoriginality' in Ivimey's score. The satire was at the expense of Bernard Shaw, H. G. Wells, and the Fabian Society, 'though not trenchant enough to rouse any political excitement.' The setting was Rottenburg's usual imaginary Cambridge location, 'St. Botolph's Hall.' The conversation of three undergraduates in Act I helps to set the scene.

Programme 1910.

Fabb & Tyler, Limited, Printers, Cambridge.

1910

Edward is the son of a miner, and therefore anti-socialist,
Lord Bertram Belmont, being an Earl, is exactly the opposite.

GEORGE: There's no question about it, the College has
got into a rotten state and we must buck up and make
things go better.

EDWARD: I quite agree. Everything is going to pot.
Look at the boat for instance.

BELMONT: I'd rather not, thanks! They're absolutely
awful.

GEORGE: I'm sorry to say I agree with you. We're
simply going to bits. And then there's the Eleven. They
aren't any better.

EDWARD: Well we only lost four matches after all.

BELMONT: And scratched the rest because you couldn't
raise a team.

GEORGE: Steady B. B.! Your beastly pat-ball game only
requires six for a team, and you wouldn't get *them* if it
wasn't an afternoon tea sort of sport and fashionable.

EDWARD: There's absolutely no keenness in the
College. No *esprit de corps*. There's one Club going
rather strong. Its called the [Fabian, crossed out in the
manuscript] Knavian Society, I believe.

GEORGE: A lot of dreamers who think that subdividing
success equally will increase the total.

BELMONT: I fancy Euclid says something about that in
the Little-Go. Am I right . . .?

A life of ease by the rolling Cam
Is the life that most suits us,
No lectures to nag us or tutors to rag us
Or chance of proctorial fuss.

I've brekker at ten and lunch at one
And a punt that just holds two,
A shady nook out of reach of the sun,
And a chair and a pipe when the day is done
And that's how I worry through.

Opening chorus *The Socialist* 1910

The Socialist, 1910

This conversation should be compared with the undergraduate backchat of 1982 on page 184.

The promising situation of a College threatened by Socialism is interrupted by the arrival of a Professor from Mars in his flying machine, who announces himself as Socialist, vegetarian, teetotaller, anti-vivisectionist and anti-gambling. He has, conveniently for the plot, brought his two pretty daughters with him. Under the Professor's leadership the College indeed goes Socialist and Mrs Berwick, wife of the Tutor of St Botolph's, is elected Mother of the College. Prophetically, the undergraduates vote to set and correct their own exams, and all award each other firsts.

Act II opens on the day of the College Ball, but the festivities have been thrown into confusion because the Bedmakers' Union and the Cooks have decided that, everyone being equal under socialism, they will attend the Ball, rather than get it ready. The Minister for Education arrives and takes away all the student's scholarships, because they are competitive. The situation is saved by an undergraduate who has accidentally whizzed off to Mars in the Professor's flying machine. He returns and reveals that the Professor is a fraud, and that Mars is not socialist at all. The Professor is overthrown, order is restored, and the Ball goes on.

The Socialist was thought good enough to put on as a charity matinée at the Court Theatre in London, on 12 December, but there are signs that the Footlights formula was beginning to pall. The ADC and the Footlights were now only part of an energetic Cambridge theatrical scene. The Marlowe Society was founded in 1907 with a more rigorous approach to classical theatre than that taken by the socially minded members of the ADC. The Literary Drama Society even admitted women members, although this was feasible because it concentrated on readings and lectures rather than performances. In the Town the Bijou and Rodney amateur dramatic societies were busy, and Cambridge also supported a branch of the Repertory Theatre Movement. A. F. M. Grieg reported in the *Cambridge Magazine* in February 1912: 'Besides what one may call the recognised societies, there are college dramatic societies springing up, and isolated performances on behalf of various causes, all contributing to what one may term a theatrical boom.'

Grieg also described the theatre-going habits of the average undergraduates:

They come rolling up to the theatre after hall in twos and threes, buy their evening paper at the entrance and pay their 2/6 for an unreserved stall, leave their gown on the seat they are entitled to and hie to the bar to smoke and read the paper. They don't drink – then. This is done between the acts later on, but only those fortunate enough to be out early can get a drink at the bar between the acts on a big night – (that is a musical comedy night) – owing to the crowd – a point to be remembered. I don't think on a crowded night a man could get drunk at the theatre, he hasn't the opportunity to get enough drink – not as a matter of fact that men are often drunk in the theatre.

Sometimes, however, they were, and Redfern and the Proctors had been forced to introduce a form of segregation by restricting undergraduates to certain parts of the house. As a commercial manager, Redfern was responsive to changing tastes. He wrote in November 1912:

> . . . in recent years the drama-public has evinced, at any rate in Cambridge, a desire for something different [to straight drama], and this has induced me to arrange for Variety entertainments. The announcement came as a shock to many of our patrons who looked upon the innovation as degrading to a high class theatre. By careful selection of 'turns' and artists I think I may claim that the fear of degradation has been entirely dispelled.

The Cambridge public made it plain that they were no longer diverted by 'B' touring companies in tatty productions of the year before last's musical comedies. More and more they wanted revue.

The term 'revue' (never, please, 'review') has its origins in the Parisian theatre of the 1830s, when a 'revue' of the previous year's events would be put on as a New Year entertainment. The dramatist James Robertson Planché (1796-1880) claimed to have introduced revue to England in 1825 when *Success! or, A Hit if You Like It* was played as an after-piece, but although the term crops up from time to time, it did not gain serious currency until 1905, when two shows, one of them George Grossmith junior's *Rogues and Vagabonds* at the Empire Music Hall, referred to themselves as 'revues'. In form it obviously owed a great deal to the continuous variety entertainments of songs and sketches (including short melodramas) of the music halls, but it also derived from more 'polite' entertainments, minstrel and pierrot shows and seaside concert parties. H. G. Pélissier's *The Follies* began as an amateur pierrot troupe before going professional in 1897, and performed burlesque and mime in what was to become the revue tradition. The 'potted play', ultimately derived from burlesque, was a *Follies* speciality. They played almost continuously at the Apollo Music Hall from 1908 until Pélissier's death in 1913, but they also appeared in 'legitimate' theatres. The difference between the two types of theatre was gradually eroded as music hall became socially acceptable and from a legal point of view disappeared altogether in 1911, when the halls came under the censorship of the Lord Chamberlain.

Revues, essentially miscellaneous and plotless, were well established in London by 1912, when the arrival of ragtime turned a fashion into a craze. *Hullo! Ragtime* ran for 451 performances at the London Hippodrome from December 1912; *Hullo! Tango* followed with 485 performances from December 1913. In June 1913 the *Cambridge Review* reported that the Footlights were doing '. . . something entirely new and original. At the present moment the universe seems to be giving itself entirely to "revue" – the University is the latest victim.'

> When down in the dumps
> Or afflicted with humps, Cheero! Cheero!
> And longing to cure it,
> You cannot endure it, Cheero! Cheero!
> Well do not despair
> Sing this glorious air
> Cheero! Cheero!
> You shout it every moment from the time you leave your
> bed
> Each time you meet a pal it is the final word that's said;
> In fact it seems to fairly hit the nail upon the head,
> So altogether and waken the dead.
> Cheero, Cambridge!

The opening chorus of *Cheer-Oh Cambridge!* – which as the song explains is a general greeting, not simply goodbye – was written by Harry Rottenburg to music by Ivimey; but the new style of the show was the work of someone who was to become one of Britain's leading comedy stars – Jack Hulbert.

Hulbert went up to Caius in October 1910 to read Law, but his true passions were divided equally between the river and the stage. His first part was with the ADC as Sir Anthony Absolute in *The Rivals*; he matched this with Sir Toby Belch in *Twelfth Night* for the Marlowe. He was a celebrated clog dancer at College smokers. He acted at Oxford and once filled in at a day's notice in a big part for a visiting professional company. These activities, plus being what he called an 'obsessed' oarsman, led his College Tutor to demand an explanation, as he describes in his memoirs:

CAMBRIDGE UNIVERSITY
FOOTLIGHTS
DRAMATIC CLUB.

CHEER·OH
CAMBRIDGE.

JUNE 1913

THE BOOK
OF
LYRICS.

'In the morning, I attend lectures and take notes. In the afternoon, I row and try to keep fit. In the evening I am rehearsing a new show or playing in one or performing at a concert. As I am in training for the races a lot of the term, I obediently go to bed at 10 p.m. Frankly, Sir, I am as worried as you are. What are we to do about it?'

The ball was now in his court. I waited for a hot return.

'I really must point out, Hulbert,' the glasses were now polished and back in position, 'this is a University, not a drama school.'

'If I might be allowed to refute that statement, Sir, I would say one of the best drama schools in the world.'

He rose at once to the bait.

'But you cannot get a degree in acting.'

'That's exactly it,' I replied. 'So what am I to do?'

One answer was to change his course from Law to Psychology and History, a new degree with only five under-graduates, thus making failure unlikely. Another was 'to do everything to train myself and be ready to start pro-fessionally.' That included writing as well as performing, and in February 1913 the New Theatre put on a light one-acter, *Acting to Act*, with the author in the lead. The plot has autobiographical overtones, for it concerns a young Cambridge undergraduate whose desire to go on the stage is opposed by his family. He overcomes their resistance by the skill with which he acts in the detection of a thief. His mother has the classic line, 'I want you to be a gentleman, not an actor.'

Hulbert was the model of the 'Cambridge actor' long before the type was recognised. The Footlights acknowledged his reputation and talent, and invited him to devise the 1913 May Week show. The script evidently contained a thread of plot, but unfortunately only the songs survive. J. L. Crommelin-Brown contributed this lyric on Cambridge cafés, a topic that was to turn up again in Footlights revues.

We've poets here from Peterhouse and choristers from
  King's
Down along at our old shop;
And critics come from Corpus and connoisseurs from
  Caius
Who talk of the intensiveness of the soulful Japanese
And Rupert Brooke and Futurists and funny things like
  these,
Down along at our old shop . . . .

E. G. Snaith

Jack Hulbert

1913

H. C. M. Fariner

C. M. Cuthbertson

N. M. Penzer

A. Portago

L. Hewitt

Jack Hulbert's songs, written with his regular partner, Alan Murray of Pembroke, were up to the minute with 'The Ragtime Craze' and 'The Wusky Woozle'. A more traditional object of fun was brought up to date in 'The Ragtime Proctor Man'. Alan Murray also wrote the first of many nostalgic Footlights farewells:

> Dear old River, I'm so sad I'm going down,
> You're the thing I love the most in this old town;
> Yes I'm sad, because I'm leaving,
> Now you know why I'm a-grieving,
> Gee, I'd simply love to have my time again:
> What's the use of worrying, it's all in vain,
> Still I'll sing, where'er I go,
> Whether it's Timbucktoo or Tokio. . . .

The show, and especially its 'females' dressed by a West End couturier, was an enormous success. Hulbert's last summer days at Cambridge passed in a busy burst of energy:

> Early morning run with the crew and then training breakfast together. Frantic rush to the examination hall in *statu pupillari*. Late afternoon at the boathouse and into rowing togs. Early evening, first division race. Back to the boat house, change from rowing kit. Flat out for the theatre, just in time to make up and dress for the show at 8.30 p.m. Special permission from the captain and coach to retire to bed at 11.30 p.m. instead of the prescribed time of 10 p.m. and then a good night's rest . . . .

Cheer-Oh Cambridge! set the crown on Hulbert's university career – and opened a direct route to London. On the 12 June the cast gave a charity matinée at the Queen's Theatre in Shaftesbury Avenue. Hulbert's father, unlike his stage parents in *Acting to Act*, was a keen theatre-goer, and persuaded several London managers to see the show. Hulbert had already had at least one offer of a part before he left Cambridge; after the show he had three, one of them from the producer Robert Courtneidge. 'It was well enough written, and he also showed sufficient promise in the leading part to convince me he had a future. I engaged him for *The Pearl Girl* on the spot.' His daughter Cicely was in the cast, they became engaged, and married in 1916. The musical comedy partnership of Jack Hulbert and Cicely Courtneidge ended only with his death in 1978. Cicely died in 1980.

The arcadian image of a pre-First World War Cambridge (*The Pearl Girl* played Cambridge in May 1914) is marred by the historical fact that the 1914 Footlights production

Was It The Lobster? was a feeble script by Rottenburg (complete with five tons of water in a model of the Cam) – though there may be something prophetic about the Second Act nightmare.

The outbreak of war in August 1914 brought a sudden halt to the Footlights activities, just as they were about to enter a new phase in their history. The lease on the rooms at 8 Corn Exchange Street was about to expire, but Rottenburg, who was himself a freemason, had arranged for new rooms above the Masonic Hall at 17 Corn Exchange Street. The building had housed the Isaac Newton University Lodge since 1893, but was undergoing extension in 1914. The club hired an architect to design the arrangement of their new premises, but the work was not finished until 1915. By that time Rottenburg was the only member of the Footlights left in Cambridge, and the rooms were taken over by the Red Cross. Rottenburg stored all the Footlights property, and waited for the undergraduates' return.

On the London stage however, May Week lived on. In 1916 Jack Hulbert played the part of an undergraduate in a musical comedy, *The Light Blues*, set in June 1914. Another future Footlights model was in the cast, Noël Coward.

Cheer-Oh Cambridge! 1913

above 1923, The Tutankhamen Rag: *below* Pram Races, 1923

CHAPTER III

'Reconstruction'

'There's a word in the air
Everywhere that you stare
Reconstruction!
And we find the expense
In a sense is immense
Reconstruction!'

Rottenburg kept his solitary lamp burning for the Footlights until the Lent Term of 1919, when he was able to call a meeting to consider the revival of the club. Only six undergraduates turned up, but they generated sufficient enthusiasm for a second meeting. This time twenty came and the work of rebuilding the club began. Brynsley Nicholson of Trinity, whose career, like that of so many others, had been interrupted by war service, was elected President. Nicholson had gone up in 1912 and played a small part in *Was It The Lobster?* before volunteering for the Royal Naval Division in August 1914. Three other undergraduate actors of 1914, now respectively a Major, a Major and a Captain, rejoined the club. Rottenburg spent a fortnight at Swanage during the Easter Vacation writing a script and Ivimey was called on for the last time to write the music.

When Rottenburg reconvened the Footlights in March 1919 Cambridge was still only half its pre-war size. The academic population consisted of 650 dons, 1,500 undergraduates, plus 400 girl students. A sizeable — and very distinctive — part of the student body consisted of Naval Officers and Naval Cadets, for the Admiralty chose Cambridge as 'an intellectual dispersal camp' for their demobilised personnel. Until 1923 the University was host to naval officers who were sent on short courses in order to earn 'wartime' degrees. They were distinctive for the odd mixture of naval and university uniform that they tended to wear — reefer jacket plus cap and gown.

As with those from the army and air corps who also returned to Cambridge, the enforced maturity of their war experiences meant that undergraduate life would not recover the hearty, but essentially innocent flavour of before 1914. These were 'men' in a sense other than that used of the undergraduates who 'ragged' at the theatre in 1913, and they took their pleasures seriously. The writer Eric Maschwitz went up to Caius in 1919 as an ordinary undergraduate and found that four of his friends (among them the playwright J. R. Ackerley) were ex-prisoners of war. He writes of the naval officers: 'In the evenings the cloistral hush was shattered by the music of their portable gramophones and ukuleles; they drank rather a lot and knew some glorious girls.' The modern undergraduate was beginning to emerge. The authorities were no longer concerned with preventing the driving of four-in-hands or the riding of bicycles in academic dress: instead they were obliged to appoint a Pro-Proctor in charge of the use of motor vehicles.

Reconstruction, 1919.
Rottenburg stands on the left

Rottenburg returned from Swanage with a script aptly titled *Reconstruction*. His subtitle was 'The rejuvenation of Cambridge'. It opens, once again, in the rooms of an undergraduate at Botolph Hall, where Rottenburg as the bearded Faust ('alias Cambridge 1914') is discovered . . . .

> FAUST: Still it evades me this secret elixir which brings back youth. (*Looking through book*) What's this? (*reads*) One of the most successful methods of becoming young again is to wear short skirts and — wear short skirts — no use. It's only for women. I must start afresh. (*Looks at other books.*) Hullo. 'The Loom of Youth'. Surely this must contain the secret. (*Starts to read. Then throws it away in disgust.*) That tells how never to be young — I'm foiled again. I've consulted my hairdresser, my chemist and my tailor — all no use.
> *Enter* MRS BINKS, *his Bedmaker.*
> BINKS: Lor Mr Fust, still at it? Still readin! You know yer overdoing it. T'ain't good for you. Why it's made you look twenty years older this term already. . . .

Faust summons up Mephistopheles, The Spirit of Reconstruction, who, with a variation on a music hall shaving sketch, turns Faust into a beardless youth in grey flannel trousers and naval jacket. After informing Faust that Cambridge now has a jazz band, the title song 'Reconstruction' leads into a series of loosely connected sketches featuring the difficulties of the Peddielux Club in mounting a musical comedy about German spies. The numbers hit at War Profiteers (represented by Peter Tildsley, who, under the professional name Peter Haddon, was to play many 'silly ass' parts in the twenties and thirties), the censorship of the Defence of the Realm Act, the Honours System and the modern girl:

> I'm a flagrantly flippant and flighty young flapper,
> I flirt and I flutter and flit
> I think I should like
> Just a nice motor bike
> With a side car and officer. . . .

The sketchy plot also features a recurrent theme of Footlights shows in the 1920s: an obsession with the spread of Bolshevism. Complete with axe and detachable red beard the Bolshevist leader Whatsky (played by P. H. Cox) burgles the University Chest, only to find it empty. The theatre, as ever, is another steady theme:

> I love producing, he loves producing
> We love producing any plays.
> And when the drama's bad, and things are wrong
> We simply introduce a comic song . . . .

Reconstruction was well received, but the quality of the material is summed up best by the report of the Lord Chamberlain's reader, Ernest Bendall: 'This is a very amateurish burlesque of ministry "Reconstruction", apparently for performance by undergraduates. There is a certain amount of rough technical fun in the outcome of high spirits; but there is very little humorous point. Fortunately there is no offence whatever. . . .'

Thanks to Rottenburg's Freemasonry the Footlights were able to move into the new rooms they had originally decided to lease in 1914. The Isaac Newton University Lodge in Corn Exchange Street housed a private temple and a large hall for social events, but above them were the Footlights rooms, approached by a separate entrance and staircase. At the top of the stairs on the right was a kitchen and small bar; to the left, past a small office, was the main room, with a stage at the far end. The stage was so narrow that the piano had to be kept on a small platform in front of the prompt side. Behind the stage another door and flight of stairs (nominally the fire exit) led down to a series of small rooms used as dressing rooms and a costume store. The stage was furnished with curtains, and there was a system of stage lighting (part of which blew up to the detriment of a committee member H. E. R. Mitchell in 1927) controlled from a cubby hole above the bar room, to which access was gained by a ladder. (This cubby hole was used for amorous purposes from time to time.)

17 Corn Exchange Street was to be the Footlights' home for the next twenty years. Apart from the regular series of smokers, the club functioned mainly during the day time. From June 1919 the main room was furnished with tables and chairs '. . . to accommodate parties wanting light luncheons, teas etc.' In November 1920 the committee agreed that 'Lunch without sausages' would cost 1/–, 'Two sausages, mash and two rolls' also 1/–, and 'Ditto plus cheese, marmalade, biscuits etc.' 1/6d. A telephone was installed by 1922 and the club had its own gramophone and records. The walls were hung with photographs of past members and past productions.

There are several signs that the club was conscious of its traditions. Looking outwards, the club decided in October 1919 to buy copies of all the music from London productions as it was published; looking inwards, they agreed that £25 should be spent on compiling a history of the club, though regrettably it never appeared. In February 1920 Rottenburg proposed that 'a Cinema film should be taken of a play produced by the Club', though again sadly nothing resulted.

In a sense, the club needed to be aware of its tradition and position in Cambridge life for it was an expensive institution to run. The rent agreed in 1914 was £100 a year, post-war it may well have been more. There were staff to pay – Suttle, now an ex-Sergeant-Major, continued in service – and there was also the cost of financing smokers and the annual May Week show. The club quickly encountered what was to be a recurrent dilemma: it had to have a large enough membership for the subscription income to cover the cost of running the club rooms; but membership was by election, and nominally at least called for some talent on the part of the would-be member.

In October 1919 the committee decided to limit membership to a hundred; in January 1920 it derestricted membership, then in April 1922 limited it again to a hundred and fifty. In October 1920 the entrance fee was raised from a guinea to one and a half, although naval officers, who were joining in large numbers, were exempted. (Sub-Lieutenant C. G. W. Penn-Curzon, who appeared in *Reconstruction*, later became the actor George Curzon.)

The club thus acquired a substantial number of subscribers, but there was still the problem of attracting talent. In January 1921 Rottenburg suggested that 'acting members' should be charged only a guinea and this was accepted. In the same month the Footlights held a 'novices' smoker for the first time, establishing a tradition that has lasted on and off to this day, of membership by audition.

The committee also looked to its own glory. The colours were agreed for a new club tie and smoking jacket (brown velvet, with scarlet cuffs and collar and light blue facings), and new sashes were ordered for committee members. (The earliest mention of these is in 1897; the conductor wears a sash in the photograph at the beginning of Chapter II.) By October 1921 Rottenburg was able to report that the club was 'in an eminently satisfactory financial position', even though E. Hay-Plumb, the producer of the 1921 May Week Show, had left Cambridge without settling his landlady's bill. The committee decided to celebrate by making oysters available on Saturdays, except at smokers. In January 1922 an investment was made in Government War Loan stock.

The Footlights continued to attract members who had an eye on the professional stage. Claude Hulbert's membership from 1919 to 1922 confirmed the traditions of his elder brother Jack, who regularly brought up parties from London (including Phylis Monkman, Beatrice Lillie and Gertrude Lawrence) to see the Footlights perform. A would-be member of 1919 was Eric Maschwitz:

> To belong to the 'Footers' one had to be able to sing, dance, or play some instrument; to qualify I spent £15, won at Newmarket on the Cambridgeshire, on a banjo and printed 'tutor'. After six weeks' practice my rendering of 'Camptown Races' was so enthusiastically inaccurate that when I went to Mill Lane to give my audition the whole committee burst into roars of laughter, but none the less elected me.

Maschwitz's account of election is inaccurate. He might not have written so warmly of the Footlights in his memoirs had he seen the committee minutes, which reveal that the first time he applied he was black-balled. He was however elected in January 1921.

Norman Hartnell, who went up to Magdalene in 1920 and was elected the following March, found the influence of 'non-acting' members was beginning to affect the character of the club.

> It was a club largely made up from the current polo-playing, gambling, sporting set to which I did not belong. Nearly all of them had money; I had not, but my

Claude Hulbert

At the 'Varsity Rag, everyone's excited
At the 'Varsity Rag everybody's there –
Trip-men, gyp-men, all the jolly lot,
Have got to learn the 'Proctor's jazz', and do the
   'Buller's Trot'.
At the 'Varsity Rag, everyone's excited –
Music everywhere.

Claude Hulbert *His Little Trip* 1920

Norman Hartnell in *Folly*

enthusiasm made up for it. I tried to make myself useful, designing poster and programmes, scenery and dresses. I even contributed songs, both the lyric and the melody, accompanied on the ukelele by Lord Ashly.

These talents were evidently recognised, for Hartnell played the part of 'Kitty Fenton' in *What A Picnic* (1921), and he is credited with a substantial part of the script for *The Bedders' Opera* in 1922. The sudden collapse of his father's income meant that he could not afford to spend a third year at Cambridge, but the costumes he designed for *The Bedders' Opera* were noticed by a fashion journalist who saw the Footlights charity performance at Daly's Theatre in London. A favourable paragraph led to various introductions and Hartnell was launched on his career as a fashion designer. He was obliged to go down in 1922, but he kept up his connection with the club, and as 'Gwendolyn' was very much the star of the 1923 show, *Folly*. The *Cambridge Review* wrote, '... for the girls' dresses there is only one word – unique! Such creations as those worn by Messrs Hartnell and Schofield are masterpieces, and deserve to be put on a statutory basis.'

Lyric Book, 1922,
design by Hartnell

1923

Folly in London

Eric Maschwitz, meanwhile, who went down in 1922, lasted four days as an Assistant Stage Manager at Her Majesty's Theatre, before taking up a job in publishing. His ambition was to be a writer – a novel, *The Passionate Clowns*, written at Cambridge, was published in 1925 – but he became caught up with the infant British Broadcasting Corporation. In 1926 he was made editor of *The Listener* and then in 1933 became the BBC's first Head of Variety, a position helpful to former members of the Footlights, as we shall see. In the 1920s he was briefly married to Hermione Gingold; the couple were to have an unexpected reunion backstage after a Footlights show in 1947.

Rottenburg described *Reconstruction* as a revue, but the thread of plot and playlet-length sketches suggest that it, like *Cheer-Oh Cambridge!*, still harked back to musical comedy. The 1914-18 war changed the character of commercial theatre; the old style actor-managers, who leased their own theatres, were driven out by the demand for entertainment, above all else. They were replaced by managements that treated theatres, actors and plays equally as commercial property. Conglomerates began to form around control of the key theatres. The profession of agent emerged; while the Actors' Association formally became a trade union in 1919. The war had cut short the vogue for Viennese operetta; in the post-war boom of 1919-1924 musical comedy ruled supreme; operetta, variety, vaudeville and revue provided alternative forms of easy entertainment. Fit-up revues proved the saviour of the provincial music halls, but even before the war these were beginning to be turned into cinemas. The West End did not feel the pressure of competition from this new medium until the arrival of the 'talkies' in 1927.

Revue was beginning to evolve into two separate styles: the 'spectacular' revues mounted by André Charlot, where the emphasis was on colour, costume and girls, and the 'intimate' revue, where verbal wit substituted for the expensive production values of Charlot or C. B. Cochran. The Hulberts starred in a series of 'little revues' at the Little Theatre throughout the 1920s. The intimate form was more accessible to the Footlights, although, probably under Rottenburg's influence, they stuck to a mainly musical comedy line. That did not prevent them from satirising contemporaries like the Co-Optimists in *What A Pic-Nic*, of 1921:

Walk up and see the May Week pierrots
   You must pay a visit
   You must never miss it.
We are the very latest heroes.

> Sit down before us
> Hear us sing a chorus
> All the oldest songs out of a last year's revue
> Everything you've heard before and nothing that's new.

The Bedder's Opera of 1922 (*The Beggar's Opera* played at the New Theatre in London in November 1921) ingeniously exploited the play within a play, and reused that long standing figure of Cambridge fun by presenting the play as having been written by Mrs Higgins, the bedder. She is introduced in a prologue by Malcolm Lyon (President 1920-22): 'The Footlights having no talent whatsoever among themselves, always encourage it wherever it is found.' The scene rapidly shifts to the garden of the Limelights Club, Cambridge, where a rehearsal is in progress.

> Irrepressible Limelights we
> On our annual May Week spree;
> Sunshine and laughter pervade our play,
> Banish trouble and care away.
> Our rehearsals are full of pep,
> Though we find that we can't keep step.
> Hope springs eternal
> We hope this infernal
> Old show will go.

The plot turns on the stock (but true-to-life) situation: will the May Week production be ready in time? The stars of the show have been sent down, or are otherwise detained, while the club President is faced with a romantic and financial problem of the utmost complexity. There is still time, however, to explain May Week in lyrics by Rottenburg:

> Trixie had a brother, a cousin, or a friend,
> Who invited her to Cambridge for the May Term's
>   festive end.
> She asked him what the programme was; what dresses
>   she should bring
> He looked a little puzzled, then he started to sing,
>   Lunch at one! Tea at five! Dine at eight!
>   Then a ball you must not be late!
>   Dance from ten to half past twelve
>   Sup and revive yourselves
>   After one dance like fun till four;
>   After soup join a group at the door.
>   Sleep till ten!
>   Breakfast then!
> With a few nice girls and men,
> And you're ready to start one more. . . .

Act II follows the play within a play a stage further by introducing two independent *grand guignol* sketches, short horror plays of the kind that were enjoying a brief fashion in London at the Little Theatre. (The Sketches, the second partly written by Maschwitz, were so long that one of them was subsequently cut.) Part of the overall plot involves the activities of a mysterious communist newspaper, *The Free Cambridge*. Editorship is traced to the Club Steward, one Scuttle:

> The aristocrat
> With his car and flat,
> I'd hurl from the highest mountain.
> And rich young boys
> With their gilded toys
> I'd drown in a public fountain. . . .

1924

However Scuttle's hatred for the members of the Limelights (his description echoes that of the show's part-author, Norman Hartnell, in his memoirs) turns out to be a further blind. He is a true conservative and wishes to demolish communism by causing people to laugh at it. (The actual Suttle was by now earning three guineas a week.)

Following the Presidency in 1923 of Baltimore-born Francis Powell, the first American to be President of any Cambridge club, in June 1924 the Footlights turned once more to revue with *Bumps* (a suitably Cambridge title), which follows the style of a Cochran show.

> We've been rehearsing at red-hot speed for a month or
>   more,
> And now we hope to amuse you all as of yore, as before;
> Hair well-dressed and figures neat,
> Pleased to dance on anyone's feet, and
> The name of the show is *Bumps*
> Yes *Bumps*, Yes *Bumps*,
> It sure will cure your humps . . . .

Unfortunately the social pleasures of club membership seem to have distracted the creators of *Bumps*. The *Cambridge Review* complained: 'As a whole *Bumps* is not very good. Too often we are given not a burlesque of revue but a reproduction. True, the reproduction is as good as can be seen on the Music Hall stage but Cambridge expects more from the Footlights. Mr Barradale at the piano in his own compositions is not very good and should be, as he takes himself seriously.' The one talented performer was Harold Warrender of Magdalene, but he had already made his mark in December 1923 with the ADC, in their parody of musical

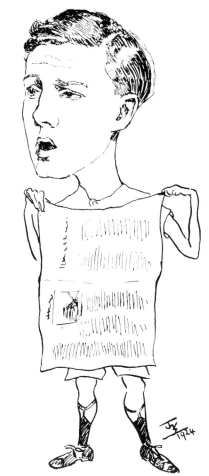

Harold Warrender

Cecil Beaton as Princess Técla

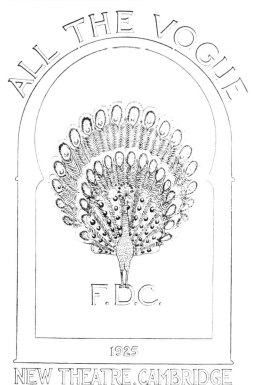

comedy *The Gyp's Princess* (set in the Throne and Ballroom, Rottenburg). The scenery for *The Gyp's Princess* was designed by a St John's undergraduate who also played the Princess Técla, Cecil Beaton. The ADC had begun to put on Christmas pantomimes in 1921 and they proved a serious challenge to the Footlights reputation. (Some, though not the majority, of ADC members were looking ahead. In March 1925 a special general meeting tried unsuccessfully to enable women to act with the ADC.)

In 1925 The Footlights show was titled (prophetically for one performer) *All the Vogue*. The *Cambridge Review* pointed out the Footlights' weakness. 'The best acting of the show must be placed to the credit of augmented talent from the ADC. Mr Beaton was brilliant...' *Granta* agreed. Beaton wrote the lyrics for his own torch song:

> Every time I back a horse
> He turns out like a bad divorce.
> I can't sew or darn or knit,
> Not that I want to; not a bit.
> Bridge or poker, not my game,
> Tennis, dancing, just the same
> However I
> Will do or die
> For I'm called Vivacious Vi.

Cecil Beaton, 1925

Beauties of "Bumps": "Ladies" of the Footlights Club.

WEARING ONE OF THE HEAD-BANDS OF THE MOMENT: MR. G. S. ALCOCK AS PAULA.

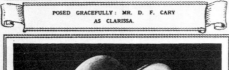

POSED GRACEFULLY: MR. D. F. CARY AS CLARISSA.

SHOWING THE LARGE PICTURE HAT OF TO-DAY: MR. D. F. CARY AS JANET.

IN A WEDDING GOWN OF LACE: MR. D. F. CARY AS THE BRIDE.

The Footlights Dramatic Club production for this year, at the New Theatre, Cambridge, is an original revue written by members of the Club, and entitled "Bumps." It is an excellent entertainment, and is not nearly so local in its humour as some of its twenty-four predecessors, while the "ladies" of the cast, who include a most attractive beauty chorus, are a really elegant "bunch," some of whom are shown in our photographs. One feels certain that, at first sight, no reader will observe that these charming "ladies" are really members of the sterner sex, for at Cambridge men undergraduates always play the women's parts.—{*Photographs by Scott and Wilkinson.*}

The Sketch,
18 June 1924

Harold Warrender, 1924

Part of the disappointment felt by Cambridge reviewers of *All the Vogue* was probably caused by the complete absence of references to proctors, bullers, bedders and so forth. Harold Warrender as President had his eyes on the London stage, which was already beckoning to him with offers of work. The scenery was borrowed from André Charlot, and the sketches, parodying Noël Coward, Aldwych farce and musical comedy would have entirely suited a West End audience.

Harold Warrender turned professional and had a reasonable career as a middle rank character actor. One of his last film performances before his death in 1953 was as Dr Wilson in *Scott of the Antarctic* (1948). He kept up his links with Cambridge and during the mid-Thirties ran an actors' club off Leicester Square. The club put on smokers and Footlights performers appeared there. Cecil Beaton (who kept a detailed diary of his Cambridge theatre days, but did not publish it) got as far as an interview with C. B. Cochran, but had to bide his time in the London office of a Danish cement firm before his moment as a stage designer came. He did eventually work for Cochran, designing the costumes for *Streamline* in 1934.

The utter conviction of the female impersonations of Beaton, Hartnell and others did not go unnoticed. By the mid-1920s Cambridge was thoroughly enjoying the pursuit of pleasure and the cultivation of decadence that followed the end of the war. On 5 October 1925 the *Daily Sketch* ran a scandal page on 'The Girl Men of Cambridge.' 'Nowhere else in Britain, except in London or, perhaps, Oxford, will you find so many soft, effeminate, painted, be-rouged youths . . .' The temptation to laugh at this is tempered by the words of a local resident who is described as having left the University in 1913. 'Men in caps and gowns carrying umbrellas are other monstrosities one sees now. Some of these youths have played parts in University theatricals, and I think this has encouraged their loathly effeminacy . . . sometimes one longs for a gun.'

Granta pointed out that the *Sketch* reporter had made his visit to Cambridge before term started, so the painted creatures he allegedly saw were not necessarily under-graduates, but Cambridge theatre, as a microcosm of the theatre at large, attracted its proportion of homosexuals, and the Footlights, as the most bohemian of the leading clubs, always had room for their talents.

William Redfern died in August 1923. His assistant manager Percy Adams became General Manager of the New Theatre, while Redfern's place on the board was taken by the Master of Pembroke, Dr W. S. Hadley, a move interpreted as strengthening the links between the University and the theatre. Sadly, however, the New Theatre was entering a period of slow decline.

In 1926 Cambridge became the site of a theatrical experiment. The Barnwell Theatre, having briefly changed from mission hall to boys' club, became a theatre once more under

Auditorium of the Festival Theatre

the direction of Terence Gray. Gray, a wealthy Egyptologist, was a theoretician rather than a theatre manager. His intention was to challenge the received notions of British theatrical style, that is to say its thoroughgoing naturalism. To that end he removed the Barnwell's proscenium arch entirely, constructed a stage revolve and built a permanent flight of steps from the stage into the auditorium. His founding partner was a metallurgist, Harold Ridge, a keen amateur actor who installed the most advanced system of stage lighting in the country. (Later he equipped Stratford Memorial Theatre.) There were other touches: transparent programmes that could be read in the dark; unusually comfortable seats and a good bar. From 1927 the Barnwell, renamed the Festival Theatre, boasted the best restaurant in Cambridge, the Festival Grill. Gray was a connoisseur of wines (he enjoyed a later career as a wine grower) and therefore banned beer and spirits from the theatre's catering, hoping to improve undergraduate palates.

Gray's revolutionary Shakespeare productions that followed his opening *Orestian Trilogy* (the chorus directed by Ninette de Valois) did not always appeal to Cambridge taste, and the Festival found itself renowned across the world, but unprofitably ignored in Cambridge. Gray's temperament did not suit his assistants, who rapidly left. His second stage-director, Norman Marshall wrote in his book *The Other Theatre*: 'Gray's lack of any real ability for

1926

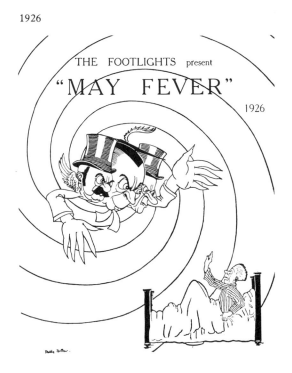

Victor Stiebel, 1927

leadership soon became obvious.' Gray's tenure of the theatre was interrupted a number of times. Anmer Hall, who was to become the dominant figure at the Westminster Theatre during the 1930s, took over for four seasons in 1928 and 1929, and gave early opportunities to Tyrone Guthrie, Flora Robson and Robert Donat, among others. Norman Marshall took over for a season in 1932. Marshall went on to take over the Gate Theatre in London in 1934, where the Gate revues featuring Hermione Gingold became the leading model for intimate comedy. Marshall and Gingold worked together at the Festival Theatre in *By Degrees* in 1933, and Marshall used local Footlights talent, in particular the song writers Ronald Hill and Geoffrey Wright.

In the late 1920s the Footlights continued on their pleasure-loving way, though gambling, fast cars and drinking attracted them as much as the theatre. That was the impression gained by Richard Murdoch when he went up to Pembroke in October 1925. As the most senior surviving former member of the Footlights to make a career in comedy, Richard Murdoch neatly punctures the Footlights myth: 'I think we all thought we were a lot better than we were . . . actually we were all drunk at the time.' Murdoch's uncle, the Reverend George Scott was a keen theatre-goer who remembered the Footlights from his own Cambridge days. The 1925 President Harold Warrender came to see Murdoch: ' "Your Uncle said I ought to make you a member," he said. Really I was just a drinking member. We had a good club room, and I spent most of my time there. There were about a hundred members, though most weren't very active.'

Murdoch was given a small part in the large chorus for the 1926 revue *May Fever*: '. . . the title was the best thing about the show. . . . It was pretty awful.' He wore a dress designed by Victor Stiebel, who like Norman Hartnell was to go from the Footlights into fashion. Murdoch only lasted a year at Cambridge: 'I spent too much time in sport, not without distinction. Secondly, I spent too much time with the Footlights . . . If I never did much work at Cambridge, it was because the theatre fascinated me.' His uncle came to the rescue and he landed a job in the chorus of *The Blue Train* at the Prince of Wales. The director was Jack Hulbert.

The low standard of *May Fever* contrasts with the success of the ADC's 1926 *Xmas Revue*, with material from Dennis Arundell and Victor Clinton-Baddeley, and Francis Wormald and Frank Birch in the cast. Some of this material was seen in Clinton-Baddeley's *Behind the Beyond* at the St

Martin's Theatre in January 1927. The *Cambridge Review* summed up the Footlights' 1927 offering *Please Tell Others* with '. . . we will be forgiven if we do not entirely accede to this request.' The *Granta* critic did not disguise his boredom:

> Opening chorus of 'women' – sketch by H. Rottenburg . . . you couldn't have a revue without a husband-wife-lover-sketch could you? There would be a crisis on the stock exchange or something . . . My God! A sentimental song. *Must* they have sentimental songs at the Footers? . . . Oh, another 'Sandford at Merton' sketch . . . Now a South Sea sketch. Knew they couldn't get through without it. It's not too original, is it? I wonder if the Ladies will keep their leaves on . . . .

The revue did, however, feature a future Hollywood actor, Michigan-born Phillips Holmes, son of the actor Taylor Holmes. Holmes spent 1926/7 at Trinity but was sent down, like Richard Murdoch, for failing his Part I exams. His film career began, suitably, with *Varsity* in 1928. He continued to act in films throughout the 1930s, but became an alcoholic. He died in 1942 at the age of thirty-five.

The redeeming feature of the Footlights shows in the late 1920s was the performances of the Quinquaginta Jazz Band. The 'Quinq' originally served as the band that played for a ballroom dancing club whose membership, as the name implies, was limited to fifty. The arrival of the Original Dixieland Jazz Band in London in April 1919 launched a craze for jazz in the dance halls that were then rapidly opening up all over the country. The Quinquaginta played regularly at dances at the Masonic Hall, so it was natural that there should be an informal link between the band and the Footlights. The 1922 revue featured 'Saul Blackman and his band', a play on the name of the leading white jazz leader, Paul Whiteman. In 1925 there is an appearance by 'The Quinquaginta Isle O'Blues Band' which according to the programme '. . . is also the Footlights Band.' In 1926 it is The Quinquaginta Band. On saxophone is one Manuel Elizalde, the younger son of a Spanish sugar magnate. Manuel's enthusiasm for jazz had diverted his elder brother Frederico from his training as a classical pianist. In 1925 the Elizalde brothers were in Los Angeles where they played professionally and made recordings, but their parents disapproved and Manuel was sent to Cambridge. Evidently Frederico followed on, for Richard Murdoch recalls Manuel singing the praises of his piano-playing brother: ' "When you hear my brother," he said, "you will absolutely buzz out!" '

Cambridge proved no cure for the brothers' addiction to

NEW THEATRE, June 6-13, 1927

1927

Phillips Holmes, 1927

George Monkhouse and
his Quinquaginta Ramblers,
1930

The Quinquaginta Ramblers, 1928

'The Footlights Band', 1937,
photographed in the Club Room

jazz. Although only Manuel played in the 1926 Footlights revue, 'Fred Elizalde and his Varsity Band (from the Quinquaginta Club, Cambridge)' made two recordings for Brunswick in May 1927, and 'Fred Elizalde and his Cambridge Undergraduates' (with the same personnel) recorded for His Master's Voice in June. In the Autumn of 1927 the Savoy Hotel in London decided to hire a jazz band to share the bill with the Savoy Orpheans, and Fred Elizalde opened there in mid-December with a professional band, including his brother, staying there until 1929.

The departure of the Elizalde brothers from Cambridge threw the Quinq into confusion and the Footlights General Meeting in October 1927 decided '. . . to try to elect a committee for the Quinquaginta Club, and to start them off again.' It was agreed that band members should be honorary members of the Footlights when playing at smokers and, although a formal amalgamation was never carried through, the Quinq and the Footlights remained in close co-operation.

At least two former members of Elizalde's Cambridge band stayed on to form the 'Quinquaginta Ramblers', George Cosmo Monkhouse, and Jack Donaldson, a saxophonist. The *Cambridge Review* found the Ramblers one of the few things to like about the 1928 revue, and added 'a word of praise for Mr Donaldson's step-dancing.' J. G. S. Donaldson, from Eton and Trinity, became a Life Peer in 1967, and from 1976 to 1979 was Minister for the Arts.

The Ramblers also played in the 1929 revue (though without Monkhouse or Donaldson) and then returned in 1930 as 'George Monkhouse and his Quinquaginta Ramblers'. Albeit with several changes of personnel, Quinquaginta dances remained a regular feature of Cambridge night life until 1937. They reappeared in the Footlights programme in 1934 as 'The Quinquaginta Four', at which stage they seem to have become a tango band. The guitarist, Malcolm Macdonald of Trinity, later became Chief Bandmaster of RAF Bomber Command. A rival organisation, the New Arimatheans, appeared in 1936, again as the band of a dance club. The Quinq ceased to function by October 1938, while the Arimatheans were referred to as the Footlights Band. In March 1939 *Granta* reported: 'As a club rule demanded that band members be club members, difficulties arose in augmenting the band, and within the last few days, the band returned to its former status of Arimatheans.'

In April 1928 the Footlights Treasurer, H. F. Shaw of Christ's, sounded a warning. He announced that the club finances were '. . . in a bad state, and urged that more people should become members of the club.' The 1928 revue, *This Week of Pace* (Cochran presented Noël Coward's *This Year*

1928

This Week of Pace, 1928

of Grace earlier in the year), was not a success. *Granta's* critic complained: 'I should have thought that a revue written and produced by an undergraduate dramatic club would best be able to justify itself by localisms, topicality and May Weekality. The Footlights Club evidently does not think so.'

Shaw repeated his warnings in October 1928 and a 'sub-committee on economies' was set up. The committee heard in April 1929 that '. . . the great difficulty in the Club at the present time as regards funds was due to the slowness of some members to pay their bar bills and subscriptions.' The position improved after the 1929 May Week show, and £100 was invested in War Loan stock, but *The General (S)election* (1929 was an election year) failed to please *Granta*:

> . . . The 'women' are a complete failure. . . . It is difficult to understand why two unfortunate members must be found every year to be powdered and dressed up like West End leading ladies without the remotest hope of ever looking or behaving like them; it must be very embarrassing for them, and it is certainly very embarrassing for the audience so long as it is not expected to laugh at the result. Surely the Footlights revue is a heaven-sent opportunity for burlesquing the chorus and leading ladies of revue, not for imitating them.

The female impersonators appear to have been taking their roles too seriously.

In January 1930 bar credit was stopped and debtors were banned from the club. (Subscriptions then stood at a guinea a term, with the remittance of a guinea for any performer in the May Week show.) The club was suffering a decline in membership. The minute book shows that from 1927 elections were becoming less frequent, while there was a more rapid turnover in the offices of the club. In particular, the club was not attracting performers. Norman Jones of St Catharine's, who was elected in January 1929, records that the club appealed only to rich undergraduates, particularly Americans: '... it was a poor period. There was little appreciation of the Cambridge that was so alive at that time; members were snobs and joined because of a certain prestige. There were few memories of the Hulbert brothers and Dave Burnaby.' Jones, who became an educationalist specialising in drama, a job he 'owed entirely to the Footers' may have been prejudiced by being one of the few members who combined membership of the Footlights with that of the Labour Club, but his impression is confirmed by Ronald Hill, who joined in the Spring of 1930. 'It was a closed shop in favour of racing men.'

Norman Jones

The standards of smokers declined with those of the revue. Norman Jones records:

> The kind of sketch was the smutty joke in a 'tableau vivant' – for example – the young girl aspiring to stardom – first seen with the office boy doing up his braces – was he satisfied? Yes, but she must satisfy the camera man, and so on to Samuel Goldwyn himself – this time in bed. Yes, he was satisfied, but she must satisfy the British public – this stays vividly in my mind – R. S. Hill was the starlet. The concert was an excuse for much drinking – and, of course, no women.

The club committee tried to restore the reputation of their smokers. In November 1929 they issued new rules, forbidding entrance to anyone without a ticket and not wearing a dinner jacket. Only committee members and performers were allowed on the stage, and

> (iv) That since despicable members and their guests have at times indulged in promiscuous urination other than in the lavatory alloted for that necessity, a large notice indicating the situation of the aforesaid should be displayed for the benefit of short sighted and rude members.

Ronald Hill

Both Norman Jones and Ronald Hill appeared in the 1930 revue, *Say When*. The director was a professional, Ronald Brandon, who shared the job with his wife. Jones: 'They

Say When, 1930

1930

came up in the May Term and tried against terrible odds to produce the show. I fear the standards of material, choreography and sketches were those, to quote Betjeman, of "the lesser Co-Optimists down at the pier". It was hell for him and his wife. . . .' Hill: 'There were an awful lot of Eastern princes who could do one little act and had to be brought in. Mrs Brandon was appalled at the "talent" she had to work with. She couldn't believe that half the cast could be drunk at the dress rehearsal. One man had a solo act, and he was "angry drunk", so we daren't interrupt him.'

Ronald Hill was one of the few members of the Footlights at that time who joined with an eye on the professional stage. He was at Cambridge only under protest, since he had wanted to go straight into the theatre. 'I hoped and assumed that the Footlights would do me a great deal of good in the theatre – which of course it didn't.' Hill was brought into the club by Richard Philpott, pianist and arranger for the Quinquaginta Ramblers, and both were able to use the Footlights to launch their professional careers. Though 'bitterly disappointed' by what he found when elected, Hill became President in October 1930, 'literally because there was no one else who would get down to putting a show on.'

Hill and Philpott wrote most of the songs for the 1931 revue, *Once Again*. Philpott recorded 'Flight of Fancy' (the original title for the revue) for Parlophone and the sheet music was on sale at the theatre, but they had forgotten to make a deal with the programme sellers and not a single copy was sold.

Once Again was better received than its predecessors, although the projected London matinée was cancelled because of lack of interest. *Granta* complained of the Footlights' 'smug self-satisfaction'. Philpott and Hill were however noticed by Normal Marshall, who was preparing to take over the Festival Theatre for a season, and both contributed to the opening revue in January 1932. Ronald Hill left Cambridge without taking a degree; he, too, was later to work with Jack Hulbert. Philpott had a somewhat desultory career as a pianist and arranger in the 1930s, before becoming an agent. Among their generation Roy Spear joined the BBC, G.C. Langdon became a thriller writer and Wynyard Browne a playwright.

The autumn of 1931 opened with the club deeper in debt, having made a loss on the 1931 revue. Members showed no great inclination to settle their bar bills. The new President, Peter Lyon (he and Ronald Hill were to produce a revue in a tank hanger during World War II) found himself facing a revolt at the General Meeting on 26 October.

> The meeting was convened to discuss certain complaints concerning the President. Various gentlemen expressed their opinions, and the complaints was found to be that the President was not 'an all round fellow'. No reply was

Sheet music, 1931

Once Again, 1931

Poppy Day, 1931

forthcoming when Mr Browne demanded a definition of the phrase. The President resigned and was re-elected. Exception was also taken to his dog and he agreed to keep it away from the Club premises in future. Two members then resigned and the meeting broke up.

The clash of personalities exacerbated worries about finance. In 1927 the club had had a balance in its favour of £1,028, but the May Week profits were declining steadily: in 1929 £343, in 1930 £78, in 1931 £62. In 1931 a former Senior Treasurer, R. H. Adie, returned to his post. On 10 January 1932 he '. . . explained the serious nature of the Club's condition and suggested that the only effective way to deal with this was by substituting a deposit system at the bar for the credit system now obtaining. This was agreed and a financial committee was appointed consisting of Mr Rottenburg, Mr Adie, Mr Budd, Mr Howard Curtis [all resident MAs], Mr Bate [Junior Treasurer] and Mr Lyon to follow the financial progress of the Club.'

Desperate measures were called for and at the same meeting it '. . . was decided to return to the old custom of producing musical comedy.' This was 1932, however, and the old customs could not be reverted to entirely. 'The subject of the inclusion of women was hotly debated, and not concluded by any means.' This revolutionary suggestion caused an uproar in the club, but there was a precedent. In 1929 Alistair Cooke (the journalist and broadcaster, then an undergraduate at Jesus) had launched a third major drama club, The Mummers. However, once he had persuaded the Vice-Chancellor that it would not be 'unnatural' for men and women to appear together on the stage, membership was specifically opened to both sexes.

Pressure for an end to the Footlights' forty-nine year old tradition appears to have come in part from a recent member, Roland Gillet, who had become a professional actor. (He had leading roles in the May Week shows of 1927 and 1928, was assistant to Rupert Rogers in 1929 and had directed *Once Again* in the previous year, for a 'nominal fee' of £50.) While back in Cambridge in 1931 he had a runaway romance with the Australian actress and heiress Naomi Waters. He may have had an eye on his wife's future when he attended another Footlights General Meeting on 4 March 1932:

> . . . the much discussed question of whether women should be invited to take part in the May Week show reached a conclusion at last. Mr Lyon proposed the matter remarking that the time had come to take a new step owing to the unfashionability of burlesque and the change in humour during the last five or six years. Mr Howard Curtis suggested that this step was against all tradition but that if the exigencies of the situation demanded, it would be better to use local talent, under-graduates, rather than professional actresses. This emendation did not seem popular. Mr Bate raised the question of the additional expense of such a step in these times of financial stringency. He was informed by Mr Lyon that their services, except for expenses, would be free. Mr Gilette (*sic*), who was present, then gave suggestions for the plot of the show, and a vote was taken on the matter. The project was carried, with only one objecting vote.

Naomi Waters, 1932

The club nonetheless continued in dissension; at a further General Meeting on 24 April '. . . it was decided that owing to the inactivity of certain members of the committee, this body should resign, and a smaller committee be appointed in their place.' Only Lyon and Bate, as President and Treasurer, kept their posts.

> Suggestions were then invited for the May Week Show, a suitable story being unfound. A farce story was put up by R. Gillet, an old member, and another by Alwyn Bolton. It was then decided on a show of hands that the President proceed to build a story round the ideas of the latter. The President then walked out of the club, and accepting this as a sign that the meeting was adjourned, members then rose.

Although the book from which these quotations come is only half full, this unsigned minute is the final, somewhat bitter entry.

Our destiny takes us, and binds us and breaks us,
Leaving life confused and hating the sun.
Our responses are musty, our Shakespeares are dusty,
The need we brought to seek for beauty has gone.
I sit and murmur word for stupid word,
Hoping I may not be overheard

For this is the music that's within my soul,
I know I can't express it as a whole:
It's just simple music that my soul has seen,
That's what I mean.
I was always dreaming when the day was done,
My childhood broke through chords of music and of
    sun,
Dreaming of the might-have-been and used-to-be;
That's what I mean.
If I could tell, I'd tell you just what then befell:
But night and day I hide – it's courage and pride.
Now if you solve this beauty you would see the man
Behind all that I try to say and never can,
And share the simple music that my soul has seen:
That's what I mean.

'That's what I mean'
Malcolm Lowry *Laughing at Love* 1932

As a finishing touch, the Footlights advertised *Laughing at Love* as their 'jubilee production', anticipating their anniversary by one year. The book is credited to the President, Peter Lyon, but he had two unusual literary collaborators, John Davenport and Malcolm Lowry. John Davenport, who later went to Hollywood and on his return to England co-wrote *The Death of The King's Canary* with Dylan Thomas in 1940, was briefly an undergraduate at Corpus between 1931 and 1932. He became a celebrated figure in the University – *Granta* described his gold monocle as 'The Eighth Wonder of Cambridge.' Malcolm Lowry, the future author of the alcoholic masterpiece *Under the Volcano*, had been a schoolboy at the Lees School in Cambridge, where he and Ronald Hill had formed a song-writing team. Since then he had run away to sea and the experience had changed him. Ronald Hill tended to avoid his former partner.

There are signs of future literary greatness in Malcolm Lowry's lyrics for the song 'That's What I Mean' (for which he also wrote the music). But there is nothing original in John Davenport's dialogue. The play opens in a nightclub, where the traditional comic servants are in lively debate with Herbert, waiter and Communist. The club gradually fills with upper-class clientèle, among them Lord George Hellvellyn, aged twenty-four, broke and in love with the cabaret artiste Joan Davids. The entrance of the cabaret performers (among them Malcolm Lowry) is an excuse for the title song:

> We're laughing at love, it's better that way
> We keep right above the others who say
> 'Believe in the thing' for we believe
> In the wise man's creed,
> A Sense of Proportion.
> Philosophers say that's what you need
> When love comes along you're sure to succeed
> Let us meet the man, we'll quickly prove
> The Wisdom of Laughing at Love.

The plot turns on what all are agreed is the social *mésalliance* between the peer and the artiste. The Hon Edward Vivasour (an 'Edwardian', played by Wynyard Browne) conspires with the Communist Herbert to restore the principle of 'Class with Class' by getting Hellvellyn (played by an actual peer, Lord Duncannon) back with his fiancée Lady Nancy Verry (Naomi Waters) and Joan back with her cabaret partner. This is done partly by a complex plot involving a 'stolen' ring and partly by making Hellvellyn make a silly ass of himself working in a gramophone shop. (The shop provides an opportunity for the real girls of the chorus to show their paces.) The plot succeeds and 'Keep Class to Class' is enforced to everyone's satisfaction.

Laughing at Love gave little satisfaction to Cambridge, as Albert Robinson (now Sir Albert Robinson), who became President in 1939, later explained: 'The townspeople were disappointed, because they liked seeing undergraduates dressed up as girls and playing feminine roles. The University were disappointed, because they were led to expect a polished West End production, and the show did not reach those heights.' The show did however begin the career of the actress Anna Lee. Half the music was written by George Posford, who later teamed up with Eric Maschwitz to write *Goodnight Vienna* (1932), *The Gay Hussar* (1933) and *Balalaika* (1936).

The club's profits from *Laughing at Love* came to £45. The club had sold its investments to pay for the production and now faced £350 of debts. According to Lord Killanin, who came up to Magdalene in October 1932, the Footlights were '... down and out, the club had gone to pieces.' A General Meeting held on 9 October was attended by only ten people, who heard Rottenburg announce that the sale of the remaining assets, including the lease on the club rooms and the piano, would raise only £250. Rottenburg and the two surviving members of the emergency finance committee resigned. Rottenburg told the *Daily Telegraph*: 'Tragic as it may be, the famous club appears doomed.' Almost as a final insult, the Director of the London Pari-Mutuel Tote Clubs Ltd. wrote to the Footlights offering to take them over.

Lord Duncannon, 1932

Anna Lee, 1932

Rottenburg, our witness to the crisis of 1895, seems to have been re-enacting the part once played by Oscar Browning. But as in 1895, the club rallied.

> There are no more women in the Footlights show
> There are no more women here
> They were awfully pleasant little girls to know
> So we tried them out last year.
> But we've no more women in our May Week show
> As will presently appear,
> Last year they were a flop,
> So we thought they'd better stop,
> So we've no more women here.

The title song of the 1933 revue, *No More Women* speaks for itself. The show was a conscious return to parochialism and the Footlights tradition. In October 1932 the few remaining members pulled themselves out of their lethargy and set to to redecorate the club. They were joined by the new recruits like Lord Killanin (he had succeeded to the title

Rehearsing *No More Women*
in the Clubroom, 1933

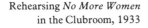

in 1927), who was made business manager of the 1933 revue. It was a sound appointment, for Killanin was interested both in theatre and film production and journalism, beoming Literary Editor of the newly founded University newspaper *Varsity*. Good connections between the stage and the press were essential, even for the nominal amateurs of Cambridge, if the Footlights were to restore their credit with University opinion.

No More Women said it all, and proctors, bulldogs, hungover undergraduates and a fashion parade by the Senate of the University of Bletchley (the railway interchange between Oxford and Cambridge) reassured the undergraduates that the old jokes were still the best jokes. Lord Killanin personally delighted the townspeople with his appearance as 'She'. Rottenburg, who had transferred most of his energies to the magicians' Pentacle Club, produced another of what had become famous as 'Rottenburg's Remarkable Tricks'. The show was held together by a running caricature of Terence Gray and the Festival Theatre (though not credited, Humphrey Jennings, the film maker and surrealist painter, who was working as a designer at the Festival, had a hand in the set). The opening number was a verse drama, directed by 'Plautus Green' of the 'Carnival Theatre'. 'Green' has decided to close down and, together with the sole member of the Carnival Theatre's audience, sets off in search of suitable material in order this time to give the public what it really wants. . . .

The satire was nearer the mark than might be supposed. In 1933 Terence Gray did give up his management of the Festival Theatre. The declining fortunes of the Footlights in the late Twenties and early Thirties matched the crisis in the commercial theatre as it succumbed to the twin pressures of competition from the cinema and economic depression. By the end of 1933 Cambridge was almost without a theatre of any kind. In July the New Theatre, which had been taken over by Prince Littler's theatre chain, was leased to a local cinema group, and began to operate as a 'theatre cinema', alternating stage shows like pantomime and the Footlights revues with film programmes. (It closed in 1938, reopened after the war with variety and 'nude revues' and finally closed in 1956. The building was demolished in 1960.) The management of the Festival Theatre passed to Gray's stage-manager, Joseph Gordon Macleod, who tried unsuccessfully to run it as an ordinary repertory. Sporadic attempts to revive it lasted until 1939 when the theatre went dark for ever. To complete the destruction, in the early hours of 10 November 1933 the ADC's 200-seater private theatre in Park Street caught fire. The backstage area, up to the fire curtain, and including Lord Killanin's sets for Beverley Nicholas' *Avalanche*, was entirely destroyed.

It did not reopen until 1935. The sudden crisis in Cambridge's theatres prompted J. M. Keynes, the economist and Fellow of King's, into action. He set about building an entirely new theatre on a constricted site in Peas Hill; and in February 1936 the Cambridge Arts Theatre opened its doors. Although senior members of the University were much involved, the theatre had no official connection with

Auditorium of the Arts Theatre, 1936

After the fire at the ADC Theatre

the University, and it remains in the hands of a private trust. With six hundred seats, the Arts holds less than half the audience of the New Theatre and is hardly an economic size. In the mid-Thirties however, Keynes may have felt justifiably cautious in building a small-scale theatre. *Granta* editorialised on the occasion of the Arts' opening:

> For many years Cambridge had been well-known among the members of the professional stage as the town that provides the worst audiences in England. Jokes are made about the people of Wigan; but the people of Cambridge are beyond a joke. This reputation had been acquired owing to the rowdy behaviour of a large and changing body of undergraduates, who consistently use every performance whether of a film or of a play as a means of displaying their own doubtful witticisms. The result has been that the drama in Cambridge has been sadly neglected. The New Theatre has become the Theatre Cinema, and offers us a weekly mixture of films and music-hall turns; the Festival Theatre has seen changes of management and changes of fortune, until now it makes no claim to any sort of theatrical originality . . . and certainly it is not well supported.

Student attitudes, however, were changing. *No More Women* found room for a comment on the rise of Hitler by presenting German proctors and bulldogs in Nazi uniforms. Writing in the *Cambridge Review* in January 1934 C. W. Guillebaud notes: 'In recent months there have been unmistakeable signs of an increase of political consciousness amongst the undergraduates of Oxford and Cambridge, and also in provincial universities.' The well organised large scale rags of the 1920s (such as pretending that the public lavatory in Market Square was the Tomb of Tutankhamen) gave way to political demonstrations. In 1934 a pacifist meeting on Armistice Day was broken up by other students who supported Oswald Mosley's blackshirts. The make-up of the undergraduate population was changing; there were fewer of the very rich to be seen and more people on grants. The Liberal Club was almost defunct, the Conservative Club, though numerically the largest, had a mainly social function, but both Labour supporters and the Communists were active. As Guillebaud summed up: '. . . in comparison with pre-war conditions there has been a decided swing from the right to the left.'

The majority of undergraduates, as always, ignored politics in favour of sport, college societies and working for a degree. The student greeting was now 'What cheer!' Most people – the 'scugs' – wore light grey flannels and elbow-patched sports jackets, although the sports clubs went in for considerable finery. In 1933 the Proctors introduced a note in the *Compendium of Regulations* issued to every freshman, reminding undergraduates that gowns must be worn after dark, even with evening dress, and that blazers '. . . other than those made of plain black or dark blue may not be worn after dusk' – except when attending a club dinner. Aesthetes – who *never* said 'What cheer!' – distinguished themselves by turtle neck sweaters or green or red ties.

Women had come to play a much larger part in University life. Although still not members of the University, since 1923 they had been allowed to use degree titles as well as sit exams. (The decision provoked another student riot.) The Footlights continued to exclude women, though the Mummers allowed them in as a matter of course. In 1934 the Marlowe presented *Antony and Cleopatra* with women performers for the first time and the ADC followed with *The Servant of Two Masters* in 1935. It was however agreed that girls '. . . invited to take part in such productions shall not be deemed members or temporary members of the club, nor shall they be allowed the use of the club room at any time.'

Lord Killanin in
No More Women, 1933

In October 1933 Killanin became President and proceeded to put the Footlights' house in order. The crisis of 1932 had attracted the attention of the Vice-Chancellor, who reminded them that scripts had to be submitted for his approval, and of the necessity of having an MA as Senior Treasurer: '. . . considerable financial risk may be involved and it is desirable to secure a continuous management of finance.' The rules were altered; the entrance fee was lowered to two guineas and membership was no longer dependent on personal acquaintance with the committee. The club printed a recruiting leaflet, extolling the virtues and facilities of the club room – open from 10 am to 11 pm, providing lunch, tea and snacks and a fully licensed bar – 'one of the cheapest in Cambridge.' The pamphlet also plays on the Footlights' professional reputation and lists its stars – George Posford, Ronald Hill, Davy Burnaby, Claude Hulbert, Harold Warrender, Jack Hulbert, Phillips Holmes, Norman Hartnell, Cecil Beaton – and boasted: 'It is nearly impossible to pick up a London theatre programme without finding the name of an old member.'

The club also decided to do something about its own professional skills by mounting productions of one-act plays (as has been the practice in the 1890s). The club defended its actions in *Granta*:

A certain mild controversy has arisen in the University around the fact that a club with so frivolous a

Lord Killanin, 1934

reputation as the Footlights should take the drama so seriously. Hitherto the club's activities have been limited to their May Week Revue and a few spasmodic pornographic smokers in the course of the year. Their virtue did not lie in the fact they they amused dreary May Week visitors, but in that the Footlights permitted any undergraduate with enterprise and personality to come to the fore.

The 1934 revue, *Sir or Madam* benefited from the new attitude. Killanin brought in a BBC Drama Producer, John Chaplin, to direct; the stage manager Philip Godfrey was a professional; and André Charlot's Ballet Mistress, Carrie Graham supervised the choreography. The cast put on a matinée at the Comedy Theatre in London, where Killanin had had a hand in finding finance for *Ballyhoo*. Much of *Sir or Madam* was written by David Yates Mason, who began writing professionally the following year. Geoffrey Wright, who both wrote music and designed the sets for *No More Women*, had begun to contribute to Norman Marshall's Gate revues.

Humphrey Bourne in *Sir or Madam*, 1934

Sir or Madam?
Guess if you can
Aren't you longing to know
Why we have kept to our usual plan
With a masculine show.
We can only hope to explain
By tonight's revue
Why the Footlights beg to remain
Sir or Madam to you.

(women:)
We are the girls
Don't you adore us?
Varsity pearls
Gracing the chorus.

(men:)
As you can see
Make-up enables
Us to be
Young Clark Gables,
    – and so

Sir or Madam
Listen to us
We'll endeavour to raise
Your dull spirits from trouble and fuss
Laugh and loosen your stays;
Don't let dull repressions restrain
Take from us your cue
While the Footlights remain
Sir or Madam to you.

Opening chorus *Sir or Madam* 1934

Although there were Footlights who saw the club as a stepping stone – Lord Killanin recalls among his contemporaries Hugh Latimer, who was intent on becoming an actor (and did so in 1936), and Robert Hamer, the future director of the Ealing Comedy *Kind Hearts and Coronets* – it still had the reputation of being a rich, if bohemian group. Its politics were catholic; members ranged from the future staunch Conservative MP Nigel Fisher to Andrew d'Antal, who was a member of the Communist Party. Nigel Burgess, brother of the future spy Guy Burgess, directed the orchestra for *No More Women* and contributed the song 'He's Nice, He's Clean, He's British' in 1934.

As 'one of the cheapest' drinking places in Cambridge, the club had a number of hangers-on from the town, odd characters like a failed solicitor turned debt collector who at one time looked after the club's finances. Howard Curtis, a dentist, was a long standing member. Several were jazz enthusiasts – Reggie Forsythe, a coloured player who worked in Chappell's music shop, and the clarinettist Rudolf Dunbar, who gave concerts in the club.

The club's homosexual reputation also stuck, as *Granta* more than hinted in November 1934:

> I am a Footlights fairy, so in terse
> But not too polished couplets, speak in verse
> You wish to join Sir? Are your tastes aesthetic
> Have you long hair, or do you use cosmetic?
> Can you compare with types from Ethel Mannin
> (McCl*nt*ck B*nb*ry (Hon.) and Lord K*ll*n*n)?
> Or do you shine at *intime* little parties
> From which are kept all trace of *horrid* hearties?
> (Why was that Attic Ladder ta'en away? –
> It proved *so* useful on a rainy day!)
> We social stars attract a num'rous flock,
> Who cannot tell a Buskin from a Sock
> Confusing Clowning with the Art of Grock,
> Who think that *floods* are liquid, and – what's odd –
> A *cyclorama* is an Act of God.
> 'Ars est celare artem' is our care
> Though it's hard to find what isn't there.
> But you Sir! Can the Gollywhoebbles name be met
> Within the hallow'd pages of *Debrett*?
> It can't? Then have you any high powered cars?
> Or lots of cash? Or both? You've not! My stars!!
> You merely act, but have not *one* of these?
> What impudence! Remove this person please!

Nuts in May in June 1935 (ingeniously promoted by free bags of peanuts bearing the name of the show) was the last appearance of the club at the New Theatre, by then better

One day I was having lunch in an army club
The luncheon was a good one, but the members they're the rub.
For no one looked, and no one winked or made a pass at me,
But sat and talked of India back in '63.

I know a man who thinks it's grand
Just to hold a lady's hand,
He's nice, He's clean, He's British.

I spent last night with him alone
But we listened to his gramophone
He's nice, He's clean, He's British.

He's been to Jamaica, He's been to old Yazoo
But I wish he'd manage to go to Paris too.

He had an idea that a date,
Is just another thing one ate
He's nice, He's clean, He's British.

He doesn't know that at a ball
One doesn't have to dance at all
He's nice, He's clean, He's British.

He never really understood
Why cars break down outside a wood
He's nice, He's clean, He's British.

I said when you were at Cambridge what ladies did you know?
And he looked surprised at me, and said 'I used to row'.

He has a chicken farm he tends
They are his only feathered friends
He's nice, He's clean, He's British.

'He's Nice, He's Clean, He's British'
Nigel Burgess *Sir or Madam* 1934

Let's turn over a new leaf
   Let's be clean
Life's a big bed of roses
We're all sweet seventeen
Nothing like *Razzle* and no *Ballyhoo*
Ours is a show that's too good to be true
Just like the *Granta* and the *Cambridge Review*
   Let's be clean.

Opening chorus *Turn Over A New Leaf* 1936

George Rylands, 1936

Robert Helpmann, 1936

known as the New Theatre Cinema. In February 1936 the Arts Theatre opened with a gala performance by the Vic-Wells Ballet, whose origins can be traced to Ninette de Valois' work with the Festival Theatre. In June 1936 the Footlights' long association with the Art Theatre began with *Turn Over a New Leaf*.

Neville Blackburn in *Turn Over a New Leaf*, 1936

It was a good title, for the Footlights now took their responsibilities seriously. The director was George Rylands, known to generations of undergraduates as 'Dadie', an influential figure in Cambridge theatre ever since his under-graduate Presidency of the ADC in 1922. Rylands was a close friend of his colleague at King's, J. M. Keynes, and they worked together on the creation of the Arts. Rylands did better than Charlot's Ballet Mistress: he brought in the principal dancer of the Vic-Wells Ballet, Robert (now Sir Robert) Helpmann, to supervise the Footlights' choreography. Sir Robert found the atmosphere '... frightfully professional, they were very serious about it all, and they worked like mad.'

According to Helpmann, the club was still 'a fairly exclusive privileged group, very much the upper crust of Cambridge. It was elegant, but *not* decadent.' Helpmann found the club's hearty footballers ideal material for his *corps de ballet*. 'In the 1937 revue I did a potted version of *Les Sylphides*, which we had done with the Wells at the Arts. I taught them the actual steps, and Peter Eade, who was the ballerina, actually got up on points. We played it absolutely straight, but I chose all the big football boys, with great big hairy legs and hairy arms. The audience got absolutely hysterical.' (Peter Eade has since become a leading theatrical agent.) For *Turn Over a New Leaf* Helpmann created a cabaret scene featuring the then novel dance, the rumba. His dancers were two Panamanians, Theo and Tito de Arias. Margot Fonteyn, as a member of the Wells company, came to see the show. She married Tito de Arias in 1955.

Helpmann choreographed the Footlights revues until 1939, and recalls the summers in Cambridge as a very happy time: 'there was a party every night, we seemed to spend our time climbing in and out of colleges, or falling into the river drunk.' George Rylands directed again in 1938, while another Fellow of King's, Donald Beves, directed in 1937 and 1939. There were outside contributions in the form of sketches by Arthur Marshall (a member of the ADC from 1928 to 1931); 'A Smack at the Blacks', lightly mocking Britain's Imperial past, later appeared in one of Norman Marshall's Gate Revues. Though not a member of the club, the poet Patric Dickinson supplied the lyrics for 'Going Down Blues'. This was his third year, and his last memory of Cambridge is of drinking whisky out of a teapot with Geoffrey Wright at the party at the Arts for *Turn Over a New Leaf*. The sketches acquired a certain intellectual stiffening: the usual Cambridge jokes ran alongside take-offs of Eugene O'Neill and Chekhov. Marshall, Dickinson and Wright continued to contribute material until 1939. Another writer in 1936 was Vivian Cox, the film producer who was to mount the Cambridge comedy *Bachelor of Hearts* in 1958; Terence Young, future screenwriter and director of James Bond films, was in the 1936 cast.

By October 1936 the fortunes of the Footlights were restored. The President for 1936/7 Albert Robinson (now Sir Albert) was able to tell the *Morning Post*, '. . . the club has prospered amazingly. Our smoking concerts and one-act play performances are packed, and we have a wealth of acting, singing and dancing, and instrumental talent at our disposal. The 1936 May Week show resulted in a net profit of £250 and we have practically succeeded in wiping off all the club's past debts.' In truth the club's financial management remained imperfect: the rent due to the Isaac Newton

(Enter General Wellington Boote)
BOOTE: You're keeping a smart look-out, men? The Bedouin is a dashed slippery customer.
SENTRY B: He won't give the slip to the Fighting Fourteenth, Sir!
BOOTE: Well said, sentry. *(At rampart)* There's not a soul in sight. *(They all look left. Black head bobs up right, and vice versa)*
SENTRY C: No, not a soul.
SENTRY A: Nothing but sand.
BOOTE: Then perhaps we can hang on until the column comes. Jovers, nearly sundown. It's a lucky thing that young Rightabout's with them, he knows these desert wastes from A to Z.
SENTRY B: What's that cloud of dust not a stone's throw from the fort?
SENTRY C: It's men, marching men.
BOOTE: An Arab attack; double the watch. *(distant drums heard)*
SENTRY B: That's not Arabs, Sir, it's far too slow for Arabs. Besides, I can spot the glint of a Lee-Enfield.
BOOTE: Let's see what these old eyes of mine will do.
SENTRY B *(aside)*: They called him 'Hawk-eyes' up in the hills.
BOOTE: It's men, all right, white men, too; it's – it's – the column!
SENTRIES: Hooray! Hooray! Saved!
BOOTE: Open the lower gate – run up the flag – warn Cook – look sharp, men, they're here.

(Military noises off. Enter, singing marching song, the column, led by ROY RIGHTABOUT)

Love and War
These are the games worth playing
No man can ask any more
When the bugles and trumpets bray
Love and War
Open adventure's door;
All that men sigh for, live, love and die for
Love and War.

'A Smack at the Blacks'
Arthur Marshall *Turn over A New Leaf* 1936

University Lodge was rarely paid on time, and there was a general vagueness about bar bills. This played into the hands of Suttle's successor as Steward, one Wilkinson, who was not honest. The committee noticed something 'fishy' about the accounts and Wilkinson resigned in the Easter Term of 1938. The President, Peter Meyer, explained in a letter to the Senior Treasurer:

> It appears that nearly everybody's bill last term was much less than it usually has been, and, as somebody pointed out, nothing could be easier than to add any sum of money to the bill; nobody knows how much he has spent and there is no check. The inference is of course that he was rattled by the inquiries that were going on.

At a higher level of finance the formation of the Arts Theatre Trust in 1938 put the Footlights and other leading amateur groups on a much more professional basis. The trust took over the theatre from the private administration set up by Keynes: once a budget was agreed the trust funded the revue and split the profits 50/50 with the club. This relieved the club of having to capitalise the show, and gave them access to the professional expertise of the staff at the Arts. Judy Birdwood, for instance, costume mistress of the Arts, has dressed every Footlights May Week show since 1938. Her hearty laughter at dress rehearsals has been a valued asset.

Full Swing, 1937

The opening scene of *Full Swing* in 1937 is a self-portrait of the Footlights – the organised chaos of a rehearsal.

> *The Chaos will take the following order.*
> *Tito* is parading before a mirror dressed as woman –
> 'How to I look boys?'
> *The Ballet* are exercising – stretching their legs, etc.
> *The Orchestra* in the pit are tuning up. Now and again
> members of the cast shout to Bill Trethowan or Geoff
> Kitchen to shut up or to 'Try this number'.
> *Paul Kramer* is being instructive. 'Yeah but in the
> States they pronounce it Ma-ammy!'
> *The Press* is snooping – asking questions. 'How many
> miles of ribbons did you say Mr Meyer?' Maybe there is
> a photographer.
> *Peter Meyer* is worrying about costumes – 'Have you
> got your costume on for the finale Eric?' etc.
> *Wilkinson* is typing at a small table. He takes no notice
> of anybody.
> *The President* is fuming. Now and again he steps back
> to the footlights with his back to the audience and says
> 'That's lousy' etc.

At this point a telegram from the Lord Chamberlain's office arrives, and the President, Albert Robinson, intervenes:

> Sorry fellers, you'll have to rewrite. We're not allowed
> to mention Hitler (*semi-collapse of writers*) [This wire
> from the Lord Camberlain says we can't mention Hitler
> or Mussolini or Spain or Abyssinia or Anthony Eden.
> Take that moustache off, Mike. (*Someone who has been
> dressed as Hitler wrenches off his moustache and
> Swastika*)] This letter asks us not to mention Boris Ord
> or King's choirboys. And here's one saying Striptease is
> out.

The irony is that the Footlights were indeed not allowed to mention Hitler – the Lord Chamberlain's blue pencil has cut out all references to the growing international crisis (the section within the square brackets), although the innuendo about the organist and Director of Music of King's Boris Ord is allowed to stand.

At least the Lord Chamberlain allowed them to say that references to Hitler were forbidden, for this was the theme for the revue, as two travellers are sent off in search of replacement material. The sketches reflect the styles and concerns of the time. There is a long parody of Hollywood, where a 'Cambridge' musical is in production, featuring Shirley Temple, Mae West, Joan Crawford, Greta Garbo and Charles Laughton. There is also a separate parody of a

Out at the ends of Empire
And far beyond the pale
Where men are white and always tight
They wait for the English mail.
Then they will stand and drink a toast
Down at the store
Grimed up to the core
As they open their far-flung post.

It's got out East by now
It's got out East by now
Last year's fashions from a last year's play
Are quite the thing in Quetta and bewitching in Bombay
In Singapore and in Ceylon
They know what sort of things are done
They've read the *Tatler* and the *Sketch* that's how
It's got out East by now.

It's got out East by now
It's got out East by now
Last year's dance tunes and the songs we sang
Are crooned by Chinese crooners and planters in Penang
In Rissalpur and in Rangoon
They'll have the talkies pretty soon
They'll have to like the Garbo and Clark Gable
    somehow
They've got out East by now.
It's got out East by now.

It's got out East by now
Last year's crazes and society happenings
Will be the rage with Burma's Very Bright Young
    Things
In Borneo and Sarawak
The news is slowly coming back
Of Princess Pearl and Harry Roy and how
That's got out East by now.

'It's Got Out East By Now'
Patric Dickinson *Full Swing* 1937

Western. A Paris sketch features tap dance and *cancan*; there is a send-up of Italian opera. English styles are dealt with in a skilful Noël Coward/Somerset Maugham song, "It's Got Out East By Now', and a long standing revue subject, the burlesque sea shanty – "Yo Ho for the permanent waves". A witty satire of Greek tragedy is performed in dialogue consisting entirely of English (but Greek sounding) proper names, in effect a nonsense sketch.

When Albert Robinson retired as President in June 1937 he was succeeded by Peter Meyer, a lawyer at Trinity Hall. Meyer was an energetic President who did much to spread the activities of the Footlights beyond their smokers and the May Week revue. At Christmas 1937 the Footlights supplied the cabaret for the Newnham College Ball at the Dorchester in London, which *Granta* (perhaps unaware of the earlier charity matinées) described as '...the first time that any University dramatic club has given a similar performance in town.' In February 1938 the Footlights contributed sketches and the Footlights Band to a Sunday performance at the Festival Theatre in aid of the Festival Club, which had been formed to try to keep the theatre open. The show featured the actress Sarah Churchill and was compèred by her husband, the comedian Vic Oliver. The Footlights also reverted to a much earlier tradition and began to give regular village concert parties. *Granta* commented, 'The Footlights are taking life seriously these days, what with provincial tours and cabarets.'

Peter Meyer took his duties seriously. At the end of his term of office he wrote a letter, now in the club archives, to the Senior Treasurer, Dr Riddiough. The letter (quoted earlier on the subject of Wilkinson) reveals the inner workings of the club. It stands for the kind of machinations that go on in almost any club at any time. Meyer had brought in a new rule tightening up elections for office by requiring proper proposers and seconders:

> ... the practice has been for people to propose their
> friends in a haphazard manner for any position that is
> suggested and the results are sometimes frightful. This
> year for instance two members of the committee were so
> incompetent that we had to force them to resign. We
> gave it out that they had resigned owing to pressure of
> work, but this made us pass this new rule.

Having tightened up the rules however, Meyer, like any President, was anxious to secure his succession. He therefore names five members who would make an ideal committee. 'They are all friends and not only the best actors in the club, but also the most sensible and capable ... They will get together at the beginning of the term (quite informally of

CAMBRIDGE FOOTLIGHTS.

Five years ago THE CAMBRIDGE FOOTLIGHTS CLUB—senior Amateur Dramatic Society in the University—was in none too good a way. The committee of five formed its sole membership. As a desperate expedient, for the first time in its history, women were introduced to play the female parts, to try and popularise productions. But Cambridge wanted its burlesque. So—that failing—in 1935 the Club staged a show called "No More Women"—casting no reflection on talented actresses who had collaborated, but just to show the Footlights had reverted to its old policy of an all-male cast giving topical shows with digs at Cambridge institutions. Since then it has prospered exceedingly, now possesses a wealth of talent, and has wiped off the overdraft. And gave a dinner in celebration. In Fred May's cartoon the Committee are distinguished by their "tails" and various expert performers by their instruments.

The Sketch, 3 March 1937

course) and decide what offices suit them best ... I know this sounds awfully fishy ...' Fishy or not, Meyer's plotting was successful, and four out of his five candidates took over offices of the club in October 1938.

Peter Meyer's Presidency was crowned by *Pure and Simple*, which managed to be a success in spite of the sending-down of several of the expected cast during the Lent

Pure and Simple, 1938

Term and the censoring of their best material. In November 1938 the Lord Chamberlain went so far as to delete these lines from the ADC pantomine:

> They can't eat their sausage and mash
> Because of one man's small moustache.

The owner of the moustache in question was casting a long shadow across Europe. After the Munich crisis the conviction that war was inevitable began to spread. Sir Robert Helpmann recalls, 'It was obvious something was up – the atmosphere began to get a bit hysterical.' Arthur Schlesinger, *Granta's* film critic in 1939, has captured the moment:

As we watched what appeared to be the dissolution of the West, we began to understand that this was the last time we were likely to have to ourselves for a considerable period. It was the long hush, the ominous half-light, the queer silence as before a cyclone strikes. And in the hush and half-light everything became more intense, more hectic, larger than life. Never was Spring more fragrant, May Week more enchanted, gaiety more sustained and desperate, as April and May and June of 1939 passed serenely by, and the clock ticked steadily away.

The *1939 Footlights Revue* (there was no other title) began blithely enough:

> The first week in June
> Hearts like a feather
> We get together, under the moon . . .

The Lord Chamberlain (though forbidding references to Queen Victoria) now permitted topical allusions, and with hindsight there is a sense of contemporary menace in this chorus from the finale (a parody of Verdi's *Aida*):

> Oh Hitler, Franco, Mussolini
> Give peace in our time we beseech ye,
> Stalin, Beck, Roosevelt, Chamberlain
> We pray that you will play the game
> We pray that you will play the game.

The Footlights also made one of their rare journeys into sentiment, with an excerpt from *Tom Brown's Schooldays* and a song from a Pavement Artist. Cambridge bedders were still a target, though there were more intellectual jokes about F. R. Leavis's critical magazine *Scrutiny* and the poets and writers of the day, Auden, Spender, Eliot, Huxley and Isherwood. Sketches were getting shorter and there was more knockabout than 'sophisticated' material.

The revue featured a remarkable music hall turn by a freshman, J. K. O'Edwards, who stepped out of a *tableau vivant* of the painting 'I Dreamt I Dwelt in Marble Halls' and proceeded to lecture on how to play the trombone. The performer is better known as 'Professor' Jimmy Edwards and the sketch, which was first performed at a smoker after Edwards had been spotted playing with the Arimatheans, later acquired a repertoire of RAF slang and became a basis of his post-war act. Part of the joke was that the trombone was full of water, which Edwards emptied into a bucket. His aim was not always good, making Robert Helpmann's choreography in the following ballet number even more difficult to execute. According to Helpmann the funniest man in the show was Peter Rawlinson of Christ's: '... he had a marvellous sort of zany quality, and he should have gone on the stage.' Instead he chose a legal and political career, was Attorney General from 1970 to 1974 and was made a life peer in 1978.

Another 1939 performer, Ronald Millar, did go on the stage. He appeared with Hermione Gingold in *Swinging the Gate* at the Ambassadors in 1940. After service in the navy he went to Hollywood as a screenwriter, returning to England in the mid-1950s. He wrote farces for the Hulberts, and gained a reputation as a stage adaptor of the novels of C. P. Snow. But a political career still waited. Since the 1970s Millar has been a political scriptwriter for the Conservative Party and, as Sir Ronald Millar, he is a speech writer for Margaret Thatcher.

In June 1939 an ARP sketch, 'Purely Academic Precautions', ended with the interruption of an air raid. Although no bombs fell on Cambridge that year, the outbreak of war just before the start of the Michaelmas term changed the life of the University as drastically as it had in 1914. The Footlights gave up their premises in October; the Masonic Hall became a drill hall and the club rooms were taken over as a canteen for Sayles department store. Later they became the Civil Service Club. The Footlights properties and records were stored in the cellar.

The club managed to maintain a shadowy existence, with Jimmy Edwards acting as unofficial secretary. Their main occupation was giving concert parties in village halls for evacuees and visiting nearby RAF stations and troop camps. During the vacation they were invited to Sheffield and performed in village halls there. They offered their services to Basil Dean's troop-entertaining organisation ENSA, but were turned down because '... we do not include amateur companies in our work.' On 4 February 1940 the 'Footlights Concert Party (Bottled)' closed the first half of a Variety Concert at the Cambridge Guildhall in aid of the Red Cross. One member of the party was Donald Hewlett, who went to RADA after service in the Navy. He is best known for his performance as Colonel Reynolds in the army-concert-party television comedy *It Ain't Half Hot Mum*.

On 14 and 15 March the Footlights put on a revue, *Touch and Go*, at the Houghton Hall in Hills Road, but Jimmy Edwards describes it as '... a failure – the hall was too far away from the centre of Cambridge and we didn't have the proper facilities we had at the Arts.' The Senior Treasurer Dr Riddiough had already started to arrange the temporary winding up of the club's affairs. There was no May Week Revue. Instead, on 4 June, the Footlights shared the bill for the Red Cross. After that, the blackout descended.

Footlights Concert Party
in Sheffield, 1940
Jimmy Edwards on far right

Footlights audience at the Dorothy Ballroom, 1952

CHAPTER IV

'La Vie Cambridgienne'

'... witty, intelligent, original and well above the usual run of broadcast satiricial revue'
BBC Audience Survey 1948

The wartime population of Cambridge – academic and civil service evacuees, officers and cadets on short courses, even a few young or unmilitary students – kept the Arts Theatre and the ADC alive until 1945. The Footlights were in suspension, but revues and pantomimes went on. At Christmas 1940 Jimmy Edwards, in training for the RAF, earned unpopularity with his squad when he was released for two weeks to play one of the robbers in the ADC panto, *The Sleeping Cutie*. According to those who saw it, the ADC's *Daffadown Silly* in 1941 was a brilliant mixture of pantomime and revue. Right across the world, past and future members of the Footlights put on shows in tank hangars, battleships, bomb-blasted Italian opera houses, hospitals and prison camps.

The exigencies of wartime favoured 'intimate' rather than spectacular revue. Eric Maschwitz, who had left the BBC for Hollywood in 1937, returned to London and joined the Secret Service. As a cover for an early operation he set up the 1940 revue *New Faces* (which visited the Arts in 1941). The twin stars of wartime revue were Maschwitz's former wife Hermione Gingold, who followed up her pre-war successes at the Gate with the *Sweet and Low* series at the Ambassadors from 1943 to 1947, and Hermione Baddeley, ex-Co-Optimist, and leading light in pre-war Cochran revues. In 1942 'the two Hermiones' shared the bill in *Sky High*. After the war theatre clubs like the New Lindsay and the Watergate carried on the tradition of Norman Marshall's revues. The Gate itself no longer existed. Both it and another home of revue, the Little Theatre, were destroyed in the Blitz.

As after the First War, Cambridge took some time to get back into its stride. Again, things could not be as they were before. *Granta*, somewhat hesitatingly relaunched in March 1946, declared that 'Cambridge is *quite* different from 1939.'

Above all, undergraduates (and undergraduettes) *look* entirely different. Gentlemen students look colourful and characterful, even if dons look exactly the same as they have for fifty years, except for the new OBE after their names on the Residents List. Lady students are gay and painted, even if Cambridge itself is now tatty and drear. Back in the Thirties . . . undergraduates wore flannel college mufflers, Harris Tweed jackets and chalk stripe pants. But now most of them wear wonderful creations such as bow-ties, sheepskin jackets, and stratospheric flying boots. The girls of Girton and Newnham wore suede golfing coats with a zipp, a handy baggy tweed skirt, and a jolly good sensible pair of brogues. Now even the girls cutting things up in the Anatomy Labs sport ravishing pinafores and GI type shirtlets.

Like the rest of the country, Cambridge remained for some time in the chilly grip of austerity. Though spared actual war, undergraduates had either experienced, or were not looking forward to, compulsory National Service – eighteen months or more of organised discomfort in uniform. There was no equivalent to the post-1918 Naval Brigade, but Cambridge was to be the host of the Joint Services Russian Course, an intellectual élite with only a half-hearted respect for the uniform they were occasionally obliged to wear. National Service was not necessarily phoney war: in 1951 Korea produced a fresh crop of ex-officer undergraduates, some with medals, others with mutilations.

For several years Cambridge remained drab, seedy, cold, unpainted and, because of petrol rationing, virtually carless. The food was terrible and, like clothing, rationed. It is little wonder that *Granta* should complain that '. . . nothing prankish has happened since the war . . . can't Cambridge pretend that the war is over, even if UNO can't? The proctors are shockingly under-worked.' The broadcaster Richard Baker, who spent two terms at Cambridge in 1943 and then served in the Navy, returned to this bleak city in 1946. 'The cold was unbelievable, and the food was somewhat limited, to say the least.' The undergraduate population – some 3,000 in 1946, but about to expand rapidly – was a curious mixture of schoolboys and ex-servicemen. The servicemen found it difficult to become undergraduates again. 'It was a terribly restless time, a lot of us found it very difficult to settle down. In the circumstances the theatre was much more attractive than getting back into medieval history.'

Richard Baker's main activities were with the Marlowe and the ADC, but his ability to play the piano drew him into the circle of the Footlights. Given the strength of the Footlights tradition, it was inevitable that the club would be restarted, but the revival began with a row.

The re-animators of the club were Arnold Edinborough, a research student at St Catharine's, and Jonathan Routh (later associated with *Candid Camera*) whose father had been a member. They became, respectively, 'temporary' President and 'temporary' Secretary. However a dispute broke out over the constitution. Edinborough got in touch with Dr C. H. Budd, a pre-war Honorary Vice-President who had a medical practice in Cambridge. Budd told Edinborough about the 'no women' rule, which Edinborough intended to preserve, while Routh wanted women admitted. At the same time others, including David Eady and Kenneth Poolman, were unhappy about the way Edinborough and Routh had selected their committee. At a general meeting at 11 a.m. on 9 March 1947 both Edinborough and Routh resigned. The new President was D. C. Orders, who had been Edinborough's choice as Music Director. Edinborough henceforth devoted his energies to the St Catharine's revue group, the Midnight Howlers, founded in 1922. Routh is said to have pestered the club with suggestions that it should use material by a BBC man, Roy Plomley. The club refused. Dr Budd also left the club during the row, taking with him parts of the archives that have since disappeared.

D. C. – D'Arcy – Orders was a useful choice as President. His parents ran a hairdressing business in Cambridge, so Orders, a jazz enthusiast, had seen some of the Footlights' wartime shows. His flat in Trumpington Street, above the shop, became the club's temporary headquarters. Sadly, the revival coincided with a dispersal. It was quite clear that without funds for rent or to employ a steward, the club could not return to the Masonic Hall. Anyway their premises were now occupied by the Civil Service Club, who were doubtless more reliable tenants. In the Lent Term of 1947 Orders and other members of the new committee went to the Masonic Hall to remove the club's effects from the cellars. Apparently the costumes had gone already, handed over to ENSA some time after D-Day for use on a tour of Europe. Thus Norman Hartnell's and Victor Stiebel's gowns disappeared, ending up, perhaps, in Rome or Vienna. It fell to Peter Tranchell of King's, who succeeded Orders as Music Director, to deal with the orchestra parts. Each pre-1914 show had had its material stored in tin deed boxes with the title painted on the lid. Because there was nowhere to keep them the boxes were emptied and Tranchell, much to his distress, had to throw all the band parts away. Three minute books, a few sheets of music, some programmes and lyric books, some framed photographs and the tin box from *Cheer-Oh Cambridge!* are all that survive. Some material was transferred to a cellar in the King's Parade, but that too is now empty.

D'Arcy Orders energetically set about bringing the club back to life. He printed a leaflet advertising the Footlights as 'a Social and Dramatic Club erring towards Original Light Stage Entertainment, OPEN TO MEN ONLY', and appealed for 'Actors, Musicians, Script Writers, Song Writers, Dancers and Impresarios.' He wrote to past members asking for funds; Peter Meyer and Sir Robert Ricketts were among the past Presidents who responded. There was encouragement from Davy Burnaby, Harold Warrender and Peter Haddon; Eric Maschwitz sent £5. On 6 March 1947 the club held a smoker in the Oak Room of the Dorothy Café in Sidney Street. The Oak Room had no stage, but the long T-shape of the room provided a performing space across the end. The Dorothy ('the Dot') also had a ballroom and became the regular venue for smokers and club dinners. Orders also got in touch with pre-war senior members of the club. Rottenburg, in retirement, suggested that they revived some of the club's past successes, which did not fit the bill. Freddie Brittain, of Jesus, agreed to become Senior Treasurer. Brittain, who had a passion for music hall and pantomime, and was a keen supporter of the Jesus Roosters' Club (a jokey revue and debating society), had joined the Footlights in 1932 at the instigation of one of his pupils, the 1922/3 President, John Coates. Like Rottenburg, he made guest appearances in pre-war shows. After the war he kept in the background, though he was able to be of service to the club when he was asked, as Senior Proctor, to censor the May Week revue. He explained to the Vice-Chancellor that he was a member of the club. That was the reason for asking him, the Vice-Chancellor replied.

There was no time to attempt a full-scale revue in 1947. The show was rehearsed for a week in the number one

FOOTLIGHTS
DRAMATIC CLUB
(President: D. C. ORDERS, Trinity Hall)

is a Social and Dramatic Club erring towards Original Light Stage Entertainment

OPEN TO MEN ONLY

- **Actors**
- **Musicians**
- **Script writers**
- **Song writers**
- **Dancers**
- **Impressarios**

are invited to

Auditions and Meetings held

Mondays, 7-10 p.m. at 53, Trumpington Street
Tuesdays, 7-10 p.m. at Stephen Joseph's Rooms,
48, Jesus Lane

or contact The Hon. Sec. B. GRADWELL, K3, Queens

1947

1947 Revue. D'Arcy Orders, Ken Willis, Bernard Langley, John Boston, George Davis, Tony Galloway

studio of Miller's the music and gramophone shop. It was put on at the ADC theatre, the only time this was ever done. The music was played on two pianos, with Richard Baker as one of the accompanists. The Lord Chamberlain requested the removal of the chamber pots mentioned in the stage directions to the Gilbert and Sullivan parody, 'Prudence'.

'Prudence', 1947

The revue still aimed at Cambridge — its obscure terminology, its clubs and cafés — and carried a full complement of bullers, bedders and proctors. Michael Westmore guyed the latest intellectual fashions in a 'historical and empirical discussion of literature and the cinema'. Charles Parker, the future producer of 'Radio Ballads' for the BBC made a hit as a clown. The talent scouts were down from London. The play publishers Samuel French bought two songs with music by Peter Tranchell, together with a sketch by David Eady, for twenty guineas.

YANK: Excuse me porter, is Mr Bell up yet?
PORTER: Full term don't begin till Tuesday, Sir.
YANK: I know, but —
PORTER: I'll have a look Sir.
YANK: Thanks bud, — I mean —
PORTER: No Sir, Mr Bell is not down.
YANK: Good, then he's up.
PORTER: No Sir, Mr Bell is not down.
YANK: All right, that's fine he must be up. I'll go and see him.
PORTER: *(producing large book):* No Sir, if Mr Bell is not down, he's not up. *(exit)*
YANK: I'm over from the States to study higher mathematics
And I find it comes much easier than these verbal acrobatics
I think the boys are simply swell and the proctors grand,
But there's lots of things at Cambridge I just don't understand.
I always thought a fellow was a regular guy
But here they're only lecturers and terribly dry.
My tutor said the backs had got some mighty fine views,
He thought that I was crazy when I said 'The backs? Whose?'

'A Yank at Cambridge'
The Footlights Revue 1947

1947 Revue. Charles Parker,
Ben Gradwell, Ian Clements

Kenneth Poolman, who with David Eady formed an elegant clubmen-and-piano double act, was asked by Rank to try out for the film *The Blue Lagoon* opposite Jean Simmons, though he did not get the part.

The 1947 revue (there was no title) was also given a Sunday performance at the Ambassadors in London, Hermione Gingold's theatre. This was not difficult to arrange, for the Footlights producer was her son, Stephen Joseph. (Eric Maschwitz's support for the club led to the unexpected reunion with his former wife.) D'Arcy Orders recalls being firmly advised by Miss Gingold to abandon the stage: '. . . you have a marked lack of talent'. Orders followed her advice and became an accountant, but he kept up his connection with Stephen Joseph and helped him to found The Studio Theatre. Joseph, whom Baker remembers as 'a great inspirer and provocateur' was a pioneer of the theatre in the round. The Studio Theatre travelled from hall to hall on the back of a lorry, but had a summer base at the Library Theatre in Scarborough, which continues in the round under Alan Ayckbourn's direction. The Studio Theatre also spawned the Victoria (a former cinema) in Stoke-on-Trent. The Studio Theatre folded with the onset of Stephen Joseph's illness in 1965; he died in 1967.

Rehearsals 1948.
Stephen Joseph talks to Peter Tranchell (left) and John Sutherland (right)

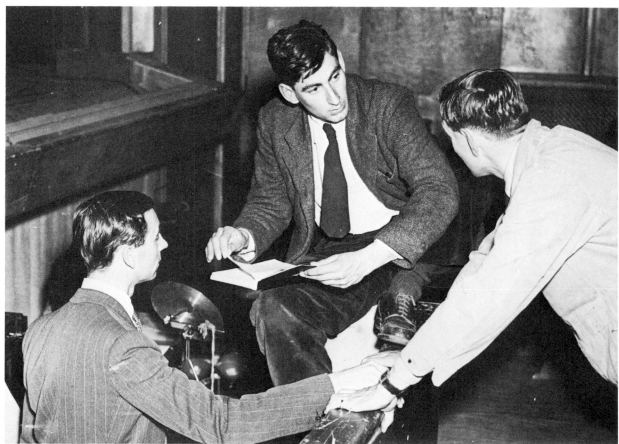

After the modest success of summer 1947 membership picked up again. Fifty-three resident members are listed in October of that year. The club lost the exclusive atmosphere of the pre-war period; instead they were pushing for members (though these still had to be elected). In the *Varsity Handbook* for 1947-48 the club is described as existing 'to cultivate the light stage and social intercourse', with subscriptions at 10/6d. They had very little money and made no great efforts to find a club room. The Dorothy did for the thrice termly smokers (the room held about 80); otherwise the members used the usual Cambridge theatrical haunts — the club room of the ADC, the Whim Coffee House in Trinity Street, the salad bar at the Arts, the bars of the Bath Hotel and the Baron of Beef. On 13 February 1948 the club held its first dinner for ten years, at the Dorothy Café, with Norman Hartnell and Jimmy Edwards as guests of honour.

The revival of the club did not escape the administrator of the Arts Theatre, Norman Higgins. Knowing that revue was a commercial certainty, he offered them £100 to put on the 1948 May Week Revue at the Arts. (When the show indeed proved a sell-out he arranged for a hundred guinea donation from the Arts Trust and passed on a fee of twenty-five guineas from the BBC.) *La Vie Cambridgienne*, again directed by Stephen Joseph, was altogether a more ambitious affair.

1948

As the title suggests, the humour still had a local focus. The distinctive atmosphere of Cambridge at that time is caught in 'Alma Paters', a song by Ian Clements and Ben Gradwell for two pram-pushing undergraduates struggling to complete war degrees.

> Rock-a-bye baby, in your first year,
> Daddy is busy, Tripos is near —
>> If Daddy fails
>> Then what will befall?
> Down they'll send Daddy, family and all.
>> Varsity Fathers
>> Husbands of the war
>> Came back to Cambridge
>> Slightly more mature.
>> We prefer
>> Academic lives,
> We're used to lectures from our loving wives.
>> Just as you'd expect
>> When baby cries
>> We croon intellect —
>> ual lullabies
>> Through the night
>> Till the blighter stops
>> Third Class in Tripos
>> But we're first-class pops!

The revue poked fun at Cambridge café life with 'Cambridge Tour' by David Eady and Kenneth Poolman – ' "Hullo Michael..." "Hullo Jon..." "Missed breakfast again, old man..." ' – and at the 'Dramatic Hangers On', the ambitious spear carriers of the ADC and the Marlowe. *La Vie Cambridgienne* took note of the final admission of women to full status as members of the University in 1948. The Vice-Chancelleuse (John Marriot) sings,

> Now the final stronghold of mysogenation
>   Has tottered in final collapse
> Now that we have won complete emancipation, girls
>   Let's be nice to the chaps.

> Full eligibility to graduation
>   Has won us our place on the maps
> We've taken the fence so damn the expense, and
>   Let's be nice to the chaps.

The Footlights' traditional skill in innuendo featured in a cleaned-up version of one of the songs written by Stephen Joseph to replace the traditional bawdy numbers sung at smokers.

> A sensible man goes as far as he can
> Up, up, up, up, – up the Cam.

'Up the Cam', 1948

La Vie Cambridgienne featured contributions from two new members from Trinity, Simon Phipps and the Trinity College Chaplain, Geoffrey Beaumont. Phipps first went up to Trinity in January 1940 and played in an ADC concert party for the troops before volunteering for the Army after Dunkirk. Following a distinguished career in the Coldstream Guards, where he won the Military Cross, he resumed his degree course in 1947. Phipps had strong family connections with revue – Joyce Grenfell was a cousin, so too was the song writer and actor Nicholas Phipps. (His friendship with Princess Margaret also lent a certain *cachet* through her patronage of Footlights revues.) Trinity College

Simon Phipps prepares
for *Always in June*, 1949

has its own tradition of college revues and, having put on
shows for his battalion, Phipps was called on to produce the
Trinity Revue. This brought him into contact with Geoffrey
Beaumont, an extraordinary character who served as
Chaplain from 1948 to 1953. He smoked too much, drank
far too much and had a fertile talent for tunes. Phipps – who
was ordained in 1950, succeeded Beaumont as Chaplain and
is now Bishop of Lincoln – recalls Beaumont's rooms as
being 'like a pub'. Beaumont was 'a deeply comic character'
and his musical skill loosened Phipp's own talent for words.
The first result of the collaboration, heard at Trinity, and
then sung in both the 1948 and 1949 Footlights revues, was
the celebrated 'Botticelli Angel':

> I'm a Botticelli Angel, and I'm bored
> At looking sweet and faintly over-awed
>   And I feel so bloody silly
>   Holding up my Eaden lily
> In that way that Botticelli so adored.
>
> My girl friend in that cloud there with a sword
> Got so sleepy at a sitting that she snored
>   And of course, that drove old Botti
>   Absolutely potty
> He was livid, and my dear, I simply roared.

But please, Mr Botticelli
Please, let me have a little fun
Immortality's all very well, I
Admit, but I am only twenty-one.
I want to see life, I want to go gay
I want to throw my halo and my harp away,
I want to go places and make a lot of noise,
Oh, and dance the hokey-cokey with the Medici boys.

It used to seem a little bit far fetched
Just standing in my nightie being sketched
   Or posing as the Muses
   With several other floosies
Or as a martyr, being quietly stretched.

Worst of all was when old Botti made us wear
Hardly any clothes, and how he used to stare
   And I've never, never been as
   Shy as in the Birth of Venus
When I'd nothing on at all except my hair.

The song with its verbal wit, cultural elegance and overtones of theatrical camp, is a classic among revue numbers. It was bought by Samuel French and, to the author's knowledge, was still being performed at Oxford cabarets in the mid-1960s.

In June 1948 the talent scouts were up in Cambridge again, and this time the BBC Light Programme broadcast a half-hour selection from the revue, with Jack Hulbert and Cicely Courtneidge contributing to the finale. (A circular from D'Arcy Orders asked for 'hearty laughters' (sic) to attend the recording.) Laurie Lister began his regular visits to Cambridge in search of sketches for the series of revues he produced in London in the 1950s. There is some division of opinion about the attitude of the Footlights to the professional stage at this time. The style of revues came from London and it was gratifying when numbers were taken up, but Phipps does not think that there was a conscious professional aim. Richard Baker (who also wrote for *La Vie Cambridgienne*) points out on the other hand that the loss of time in war service meant that a professional attitude had to be adopted: '. . . the mood was not one where one wasted time.' Certainly a steady stream of Footlights members made their way into the theatre or the BBC, and have since made their mark in radio and television. John Morley, outrageous as a temple dancer in 1948, began a career in musicals and as a cabaret performer, and since 1965 has become the country's most prolific writer of pantomimes.

Consciously or unconsciously, the Footlights revues were turning outwards, away from purely Cambridge references and 'undergraduate' humour. This was partly because these undergraduates were generally older men, but even eighteen-year-olds like Julian Slade, who came up to Trinity in October 1948, were beginning to perceive that undergraduate theatre was a direct route to the professional stage. 'It never occurred to me to be a musical comedy writer, I went up to Cambridge with visions of being Alec Guinness. I had two ambitions, to join the Footlights and the ADC.'

Slade also had, however, a facility for words and tunes, and his talent was quickly detected by Geoffrey Beaumont:

> Trinity is a very big college, and you can easily get lost there, as a personality, but Geoffrey Beaumont invited me round to his rooms for a drink – he had the capacity to invite anybody. His rooms were full every night with an extraordinary collection of people, not just undergraduates, there were policemen, tramps, even burglars I'm sure. He made me one of his entertainers, much to the horror of Peter Shaffer who had rooms above and was working for a First. There was of course a piano, and Geoffrey transcribed my music – I couldn't write music, I didn't know what a bar line was. Geoffrey made it into something.

Beaumont encouraged Slade to perform for the Footlights and the first number he ever performed at a smoker was a tribute to the current Queen of Revue:

> It really seems almost too bad to be true
> But I'm once again in *another* Revue!
> By 'another' I mean it's exactly the same
> (Though we did take the trouble to alter the name).
> After 'Sweetest and Lowest' had run for two years
> Alan Melville said 'Gingold, my pet it appears
> 'That the public will swallow whatever we brew
> 'So I'll stir up some little poisons for you.'
> Well – here's the result. It's called 'Early to Bed'.
> The Lord Chamberlain gave it his blessing and said
> 'I don't think I've ever enjoyed a show more –
> 'Why, it's *Sweetah* – and *Lowah* – than *Evah* before!'
>> We'll have the same old jokes
>> And the same old pokes
>> At the same old Theatrical crew. . . .

(Slade once sang the song in Beaumont's rooms for the other Hermione, Hermione Baddeley, who found his impersonation cruelly perfect.)

Slade had a small part in the 1949 Footlights *Always in*

1949

Summer is the time of year
When nicely brought-up debutantes appear
Upon the parquet
Of London's white-slave black market,
And mothers, with a sigh,
Contemplate, how hard they've got to try
To make their girls embody the suggestion
That suitable young men should pop the question.

Simon Phipps *Always in June* 1949

Julian Slade, Simon Phipps, *Always in June*, 1949

June as a *débutante*, with Simon Phipps (still in military moustache) as his chaperone. Julian More, the future author of *Grab Me A Gondola* and *Expresso Bongo*, made his Footlights début in the same cast. The show was stylishly produced by Phipps as President, employing the theme of the four seasons. Apparently undeterred by Julian Slade's piano playing, the future playwright Peter Shaffer contributed a neat theatrical parody, 'The Collapse, or Are You in Danger'.

'Autumn', *Always in June*, 1949

CHARLES *(blandly):* I really am glad you were all of you able to come. It makes such a change in the dreary round of work.

VALERIE: Yes, indeed, how right you are. *(aside to MARGARET)* Little does he think I know he got a Third in Part One.

MARGARET *(quickly aside to VALERIE):* A Special. *(aloud)* They tell me you work terribly hard, Charles. You certainly look peaky enough for it.

DAVID *(aside, quickly):* Cocaine!

ADRIAN *(aside, quickly):* Hashish. But I can't find out where he gets it.

VALERIE: It certainly can't be good for you to work like that. It may easily ruin your health. I'm sure David and Adrian aren't that industrious.

MARGARET *(aside to audience):* I'm damn sure they're not!

CHARLES: Ah, but they are lucky enough not to need to. For me it's effort, effort all the time.

MARGARET *(aside to audience):* A pity he didn't show a little more assembling this tea. The whole meal has been remarkably schizophrenic.

ADRIAN *(aside to MARGARET):* That is, without exception, the most meaningless aside I have ever heard.

'The Collapse, or
Are You in Danger'
Peter Shaffer *Always in June* 1949

The BBC were definitely interested in the Footlights as a source of recruits. Simon Phipps was contacted by the Chief Assistant of the Light Programme, who offered to make him 'a worthwhile proposal' if he wished to continue revue writing. The Light Programme again broadcast excerpts, though at 11 o'clock at night. A confidential BBC audience survey revealed a high appreciation index of 70 (the previous year's was below average with 54).

> The sketches and lyrics made a very favourable impression indeed. Adverse comment was sparse and diffuse; one or two thought the parody of church choirs 'irreverent' and a few complained that there were occasional allusions too local for the wider listening audience. The bulk of the comment, however, was unqualified praise; the whole show was said to be witty, intelligent, original and well above the usual run of broadcast satirical revue.

For the first time since the war the revue had an orchestra, of thirteen. The overture was a splendid potpourri of operatic themes arranged and conducted by the musical director Peter Tranchell, resplendent in a silver spangled jacket. A trumpeter burst out of a stage box to play a snatch from *Leonora* and from then on the atmosphere was set. Simon Phipps recalls, 'On the second night the Jesus Boat Club always took the first three rows. You had to get them in the first minute, otherwise they ruined the show. If you got them, they were a magnificent *claque.*'

Music, with tune writers like Geoffrey Beaumont and Julian Slade, and brilliant musicians and orchestrators like Peter Tranchell (who became Director of Studies in Music at Caius), was a strong feature of post-war Footlights revues, but then music was very much a part of Cambridge University life. King's had its own choral tradition; most colleges have organ and choral scholarships and are able to run their own orchestras and ensembles besides supplying members of the Music and Operatic Societies. The Professor of Music, Patrick Hadley, did not discourage extra-mural activities. In 1948 the teacher and composer Thurston Dart was happy to play the harmonium in the pit for his parodic arrangements of plainsong, psalm-singing and Vaughan Williams in 'Three Choirs', to words by Simon Phipps.

Julian Slade seized the musical opportunities. Invited by Geoffrey Beaumont to write a Trinity Revue he produced a 'revue opera' *Bang Goes the Meringue!* which was such a success that the ADC revived it the following term. While still contributing to the Footlights, Slade was commissioned by the ADC to write a May Week musical for 1951, *Lady May*, directed by John Barton. The administrator of the

Peter Tranchell, 1949

'Three Choirs', 1948

Arts, Norman Higgins, found him a job with the Bristol Old Vic, and it was there that in 1954 he wrote *Salad Days*. *Salad Days* begins where most Footlights revues ended, with a sentimental farewell to Alma Mater. The lovers in the story, Timothy and Jane, begin in BA gowns, 'symbols of the departing graduate', surrounded by a chorus of singing and dancing dons. They recognise the danger to which every Cambridge graduate is exposed.

> JANE. Do you realise, Tim, what we are leaving behind?
> TIMOTHY: Shall we be *able* to leave it behind?

The name of Cambridge is never specifically invoked, but the tunes and turns of the story echo Cambridge revues and smokers, filtered (and, as he says, much improved) by the experience Slade had had as a professional. Meanwhile the gap between Cambridge and the professionals was narrowing all the time.

In 1951 *A Flash in the Cam* set the style of revue towards which the Footlights had been working since 1947. The Festival of Britain made a handy thread on which to hang a series of sketches and 'point' songs on the topics of the day, from the Great Exhibition to the Gaumont British Newsreel. They did not neglect more traditional Footlights themes such as a burlesque ballet, 'The Dons Go A'Begging', featuring a 'bedderina' and dancing bulldogs. Nor did they forget to return to May Week for the closing number. There was a large cast, the music was tuneful and the sets were designed by Malcolm Burgess. Burgess, a research student at Corpus, was to have to choose between a career as a pro-

1950

The Festival of Britain
Really has begun
Don't you come to see
Our austerity
But come for the sun
And if you find it's raining
It's useless your complaining:
The visitors will find
That our posters remind
Them the sun shines most of the year.

Opening chorus *A Flash in the Cam* 1951

Our roving camera reports! *(business of aeroplane)*
Workmen on the Festival site manage to erect the
Skylon just in time. Our gallant cameraman risked his
life trying to get these wonderful pictures. *(Mime of
three men putting it up, business of it falling and being
put up again)* Cambridge during May Week. Our interviewer is standing on King's Parade. *(Business of a
couple walking down street)*
INTERVIEWER: Good morning, ah . . . I see you have been
to a May Ball? I expect you enjoyed it immensely.
GIRL: Enormously. It was tremendous fun – wasn't it,
John?
MAN: Yes – awfully – really.
INTERVIEWER: What I loved so much about it was that it
reminded me so much – of Oxford.

'Newsrevue'
Ian Kellie, Michael Miller, Peter Jeffrey *A Flash in the
Cam* 1951

Opening number *A Flash in the Cam*, 1951

fessional designer and becoming a Lecturer in Russian. He chose the latter, but continued to design some of the most elegant and colourful sets that the Arts Theatre had seen. He also contributed décor to London revues.

Malcolm – 'Malky' to his friends – also set the tone for the more effete among Cambridge theatricals. It is said that his opening lines on arrival at Cambridge were 'I'm fresh – are you?' Theatrical camp is no longer in fashion and it is hard to describe: Frederic Raphael caricatured the type in the Cambridge homosexual Denis Porson in *The Glittering*

Malcolm Burgess: 'Seaside' set design for *Tip and Run*, 1952

Prizes. Homosexuality undoubtedly contributed to the style and manner of camp, but the most heterosexual of undergraduates adopted it as a defence against, among other things, the prevailing glumness of post-war Britain. By 1951 – as the Festival of Britain was intended to demonstrate – the worst of austerity was over. Colour, gaiety (in the then innocent sense of the word) and above all a sense of style was the thing. Poise and pose were often confused, and sometimes this rebounded. John Pardoe, who came up to Corpus in 1953, recalls that one year 'Malky decided that the colour of the revue was going to be *sepia*. He was most upset when all the reviewers referred to "dung-coloured" sets.'

Style was not exclusively a Footlights concern. The *Varsity Handbook* for 1950 gave advice to freshmen on

'Etiquette in Cambridge' : 'Don't wear khaki shirts or SD trousers. No one here is remotely interested in your career as a National Serviceman.'

> The *ton* or *beau monde*, pinnacle of *arriviste* ambition, divides its time between Trinity, Miller's, Newmarket, and London; the world of the cloth waistcoat and the flat cap, mainly composed of Legal and other Smoothies, is to be found in the English Speaking Union, the K.P., or the Pitt Club; the academic intelligentsia frequents the tea-room of the University Library; the politicians may be seen boring each other to extinction in the Union; the Cambridge writers and actors (few of whom either write or act) are often to be heard in the Copper Kettle and the Whim. Don't forget that the Cambridge habits of bright bitchiness and pseudo-Noël Coward smartness must be discarded if you wish to make any friends . . . .

Varsity was hardly innocent of bright bitchiness itself, but after the success of *A Flash in the Cam* it warned freshmen coming up in October 1951 that the Footlights revue '. . . is treated as the major event in the theatrical year from a popular point of view, and seats are difficult to obtain.' The club had regained its place at the centre of Cambridge society.

A Flash in the Cam opened up two new areas of experience for the Footlights. A one hour version of the revue was presented nightly during the vacation at the Dorchester Hotel in London; there were protests from the

I'm a cuddlesome kittenish cutie
And I'm a jolly bad hat
We both talk a bogus lot of bosh
Our party patter is pat
We meet at the Ritz for tea for two
And Charleston through the night
In the morning skies are blue
And we're too utterly bright.

'Gosh, How I love My Cloche'
Julian More *A Flash in the Cam* 1951

'Gosh How I love My Cloche'. Peter Firth, Warden Miller, Peter Jeffrey and Angus Thomas at the Dorchester, 1951

Variety Artistes' Federation, but the Vice-Chancellor raised no objection, 'provided we behaved ourselves.' For the first time the club appeared on television, with a half hour broadcast for the BBC. (The only service then operating. The club had made a couple of newsreel appearances before the war. A 'Bedder Sketch' was shot for Paramount newsreel in November 1932.)

The glamour associated with television, a season at the Dorchester and a photo-feature in *The Tatler* was all part of the aura that began to emanate, not just from the Footlights, but the whole of Cambridge Theatre. Reminiscing for *Granta* in 1964 the drama critic of the *Observer* (and a former critic for *Granta*), Ronald Bryden, asked himself why the theatre, above all the professions except possibly journalism, came to be such a focus of undergraduate ambition.

> Probably it was one of the effects of austerity, lingering on like a wasting convalescence six years after the war. From rationed coal, sausage dinners and headlines about Mossadeq you could escape to the fuggy warmth of the Arts or the ADC, to hot orange lights, gold costumes and great red veined slabs of Elizabethan self-assertion. Escape was the operative word: Anouilh, of the *pièces roses* was the great name in those days, and Giraudoux, Christopher Fry, the southern rococco of Tennesee Williams. Olivier's Shakespeare films, Alec Guinness's Ealing Comedies, were ringing round the world — in this, at least — Britain still seemed to lead to something or other. It was also, in that near celibate society, a place you could see pretty girls.
>
> Whatever the reasons, everyone was theatre mad. The tiny ADC stage was busy every night of term with rehearsals, nurseries, club performances. Enthusiastic amateur groups queued to use halls and lecture rooms. There were plays in courts, Fellows' Gardens, chapels, common rooms. Visionaries discussed staging *The Merchant of Venice* on punts. Colleges would limit societies to one play a term; new clubs with identical memberships would spring up overnight. Supervisors would forbid their pupils any further acting before Tripos only to find them a week later appearing behind pseudonyms and false beards in French Club productions of Racine, Russian Course productions of Chekhov.

The ruling spirit of this theatrical whirlpool was George Rylands of King's. He had the right connections with the London world, was a Governor of the Old Vic and Chairman of the Cambridge Arts Trust. He directed John Gielgud in *Hamlet* in 1945 and he was engaged in recording with the Marlowe the complete cycle of Shakespeare plays for the British Council. The conductor Raymond Leppard, one of the Footlights' musical contributors, has described Rylands as '. . . the epitome of theatrically-orientated sophistication. He always seemed to know so much and, as we gradually found out, did; much more than we used to give him credit for at those moments of extreme exasperation at his bland, devastating demolition of our more pretentious views. Lovable and maddening at the same time, he was, I think, a true educator and the majority of our current theatrical talents owe him something; or would vehemently deny it, which comes to the same thing.' Rylands' great concern – and contribution to post-war British theatre – was for a proper understanding and speaking of the verse in English classical drama. He had as his assistant a student, and then Fellow, of King's, John Barton, who set vigorous action to Rylands' carefully spoken words. In the early 1950s John Barton and an undergraduate at St Catharine's, Peter Hall, were the twin directorial stars. Around them clustered a galaxy of greater and lesser names who were to form a fresh constellation in the 1960s, when Peter Hall became Director of the Royal Shakespeare Company and John Barton left Cambridge to become his associate.

Ronald Bryden was not exaggerating when he wrote of the proliferation of drama clubs. The University restricted each club to one production a term, so it was necessary to create more clubs to fill the demand for productions. Eight university drama groups are listed in 1952, among them the Comedy Theatre Group – which existed to perform classical comedy, Sheridan, Beaumarchais, Molière – and the University Actors, a group so exclusive that it had no formal constitution, and whose membership was defined by the invitation to appear in a production. On the lighter side the example of Julian Slade encouraged the formation of the Musical Comedy Club by Leslie Bricusse in 1953. Its membership interlocked with the Footlights; its first production, *Lady at the Wheel*, had a book by Frederic Raphael, lyrics by Leslie Bricusse, music by Robin Beaumont and Leslie Bricusse and décor by Malcolm Burgess. The following year Peter Tranchell's *Zuleika Dobson* was taken up by a professional management, although the subsequent London production was a failure. The Pantomime Club also surfaces in 1953, and later the Footlights faced mild competition from the Cambridge Light Entertainment Society.

There were almost as many revue and cabaret groups in the individual colleges as college boats. The Trinity Revue in the Lent Term was a well-established institution; St John's customarily mounted a revue during the week running up to Poppy Day, the Saturday before Remembrance Day and the

578—*The Sketch*—June 18, 1952

L. to r., the Hon. Andrew Davidson, Miss Judy Birdwood, wardrobe mistress for 38 years; Mr. M. Burgess and Miss S. Grundy. Mr. Davidson wrote much of the book and music for *Tip and Run*.

During the performance of the sketch called *Turn of the Century*, which is about the arrival of Bleriot in this country. The Footlights cast is all-male.

FOOTLIGHTS AT CAMBRIDGE

The clever young president with his parents, Viscount and Viscountess Davidson; she has just been made a D.B.E. in the Birthday Honours.

" Footlights " has acquired a special meaning at Cambridge : there is no need to add " Dramatic Club " because the yearly May Week production—which was suspended during the war — grows steadily more famous. This year the show, at the Cambridge Arts Theatre, was called *Tip and Run*. It ran to full houses for a fortnight from June 2, and the standard of writing and acting was as high as ever. Andrew Davidson, this year's Footlights president, devised and produced the revue, which was lightly flavoured with cricket—the two halves were called First Innings and Second Innings, and mad chaps in blazers were drawn jumping for joy on the cover of the programme.

By " THE SKETCH " special photographer, Harold White, F.I.B.P., F.R.P.S.

Mr. Davidson, who is studying Geography at Pembroke College, with Mr. Malcolm Burgess, of Corpus Christi, who was responsible for the settings of *Tip and Run* and is writing a thesis on the Russian theatre.

Mr. David Morgan Rees, secretary of the Footlights, was photographed in the wings after his last appearance as a Calypso singer.

Two honorary members of the Footlights : Mr. Donald Beves, Don of King's, and Mr. Leonard Thompson, taken during the interval.

Above: Mr. Peter Firth (*right*) and Mr. Robin Tuck are photographed with King's Chapel and the famous backs behind them. *Below*: they appear in a dressing-room shot, brooding over a little old wig between their appearances on the stage. Mr. Firth is junior treasurer of the Footlights and Mr. Tuck vice-president.

Above: With their costumes, outside the stage door, are Mr. Michael Young (*left*) and Mr. Kenneth Alexander, both of Trinity. *Below*: they are in Mr. Young's room with Raoul Dufy prints as pin-ups. Their respective studies are Theology and History; and Law and Science. Mr. Alexander is a son of Sir William Alexander.

Mr. Jimmy Edwards, one of the many old Footlighters now famous, helps Mr. Peter Stephens to adjust a version of the well-known moustache.

The Sketch, 18 June 1952

Dear Angus Wilson, you're so elegant
And most intelligent, we must confess.
I think I know what 1920 meant.
It holds a sentiment that I express . . . yes . . .
The night clubs, the right clubs,
Were frightfully glaring
The flappers were daring
With gay love affairs.
The Carlton-Charleston
Was terribly classy
But now it's passé
And nobody cares.
I'd put the cloche right back
But now it's too late
And golly, gosh, alack
We're right out of date.
Because the instinct's – extinct,
As dead as a Do-Do-
Vo-do-de-o-do-do
Vo-do-de-o-do.

Tony Becher *Out of the Blue* 1954

1952, programme design by Mark Boxer

one licensed Rag Day of the year. St Catharine's Midnight Howlers had been going since 1922; at Queens' the College drama society, the Bats, also attempted to rival the Footlights. 'Christ's Pieces' came into being in 1953, St John's Unicorns at about the same time; Downing College founded the Jabberwocks in 1956.

Though sometimes challenged, and sometimes machinated against, the Footlights remained the focus of comic ambition. Its committee was courted as it went from college smoker to college smoker, picking out likely members and likely material. Though no longer patronised by aristocrats and racing drivers, it had become once more an exclusive club, with an emphasis on 'elegance', and even a certain air of High Church, Anglo-Catholicism about it. Jonathan Miller recalls that in 1954 there were two novels to be seen reading: Angus Wilson's *Hemlock and After* or Kingsley Amis's *Lucky Jim*. The Footlights favoured Angus Wilson. (Later, he was made an Honorary Member.)

The intention of the Footlights was to produce a revue aimed at an intelligent, would-be sophisticated audience, a revue more literate than was possible in London, and more barbed, though the intention was to sting rather than to wound. Criticism took place within a charmed circle, and what was to become known as the Establishment indulged the rebelliousness of favoured sons. The revues of 1952 and 1953, *Tip and Run* and *Cabbages and Kings*, received contrasting treatment from their respective critics in the *Cambridge Review*. Simon Raven (the future novelist) chose to make his notice of *Tip and Run* into his own valedictory address to Cambridge. The Footlights, he wrote, had captured the true spirit of the place:

> a place of contrast, and contrast is the essence of humour. But contrast also implies poetry (life and death, love and loss, youth and age – such are the poet's main themes when all is said) and, in particular, nostalgic poetry. So Cambridge to me means humour and lyricism, the two qualities which its abundant contrasts provide: and there in the end, are the two great qualities of the current May Week production. It has caught them, it has caught Cambridge.

Raven managed to say very little about the actual production:

> Whether it was the music, the enchanting sets, the swiftness of the changes or the deftness of the costumes, whatever it was, the production realised for me the spirit of four years of misty autumns and green springs, of gaiety and neurosis, of non-existent bank balances

CABBAGES AND KINGS

	OVERTURE	The Orchestra
1	LET'S PRETEND words and music by leslie bricusse and robin beaumont	The Company
2	FOLK SONG by robin bazeley-white	Robin Bazeley-White
3	INDIA RUBBER MAN words and music by peter firth	Bernard Barr Gerald Manners
4	MANY QUESTIONS by frederic raphael and tony becher	Dermot Hoare David Conyers Peter Stephens Dennis Millmore Frederic Raphael Tony Becher Gerard Roessink
5	OLD FOLKS AT HOME lyric by leslie williamson music: traditional arr. robin beaumont and leslie bricusse	Peter Firth Leslie Bricusse
6	SOAP by peter townsend and colin pearson	Peter Townsend Robin Bazeley-White

W
I
N
E

Elizabeth R
1953

7	DETECTIVE STORY by leslie bricusse frederic raphael and tony becher	Frederic Raphael Tony Becher Leslie Bricusse Bernard Barr David Jenkins David Conyers Peter Stephens
8	WEIRD SISTERS words by colin pearson music by robin beaumont	Kennedy Thom Dennis Millmore Dermot Hoare
9	RUSSIAN SALAD words by malcolm burgess music by peter tranchell	Peter Firth David Jenkins Gerald Manners Bernard Barr
10	NO PROGRESS by peter townsend and neville hudson	Peter Townsend Geoffrey Brown Peter Stephens
11	TATTERS from an old MS.	Frederic Raphael Peter Stephens Robin Bazeley-White Kennedy Thom Dennis Millmore David Conyers Geoffrey Brown
12	FOOL by colin pearson	David Jenkins
13	CURIOUSER AND CURIOUSER words and music by peter firth	The Company

W
I
T

AN INTERVAL OF FIFTEEN MINUTES

Elizabeth R
1953

Programme designs by Mark Boxer

and vast bills, of vacuity and intensity, of love and hate: four years of contrast, four years of wit on the one hand and poetry on the other; four years, in a word, of Cambridge.

This lyricism plainly called for an answer from Raven's successor, the future historian and critic Richard Mayne (who had himself performed with the Footlights). His review of *Cabbages and Kings* in 1953 presents the other side of the coin. The revue is:

the annual reincarnation of a favourite Cambridge myth. We know that there'll be some theatrical parodies, jokes at the expense of the *Tatler* (it can afford it), some galumphing ballet, a sad little song, men dressed as women, a sentimental finale, and lots of local jokes about smarties at parties and tea at the Whim, hunting and punting, etc, with Kim. It's a myth that has

High in the hills of England's historic Ely island, near historic Sherwood Forest, home of Walt Disney's Richard Todd, stands the historic University of Cambridge in the county of Cambridgeshire, bordered on all sides by Oxfordshire, Grantchester and Girtonshire. It is generally agreed that Cambridge, which takes its name from Cambridge, Massachusetts, home of our own historic Harvard University, was founded in 1066, though some claim it was as early as the Eleventh Century.

Cambridge has many royal colleges. Here we see Queens' College, known as the Rex, and King's College, known as the Backs. A royal city indeed. Here we see Professor Sir George Daddy Rylands, affectionately known as the Seat of Learning, taking tea at the historic Whim Café, where in 1066 King Alfred burned the cakes – and by this symbol the Whim Café honours his memory even today.

Here in the River Grantchester we see undergraduates in rowboats who are known as punters on account of they have flat bottoms and their proximity to Newmarket, otherwise known as Ascot, where the historic Grand National has been run over the River Styx since its inauguration in 1066. Here it was the Sir Rupert Brooke, the Immortal Bard, who later became Archbishop of Canterbury, wrote his historic Ode to a nightingale – Florence – in 1492 when he sighted the Armada, which is now being filmed in Cinemascope by Cecil B. de Mille, an American citizen. Here too we see the historic River Cam, home of the historic boat race. In the historic olden days, three men in a boat used a row from Oxford to Cambridge via Bletchley. (So legend has it – and legend can have it.) Nowadays they row on the River Thames from Uxbridge to Aldershot, singing the Eton Boating Song, or the Rowing Blues – and the winners are known as Rowed Scholars. Rival 'Varsity Oxford is of course well known as the scene of the movie *A Yank at Oxford*, title role of which was played by Robert Taylor, an American citizen. Oxford also plays rugby football, known as rugger, against Cambridge at Lords – this is called the Cup Final – and Socby, known as Soccer, at Henley, and cricket at Twickenham, where Magna Carta was signed in 1066 – that was quite a year. . . .

Here we see cows playing Hockey, and Girton girls grazing behind King's chapel. Next we see the famous Senate House, home of the historic Cambridge Tripod exam, so called on account of the photographs taken on graduation day. . . .

'Travelogue'
Leslie Bricusse, Frederic Raphael, Tony Becher *Out of the Blue* 1954

to do with May Week, with silk scarves and cricket blazers and the pre-war *Granta* . . . the Footlights are still doing what's expected of them, perpetuating for a score of nostalgic journalists their frothy undergraduate legend of ease and negligent wit.

Where Mayne and Raven agree is that the revues did represent a self-image of Cambridge, however much that was a pose, or as Mayne says, a myth. And both point to the underlying sense of nostalgia for a Cambridge that almost certainly never existed. (Evelyn Waugh's *Brideshead Revisited*, published in 1945, has set a myth of Oxford for generations of undergraduates.) The undergraduates of the materialistic, meritocratic 1950s, products of the Butler Education Act of 1944, felt a nostalgia for pre-war Cambridge that their fathers had not felt. Much of the nostalgia, summed up in Footlights farewell numbers, was a pre-graduation nostalgia for their own undergraduate innocence. The visual impression of the revues was of bright pantomime colours, a blaze from the footlights, handsome white-flannelled youths caught in the spotlight, blue eye shadow and plenty of pancake and powder. The send-up of Pierrot shows was only half serious. After the performance the audience, in dinner jackets and long gowns, drifted away from this perfumed limbo to May Balls and parties, to their last precious hours at Cambridge. It was a world to which one was always saying goodbye; and only the tinkling tunes lingered, out in the blue:

> In our memories we never quite go down
> On a winter's day in a crowded town
> It will always be the same.
>
> Suddenly in a London thoroughfare
> Time stands still – it sometimes will –
> And so your mind has strayed
> And you're back on King's Parade.
> Cambridge days will hold your memory
> Evening punts – a lecture once –
> Or an old nostalgic tune
> That the Footlights sang in June.
>
> So let's take a last look round
> If it's going down well, it always will,
> It was Cambridge then, and it's Cambridge still
> It will always be the same.

The brittle laughter, however, still had an edge. It took professionalism and ambition to put on a successful revue, and the Footlights had both. By 1952 the rising cost of mounting the show (and the fierce competition for tickets) led the Arts Theatre Trust to extend the run from the last week of term into the first week of the vacation, with expenses paid to the cast for the second week, a practice that has continued ever since. In 1954, 1955 and 1956 the revue was also presented by professional managements in London. *Out of the Blue* ran for three weeks at the Phoenix, *Between the Lines* for three weeks at the Scala in Charlotte Street,

1955

Peter Woodthorpe, 1955

and *Anything May* for three weeks at the Lyric Hammersmith. The May Week revue was already seen as a showcase for would-be professional talent; it was an even better one if it went to London. In 1954 the President and Producer, Leslie Bricusse, began to meet his own ambitions by going off to join Beatrice Lillie in her show, *An Evening with Beatrice Lillie*. In 1955 Peter Woodthorpe (his reputation as an actor already secure) went off to play Estragon in Peter Hall's pioneer production of Beckett's *Waiting for Godot* at the (London) Arts. In 1955 Daniel Massey was immediately offered work by the director of (the then very superior) Worthing Rep. Massey, for whom playing in the revue was 'a feather in the May Week cap' lent glamour to the opening night in London when his parents, the actor Raymond Massey and the actress Adrianne Allen, took along a large party of theatrical notabilities and then threw a first night celebration.

Daniel Massey, 1955

Between the Lines, 1954

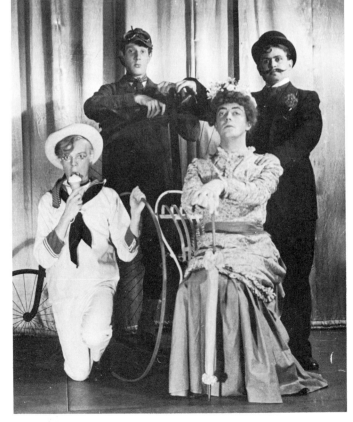

Between the Lines, 1954.
Left to right: Julian Jebb,
Jonathan Miller, Willie Eustace,
Peter Woodthorpe

We salute the five star Napoleon Brando!

EVIE: Hello Terry.
TERRY: Yeah, you talking to me?
EVIE: There's no one else here.
TERRY: Yeah. All right. Forget it.
EVIE: Strike still on down at the docks, Terry?
TERRY: Yeah. I dunno. I ain't been down for two years.
EVIE: But Terry, the strike's only been on a week.
TERRY: Yeah, that's the trouble. I'm ahead of my time.
   It's the Union, Evie, I can't work with the Union.
EVIE: Do you have to be in the Union?
TERRY: Look Evie, if I'm not in the Union, I don't work.
EVIE: But you're not working anyway.
TERRY: Do you think that makes it any easier? I dunno,
   Evie. I'm all mixed up inside.
EVIE: What's the matter, Terry?
TERRY: I dunno, Evie, I'm all mixed up inside.
EVIE: Terry, where's your heart? Where's your stomach?
   Where's your guts?
TERRY: I dunno, Evie, I'm all mixed up inside.

'A Waterfront named Desirée'
Leslie Bricusse *Between the Lines* 1955

The possibility of a London transfer altered the character of the revues by generalising their appeal. It also made the competition for a place in the Footlights cast all the more fierce. The novelist Frederic Raphael, who was in the cast in 1953 and 1954, has given a somewhat heightened picture of Cambridge theatre in his television drama *The Glittering Prizes* (the ambitious director Mike Clode was played by an ex-Footlights member of a later generation, Mark Wing-Davey). Raphael has said, 'I had a very idealistic idea of Cambridge, and in many ways I still have. In those days we all regarded it as an ante-room for success in the real world.' When Simon Phipps returned to Cambridge in 1953 as Trinity College Chaplain he noticed a change. 'The Footlights seemed to have an eye on making their way in a way that we didn't. Our work was taken up – they definitely tried to attract attention.'

The club was encouraged by the rapturous reception they received when *Out of the Blue* arrived in London in 1954, at a time when the theatre was glutted with commercial revues. Their literate wit appealed to the critics' jaded palettes.

> We're the bite in all that's biting,
> We're what's right in contemporary writing,
> Evelyn Waugh, Graham Greene,
> It's gloom, gloom that puts our name in lights,
> It's gloom, gloom, gloom that whets our appetites. . . .

The revue also attempted satire. There were sketches about the colour bar in British Hotels and the German economic miracle; and every night John Quashie-Idun (who has since had a distinguished legal career in Ghana) produced a fresh stanza for his topical calypso:

> Pandemonium reigns supreme in the Labour Party,
> So there'll be a meeting called by Mr Attlee,
> Mr Morrison will use hand grenades and dynamite,
> To rid the Labour Party of the Bevanite.

Although Harold Hobson, Bernard Levin and the rest gave the casts of 1954 and 1955 a warm glow of satisfaction, the club was nearly wrecked by its bid for professional success. The problem, as ever, was the amateur state of the club's finances. The London revues made reputations, but they also made a loss for the club: £699 in 1954, £358 in 1955 and £76 in 1956. In an attempt to warn future committees of the dangers, the Junior Treasurer for 1955/6, Clive Eckert, drew up a 'Committee Guide Book'. Eckert solemnly concluded his introduction: 'The use of this knowledge and observation of the code for conducting Club affairs, as laid

Oh! Cambridge has gone down
But it's always been this way
As soon as you get out of school
You come up here and play the fool
And only work in May
Debauched and decadent playboys
Your fathers were to blame
You never care about degrees
You seem to do just as you please
But Cambridge has always been the same.

At last we're going down
Farewell our final term
We'll think of you when we're immured
With good safe seats upon the board
Of Uncle Henry's firm
Debauched and decadent playboys
It couldn't be we've passed
But anyhow our final curtain's
Going down and this is certain
Footlights are going down at last.

Closing number
Between the Lines London 1955

down in the Constitution, will, I hope, prevent a repetition of mismanagement which has occurred from time to time and improve the administration of one of the most important clubs in Cambridge.'

It was Eckert's intention that the Guide Book would be regularly brought up to date. He would be sadly disappointed to know that it was not and the club fell back into its old ways. The volume gives a valuable insight into the running of the club. A sample budget for the May Week revue shows the rising costs involved. The production budget was £1,000, the hire of the Arts was £800, and projected box office receipts £2,800. This left a tidy profit of £1,000 to be split 50/50 with the Arts Theatre Trust. The average revenue from Club subscriptions was £150 a year, so the revue was the main source of funds. An appearance in London totally changed the picture. The cost to the club of three weeks at the Phoenix was £7,724, and their share of the box office with Prince Littler's management was only £7,761. Eckert commented, 'In 1954 the Club nearly went bankrupt through mismanagement.' Besides the losses in London, debts were overlooked and a lot of money lost in privately recording *Out of the Blue* (now a collector's item). Eckert's treasurer's report in October 1955 states that 'spending was extravagant, the accounts were badly kept and club assets not looked after.' Leading members of the club ran up large personal expenses – a similar row over such matters features in *The Glittering Prizes*.

Although the London revues in 1955 and 1956 were not so badly managed, for the club was learning how to negotiate with commercial managements, the club had to take stock of its position. One decision was quietly to remove the Senior Treasurer, Freddie Brittain, which as his successor, Simon Phipps explained, had to be done '. . . rather diplomatically. His brand of undergraduate humour – you know, the beery, unsophisticated, rowing club kind of humour – had gone out of date, so he was a bit of a menace.' The Club also decided to revise its constitution, adding this significant rule to protect club material: 'After a member has agreed that a work of his copyright may be performed at a certain club event, the member must not allow the work to be performed in public without the approval of the Committee.' Finally, having been landed with a large tax bill on its profits in Cambridge on the 1954 revue, the club decided to allow the Arts Theatre Trust to look after its revue finances, building a reserve that was to prove extremely useful when the club made its next expansion at the end of the decade.

It is an irony of the Footlights history that one of its greatest discoveries, who was to have a profound influence both on

British revue (to the extent of almost killing it off) and on the theatre at large, was never a member. Jonathan Miller was a freshman at St John's when his performance in a Poppy Day revue in the St John's bicycle shed was spotted by Leslie Bricusse, the Footlights President. Miller says that his Cambridge was not 'the bowl of piranha fish' portrayed in *The Glittering Prizes*. That may be because he had very little to do with the theatre. He acted in only one play and took no part in Footlights smokers. His was the intellectual Cambridge of the Apostles and the History of Science Society. He had an evident distaste for the theatrical camp of most of the Footlights and, although he appeared in other sketches his main contributions to *Out of the Blue* in 1954 and *Between the Lines* in 1955 were monologues. 'I just did my bits and got out.'

Jonathan Miller was the one the London critics noticed. In the *Sunday Times* Harold Hobson devoted four-fifths of his review to Miller. Other critics with less leisurely deadlines grabbed the nearest comparison with a professional comic that they could find and came up with Danny Kaye. That described the animated, long-limbed physicality of his mime in his one-man documentary on Australia, 'Colonial Report', but it did not properly reflect the world of fantasy and nonsense that his monologues created. (The sense of poetic improvisation is conveyed by the scripts submitted to the Lord Chamberlain, which are little more than lists of topics). His Third Programme parody required a certain familiarity with cultural matters, though there is still something of the clever schoolboy aping the masters in Miller's mimicry of Bertrand Russell:

> One of the advantages of living in Great Court, Trinity, I seem to recall, was the fact that one could pop across at any time of the day or night and trap the then young G. E. Moore into a logical falsehood, by means of a cunning semantic subterfuge. I recall one occasion with particular vividness. I had popped across and had knocked upon his door. 'Come in,' he said. I decided to wait a while in order to test the validity of his proposition. 'Come in,' he said once again, a trifle testily, I thought. 'Very well,' I replied, 'if that is in fact truly what you wish.' I opened the door accordingly, and went in. And there was Moore, sitting by the fire, with a basket on his knee. 'Moore,' I said, 'have you any apples in that basket?' 'No,' he replied, and smiled seraphically, as was his wont. I decided to try a different logical tack. 'Moore,' I said, 'do you then have *some* apples in that basket?' 'No,' he said, once again. Now I was in a logical cleft stick, so to speak, and had but one way out. 'Moore,' I said, 'do you then have *apples* in that basket?'

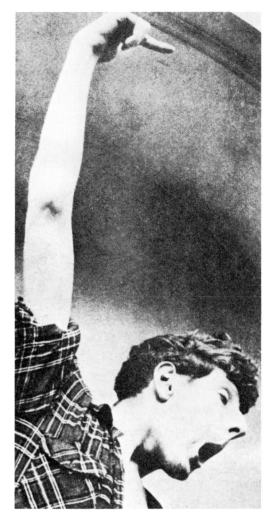

Jonathan Miller, 1953
Jonathan Miller, 1954

No nation was more perky
Than medieval Turkey
For she was always victor in the strife.
The Turk bore no comparison
To Saxon or to Saracen,
But life was pretty deadly for his wife.

Oh, there's not a man
On my Ottoman –
There hasn't been one for weeks.
There's not a man on my ottoman –
He's gone to fight the Greeks.
Or maybe it's the Spanish, or the French – I do not care
For my dreams of love all vanish, and my ottoman is bare.
There's not a man on my ottoman, and it's not fair!

But one day the crusaders decided to invade us –
And we were simply overrun with men.
They came across the Bosphorus
And didn't even toss for us.
Oh! What rape and pillage there was then.

So I got a man on my ottoman
An ever so English Lord.
Yes, I got a man on my ottoman,
But all he took off was his sword.
He talked about crusading
But I found the subject grim,
His idea of serenading
Was the very latest hymn.
Yes I got a man on my ottoman, but he's too dim.

I've had a lot of men on my ottoman
But none of them so cool,
I want hotter men on my ottoman
Instead of this old fool.
Keep sober is his motto, and I couldn't like it less.
I failed to get him blotto
Drinking fizzes from my fez.
Not a lot of men on my ottoman, won't say 'Yes'.

And if anyone thinks he isn't dum
Take it from me.
He's the slowest crusader in Christendom.

'Turkish Delight'
Julian More *Out of the Blue* 1954

Ronald Searle cartoon for *Punch*, 1954

'Yes,' he replied, and from that day forth we have remained the very closest of friends.

Miller had a number of offers from theatrical managements, but he turned them all down, and his final performance at the Phoenix was announced as the end of his theatrical career. (This is written at a time when Miller has again announced his retirement from the theatre). Miller, however, reappeared the following year in *Between the Lines*. (Bernard Levin called him 'a genius'). He and Rory McEwen (later best known as a folk singer) added to their London allowances by doing late night cabaret at the Royal Court Theatre Club, a night club run by Clement Freud in what is now the Royal Court's Theatre Upstairs. Again, the offers flowed in and Miller refused all of them, but one. Needing money to get married, Miller appeared on commercial television's 'Saturday Night at the London Palladium'. Miller, in Bertrand Russell guise, incongruously shared the bill with Yana.

The element of fantasy in Miller's monologues – refined and developed for *Beyond the Fringe* – was a sign of changing times. Absurdity has been an element in English humour since before Lewis Carroll; in the mid-1950s there was a

[*Out of the Blue*

MR. JONATHAN MILLER   MR. DERMOT HOARE

fresh burst of surrealist humour, be it Paul Jennings's 'Oddly Enough' column for the *Observer* or the violent anarchy of the *Goon Show*. There was always an element of whimsy in Laurie Lister's West End revues, particularly in the material by Joyce Grenfell and Michael Flanders and Donald Swann, but new influences were being brought to bear in revue writing. In 1955 Robert Dhéry presented some of the best material from his Paris revues in *La Plume de Ma Tante* and the choreographer John Cranko brought the *auteur* principle to revue with *Cranks*. *Cranks* was a truly surreal sequence of songs, mime, dance and word play, entirely devised by Cranko, that escaped the predictabilities of *Airs on a Shoestring* (Max Adrian, Moyra Fraser, Sally Rogers and Betty Marsden) or *Intimacy at 8.30*, with material by Peter Myers, Alec Grahame and David Climie, and music by John Pritchett and Ronald Cass.

The change of mood made itself felt in the 1956 Footlights, *Anything May*. (The cast had also altered after the 'vintage' years of '54 and '55). The producer Hugh Southern told *Granta*, 'The Footlights, with some years of excellent and fairly traditional revue behind them, to say nothing of a boisterous era earlier on, are now trying to be different.' His quest for surreal lyrics and sketches had produced 'a crop of revue turns beginning and ending with protracted gunfire, punctuated with screams and the crackle of flaming woodwork.' The *Cambridge Review* described the result as fluctuating between 'the whimsical and the macabre', and 'macabre' became the general description used by bewildered critics. The overall theme was a psychic journey from cradle to grave; for the finale the cast abandoned their traditional boaters and dressed as devils. There was still room for impersonations of Joyce Grenfell and Wilfrid Pickles, but there was also an obscure allegory about Communism and a military conscription nightmare. The pantomime colours were beginning to darken.

The year of *Anything May*, 1956, was a turning point for both British theatre and British politics, even if the timing was coincidental. The Suez crisis, although the actual invasion did not take place until October, jolted Cambridge undergraduates out of their complacency. Many of them were army reservists or about to go into the forces. In January 1955 Martin Rosenhead had complained in the *Cambridge Review* of the apathy with which three-quarters of the undergraduates viewed the political scene. There was a '. . . a distrust for any reforming zeal, a disinclination towards any change or radical modification of current standards.' Current standards still seemed to be set by the flat-capped gentlemen of Cambridge, the chinless wonders in suede car-coats, yellow waistcoats and green MGs. The *Varsity Handbook* advised freshmen in 1956 '. . . for parties, high-days and holidays nothing else will do but a suit of charcoal grey with a red tie in winter and an Italian white tie in summer. A dinner jacket is absolutely indispensable.'

The nostalgia for 'before the war' infected the literary Left as well as the Right, or so Bob Heller's 'Dirty Thirties' duet would have us believe in *Between the Lines:*

> It was very much much more exciting in the Thirties –
> Why don't the Spanish have another Civil War?
> We wouldn't find the fighting
> Particularly inviting
> But we'd put a new complexion
> On our faces.
> At Headquarters where the base is –
> That is the safest place?

The song concludes:

> It'll be so biting
> And requiting
> And delighting
> And much much more re-writing, in the Fifties.

The Suez crisis gave the Left in Cambridge an issue for almost the first time since the Conservatives came to power in 1951, and gave an impetus to the student protests that began with the Campaign for Nuclear Disarmament launched in 1958. The Cambridge Union carried a motion opposing Government policy on Suez, though in the course of a somewhat frivolous debate. A protest meeting was well attended – and broken up by pro-Government hooligans who heckled the young Anthony Wedgwood Benn and threw stink bombs, flour bags and fireworks. A City Labour Club march was similarly disrupted.

The shift in the political climate did not make itself felt in the Footlights immediately. It is not until 1959 that the influence of the New Left or CND can really be detected in the material – and the Footlights were entertainers, after all. But the change in the theatre filtered through more quickly. Osborne's *Look Back in Anger* made a critical theatre fashionable. A member from an earlier generation has said, '. . . we became infected by the kitchen sink.' London productions of Beckett and Ionesco suggested a theatre of the absurd that appealed to the fans of *Cranks*. Harold Pinter and N. F. Simpson contributed to the genre in the following years.

The shift towards a different kind of revue became more marked in 1957. In April 1957 Bamber Gascoigne, who had contributed one sketch to *Anything May*, mounted a whole revue, written and directed by himself, for the Magdalene

Zounds, 1957

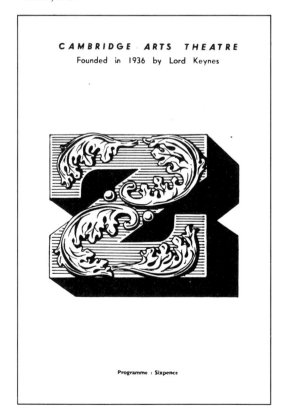

CAMBRIDGE ARTS THEATRE
Founded in 1936 by Lord Keynes

Programme : Sixpence

1957, with the first females since 1932.
Back row: Dorothy Mulcahy, below,
between Joe Melia and
Michael Collings, Ann Jones

College Bankhead Society. It ran for a week at the ADC Theatre and, to Gascoigne's astonishment, the young impresario Michael Codron bought the script. *Share My Lettuce* opened at the Lyric Hammersmith in August, and then ran for a year at the Garrick. Gascoigne acknowledges the influence of *Cranks;* he had a firm idea that a revue should produce a mood, rather than be an assemblage of sketches, and that the visual element was as important as the jokes. The title reflects the taste for whimsical nonsense and led to some confusion with Julian Slade's *Salad Days*, whose sentimental appeal was helping to break box office records.

Gascoigne has said that the success of *Share My Lettuce* made him 'too grand to write unpaid for the Footlights', and it fell to another contributor to *Anything May*, Michael Frayn, to develop the possibilities suggested to the Foot-lights by *Cranks*. The collective nature of the club prevented the imposition of a strong personal style such as Gascoigne had been able to create for *Share My Lettuce*, but *Zounds*, the 1957 May Week show, is unusual in that it is almost entirely written by Michael Frayn and John Edwards. The cast is smaller and, for the first time since 1932, includes women. Dorothy Mulcahy, an undergraduate at Girton, had appeared in *Share My Lettuce*, and Ann Jones, a locally based former Tiller Girl, appeared in several Cambridge revues. (The presence of women does not seem to have caused very much stir. After all, they were not actually members of the club). The cast also included Michael Collings, one of the stars of *Share My Lettuce*, and both shows had the same Musical Director, Keith Statham. The director, Graeme Macdonald, later became Head of BBC Television Drama, and has recently been appointed controller of BBC2.

Michael Frayn, now an established dramatist, has rather deprecated his early efforts in revue: '. . . never once did it enter my head to try (for example) doing things without the embarrassing moronic torch numbers which I felt such a damn fool struggling to write.' That may be because *Zounds* was not a great success. The opening title song – which reappeared on either side of the interval and in the closer – was very much in the Cranko mould, a nonsensical verbal-visual display in which the cast introduce themselves as 'Zounds'. The pace of the sketches was much faster, but they revolve around funny ideas rather than gags (though

Tradition is what makes the world go round
Fashions change, but we'll go on
Just leaving the world as the world was found;
Keep the torch burning, hand it on.

Keep the torch burning, one by one
We're England's glory
Her proudest story
Keep the torch burning, hand it on.

The chaps are playing the same old games,
Still all the same old things are done;
The same old places, the same old names,
Keep the torch burning, hand it on.

Whatever we do, you must do the same,
Father to brother, then to son;
With each one helping to feed the flame,
Keep the torch burning, hand it on.

And when we are dead, a forgotten name;
Nothing to show for the deeds we've done,
Remember we're part of that glorious flame;
Keep the torch burning, hand it on.

(Meanwhile the torch, in spite of all efforts to resuscitate it, and the suggestion of a salesman that they might modernise it, goes out)

'That Flaming Torch'
Bamber Gascoigne *Springs to Mind* 1958

On stage is a large board frame, like a blank hoarding, on which the notices can be hung. . . . COLLINGS *is discovered taking a sign which reads* KEEP OFF THE GRASS *out of a stack and hanging it on the frame. Enter* MITCHELL, *wearing cloth cap and army boots, with his trousers tucked up in his socks. He stops when he sees the sign, reads it slowly, and then says:* 'Keep off what grass?' COLLINGS *whips out a sign reading* SILENCE, hangs it on the frame and glares at MITCHELL. MITCHELL *shrugs his shoulders, looks a bit disgruntled, and turns away. He lights a cigarette.* COLLINGS, *who has been polishing the* SILENCE *sign, suddenly turns and notices this. He walks right round until he can see* MITCHELL'S *profile, just to make sure, then taps him on the arm, goes back to the frame and hangs up a notice reading* NO SMOKING. MITCHELL *says:* 'Oh strewth!' COLLINGS *immediately hangs up a sign saying* KINDLY MODERATE YOUR LANGUAGE *and taps it menacingly.* MITCHELL *begins,* 'I only said –'; COLLINGS *taps the* SILENCE *sign even more menacingly.* MITCHELL *sighs, throws the cigarette away. Immediately* COLLINGS *hangs up a sign saying* NO LITTER. . . .

'No Nothing'
Michael Frayn and John Edwards *Zounds* 1957

Michael Frayn

there was one torch song extinguished by a fireman). The revue was almost completely free of satirical or political content. The *Cambridge Daily News* noted its 'gentleness'. Fantasy and mime appealed to the writers, but they baffled the audience, and, it seems, most of the cast.

Springs to Mind in 1958 reverted to type, with no women in the cast, and the script assembled from the best that had been picked up in Footlights smokers and college revues.

1958, programme design
by Timothy Birdsall

JOE MELIA: Hey, what's all this? I mean, what's all this about Springs to Mind? Springs to Mind? Mind the Springs! What does it all mean then?
ADRIAN SLADE: Well, it's the effort.
GEOFF PATTIE: The Old School.
MICHAEL COLLINGS: The critics.
DAVID MONICO: The mad rush of it all.
DAVID JOHNSON: The team spirit.
TIMOTHY BIRDSALL: Personality.
FRED EMERY: Charm.
BILL WALLIS: Sex.
JOE MELIA: Oh, I see, it's the visual aspect.
SONG: It may be a question of clever lighting,
       Or the foyer crush.
       It may be a matter of witty writing,
       Satire, dance or slush.
       It's the things that spring to mind that matter,
       Not the clanking or the clatter,
       Whatever it is, we think you'll find
       It springs to mind.

       It may be a matter of finding actors,
       Gathering a cast.
       It may be the characters that attract us,
       Or the final blast.
       It's the things that spring to mind that matter,
       Lots of new ideas to scatter,
       Whatever it is, we think you'll find
       It springs to mind.

Opening chorus
John Drummond, Adrian Slade *Springs to Mind* 1958

The *Cambridge Review* found it 'predictable, unexceptional, amiable'. The revue formula had absorbed whimsical humour into the pattern of intelligent clowning, literary parody, jokes about Cambridge and a sentimental song or two. Geoffrey Strachan, who contributed a send-up of *Under Milk Wood*, comments that jokes about politics, or literature for that matter, were purely private, without aggression. (He recalls the withdrawal of an anti-South African song from a Footlights smoker because of a threat that the smoker might be broken up. Laughter was more important than controversy.) 'Revue was not about making a political point.'

Springs to Mind was at least funny, and launched the careers of actors Joe Melia and Bill Wallis, both of whom were later to take over from members of the original cast of *Beyond the Fringe* when it transferred to Broadway. They were almost the last members of the Footlights to set out via the theatre, rather than radio and television. But the amiable, predictable nature of *Springs to Mind* was not one that attracted a freshman at Pembroke, Peter Cook.

Peter Cook has variously said that when he arrived in Cambridge he thought that the Footlights 'were a load of rubbish' and that '. . . it was a tremendously élite club – I was too bashful to even consider applying for it.' The two views are not mutually exclusive and he did not audition for membership until his second year. Once elected, Cook had an enormous influence on the club, but that influence has to be seen against the mood of Cambridge at that time.

Cambridge had lost none of the meritocratic ambitiousness of the early 1950s. In 1957 the *Varsity Handbook* advised:

> There are two ways of getting into Cambridge society. Either you may have talent, or else you may know someone who has talent. If you have any talent it may get wasted because you don't get on well enough with the people at the top, but if you have no talent, you will never get to the top, though it may be flattering to your ego to hang on to the fringe of talented society.

In that respect a training in Cambridge theatre was a training for life and its informal nature was an advantage. Bamber Gascoigne returned to Cambridge in October 1959 after a stifling year at Yale Drama School. He wrote in the *Cambridge Review*: 'I now see clearly what I had always expected; that Cambridge has the freest and most stimulating University theatre possible. We even have it over Oxford which lacks a theatre of its own.' Cambridge dons, he points out, do not use University productions as 'school

Joe Melia

Melia

A mimed game of football is in progress

CENTRE FORWARD: Do you come here often?
INSIDE RIGHT: As often as not.
INSIDE LEFT: My home is in Notts.
OUTSIDE LEFT: So's mine. Can't get it straight. Kitchen's overgrown with brush. *(Coughs)*.
CENTRE FORWARD: That's a nasty cough. What are you taking for it?
OUTSIDE LEFT: I don't know. Make me an offer.
INSIDE LEFT: Wolf Mankowitz.
CENTRE FORWARD: In kid's clothing.
INSIDE RIGHT: Two farthing's a time – it's daylight robbery.
OUTSIDE RIGHT: Were they granny knots, the knots in your kitchen? Because I had a granny too – boring old idiot. We were in the same form at school – mind you, she left just before I got there – well, she was older than me, not that that stopped us going steady together, though the difference in ages – well, she was 94 and – well, people used to say 'She's old enough to be your mother', so to laugh it off I used to say 'Older. She's old enough to be my grandmother, and what's more that's exactly what she is.'
CENTRE FORWARD: 94 – that makes 103.
INSIDE LEFT *(jumping up)*: I'm afraid that's a bit above my head.
OUTSIDE LEFT: *(throwing in)*: Blood sports involve unjustifiable cruelty to animals: discuss.
INSIDE LEFT: I don't follow.
CENTRE FORWARD: Nor do I nowadays, except in the Christmas vacation. . . .

David Nobbs 'Association Word Game' *Springs to Mind* 1958

Eleanor Bron

Bron

Mathematics
Calculation
Gives erratic
Information
To err by a touch
Makes corpses of such
People as we.

'The Last Laugh'
Opening chorus *The Last Laugh* 1959

plays', as tended to be the case at Oxford; even at the Marlowe George Rylands was prepared to take a back seat to an undergraduate producer. 'Cambridge theatre retains its distinctly amateur nature, in the best sense of the word, and the paradox is true but understandable that far more past Cambridge students of English, History, Languages and the Sciences shine in the West End than past Yale Students of Theatre on Broadway.'

Cambridge could still make mistakes – Daniel Massey failed his audition for the ADC – and the senior societies had such an aura of professionalism that only the most determined quickly penetrated the magic circle. But it was possible to get in somewhere and once talent was recognised it was allowed to develop. On occasion, Cambridge producers were more adventurous than their professional counterparts. One of them was John Bird, who came up to King's in 1955. He acquired a reputation as a director and a designer, specialising in Ibsen and Brecht. In 1957 the Royal Court staged a one-act version of N. F. Simpson's *A Resounding Tinkle*, believing the full version to be unplayable. Bird proceeded to prove them wrong.

Bird chose a Newnham undergraduate to play Middie Paradock, Eleanor Bron, spotted in a 'nursery' production for the Mummers. She had seen *Zounds* in 1957 and 'fallen in love' with Joe Melia, and had arrived in Cambridge with the vague ambition of appearing in a Footlights revue, though she did not know how to set about it. Bird, however, came to her room in Newnham during the preparations for *A Resounding Tinkle* and announced that he had just encountered 'the funniest man he had ever met.' This was Peter Cook, who duly played Bro Paradock. William Gaskill, the producer of the Royal Court version, came to see the production and paid them the compliment of arranging for them to give a Sunday performance at the Court. Bird was invited to become an Assistant Director at the Royal Court and so gave up his research on European drama. Before he left Cambridge, the Footlights asked John Bird to direct the 1959 revue.

The Last Laugh was unlike any May Week show, before or since. Bird chose imminent nuclear destruction as his theme; the whole revue is set in an underground bunker where scientists await the outcome of an experiment that may bring about the end of the world. Eleanor Bron, the only woman in the cast, recalls the feeling of commitment (a fashionable word at the time): 'There really was a great anger, they really were politically aware.' (One member of the cast, Geoffrey Pattie, has since become a Conservative Member of Parliament and an Under Secretary of State at the Ministry of Defence.)

Instead of the traditional tinkling orchestra, *The Last*

LAST LAUGH	Company		Company	**WEX SIDE STORY**
John Bird			Design : George Coral	James Cornford, Martin Monico
GUILTY PARTY	Cook, Johnson, Mitchell		Pattie	**ORCHESTRA**
Peter Cook				Geoff Pattie
JUST ME	Birdsall		Bron, Cook, Slade	**FRIENDS AND NEIGHBOURS**
Adrian Slade				Peter Cook, Adrian Slade
STRANGER IN TOWN	Bellwood, Pattie		Birdsall	**REPEAT NINE**
Geoff Pattie				Timothy Birdsall, John Bird
CHIAROSCURO	Bron, Mitchell, Monico		Birdsall, Cook	**Mr GROLE**
Martin Monico				Peter Cook
POLAR BORES	Birdsall, Cook, Johnson, Mitchell,		Bron, Bellwood, Johnson,	**DON'T ASK ME**
Peter Cook, Adrian Slade	Monico, Pattie, Slade		Mitchell, Monico, Pattie, Slade	Peter Cook
THE LADY	Bron, Bellwood, Birdsall, Monico		Bron, Birdsall, Cook	**THE ABSENCE OF Mrs. CLECK**
John Bird				E. Duncansson
ENTITYTAINMENT	Cook		Company	**PETER AND THE**
Peter Cook				**WOLFENDON**
				John Bird, Geoff Wilson
SOLDIERS OF THE QUEEN	Bellwood, Birdsall, Johnson, Mitchell,		Cook, Mitchell	**THAT'S THE DRILL**
Timothy Birdsall, John Bird	Monico, Pattie, Slade			Peter Cook, Geoff Pattie
FOREVER AMBER	Bron		Bron, Bellwood, Monico	**BEATVIC**
Adrian Slade				John Bird
PHIPPS GC.	Johnson, Monico, Pattie, Slade		Birdsall, Johnson, Pattie, Slade	**FOR FOX SAKE**
Geoff Pattie				Peter Cook, Adrian Slade
LOW PUNCH	Bron, Bellwood, Mitchell		Monico, Bellwood, Birdsall,	**INTERLUDE**
Adrian Slade			Mitchell, Slade	John Read, Jackie Thompson
ONE FOOT IN	Pattie		Birdsall, Cook	**Mr. MOSES**
Geoff Pattie				Peter Cook
THE KING CAN'T HELP IT	Company		Company	**FALLOUT**
Anthony Firth, Sophocles	Music : Jackie Thompson,			John Bird
	Design : Ewan MacLeod			

Permanent setting devised by John Bird
and designed by Timothy Birdsall

All designs, except those indicated by Timothy Birdsall

All music except "The King Can't Help It" and "Interlude"
by Patrick Gowers

The Last Laugh, 1959

The Last Laugh. Peter Cook is far right, Eleanor Bron is top, Timothy Birdsall far left

GEORGE: I must say the NSPCC get my goat. I'm damned if I see why they should. I'm fed up to the back teeth with this false scent they put down. It's disgusting.

MASTER: I seem to remember last week we ended up in Woolworth's. I wouldn't be at all surprised if Jarvis wasn't behind it.

JERRY: Oh God, there is the man. Pretend we're not here. (*Business: Jarvis walks across stage and off*) I mean I couldn't care less where he comes from or what school he went to, but when a man like that tells me to get off my own land, one's got to draw the line somewhere.

GEORGE: I mean admittedly it's his land now, but it was in your family for three hundred years before he bought it. Damn it all, you saw it first.

MASTER: Take these Teddy Boys. They go around hitting old ladies on the head. They've got the right idea but they're on the wrong scent. If only this spirit of adventure were directed towards the fox, we'd be getting somewhere. The government should take away their jeans and their television, and give them a pair of jodhpurs and a horse.

JERRY: There are plenty of horses I know, for one, who need exercise, and if we're not careful, we'll have the horses watching television too.

GEORGE: It's all the same these days. These young people with too much pocket money spend it all on gramophones and motor cars. They think they can replace the horse; well, I yield to none in my admiration for the scientists, but I'm blowed if I'm going to hunt foxes in a car.

MASTER: And if we don't hunt the foxes, who the devil will?

JERRY: The trouble is with all this canned food and entertainment, people are losing the use of their own four legs.

'For Fox Sake'
Peter Cook *The Last Laugh* 1959

Peter Cook, 1960

Laugh had a ten piece jazz group. There were complicated special effects and back projections. The star was undoubtedly Peter Cook. The spirit of E. L. Wisty, the mackintoshed character with his manic drone and insanely level logic that has become Cook's hallmark, haunts the pages of the script, some of which was to appear later that year on the lips of Kenneth Williams in *Pieces of Eight*. Julian Slade came up to Cambridge to see his younger brother Adrian, who was also in the cast: 'Peter Cook made a stunning impact. He came on and did his E. L. Wisty and I really was so taken in that I thought they were just filling in because they hadn't managed to change the set. Of course, it was a very brilliant piece of semi-improvisation.'

The targets were political, but in a social and cultural rather than ideological sense. 'For Fox Sake' had some sharp points about hunting and class warfare; Peter Cook presented Parliamentary Question Time in terms of a TV Quiz. There was considerable guying of British sacred cows – Scott of the Antarctic, and a Prisoner of War film parody that anticipates 'The Aftermyth of War' sketch in *Beyond the Fringe*. Even Cambridge references were brought up to date with a parody of *West Side Story*, built around 'The Dukes' a gang representing aristocratic Cambridge and 'The Grads', meritocrats living on grants. Death and disaster – a do-it-yourself sketch on how to make your own coffin – was never far away.

The opening night of *The Last Laugh* was a failure. The show went on far too long; there are stories that it was booed off the stage, and that the manager of the Arts had to go backstage and tell them to bring the curtain down before the performance ran past midnight. The revue got very poor notices, apart from a rave for the music in the *Manchester Guardian* from Alistair Cooke. This did not deter William Donaldson, a recent member of the Footlights who had gone into theatrical management. He bought the script, changed the title to *Here is the News* and put in a professional cast including Lance Percival, Cleo Laine, Valentine Dyall and Sheila Hancock. In spite of Donaldson's faith in the production, it was not a success, and it got no nearer to London than Oxford.

In Cambridge *The Last Laugh* much improved after the first night. The script was cut and the technical effects got right. Peter Cook's reputation was made and soon people were walking around Cambridge talking like E. L. Wisty, as once they had talked like Bluebottle or Eccles from the *Goons*. There were other Cook characters to be heard in the Whim or the Arts Theatre bar, among them 'Grole' and the right wing Colonel Rutter. Eleanor Bron says that 'Peter Cook's influence became nightmarish – I began to think we couldn't speak in any other way.' Cook enjoyed a comic partnership with Timothy Birdsall, who appeared in the 1958 and 1959 revues. (Cook, Birdsall and John Bird adopted a joint writing pseudonym, E. E. Duncasson). Birdsall (who was to die of leukaemia in 1965) was a cartoonist for *Granta* and by his final year was also drawing for *Punch*. Bron recalls him as '. . . a personality just shedding delight. Tim would do a drawing, or Peter would write a caption, and they would swap. In revue there were things that had never been done before, like talking about God in that way. They had content – it was a questioning of accepted ways of looking at things.'

When Michael Codron (the producer of *Share My Lettuce*) opened *Pieces of Eight* at the Apollo in September 1959 Peter Cook's name appeared in the credits above that of Harold Pinter. *When One Over the Eight* opened in April 1961 Cook's name was above that of N. F. Simpson and John Mortimer. In both revues only Cook is credited with 'sketches by'; all the rest are merely listed as 'additional material'.

Cook was elected President of the Footlights for his final year, 1959/60 and, naturally, he wrote most of the May Week Show, *Pop Goes Mrs Jessop*. (The title comes from the

A: Good evening.
B: Oh, good evening.
A: I'm extremely interested in all facets of human life, including you. Tell me, are you a mariner?
B: No, I'm afraid I'm not; I'm an architect.
A: Oh I see, I only mentioned that you might be a mariner so that I could lead the conversation round to an interesting fact that I've accumulated. It pertains to the codfish, that's an ocean dwelling creature.
B: Yes, I've heard of the cod.
A: Yes, it's quite an interesting fact that – the codfish relies almost solely for protection on blending with the natural seaweeds amongst which it lives.
B: Goodness me.
A: It is its sole protection, whereas the sole relies almost entirely on hanging about behind shoals of cod. That's quite interesting isn't it?
B: Yes, yes, it is.
A: But not as interesting in my opinion as another fact I've come across.
B: Oh?
A: It's about the eagle; it's quite interesting that the eagle has an estimated wingspan of eighteen feet, whereas its two feet span three feet which is double the length of its tail feather and over four times the width of its beak alone. That's quite an interesting statistic isn't it?
B: Fancy that, the eagle. . . . I never knew.
A: I doubt if the eagle does either . . . it's quite interesting to think that if all the Chinamen in the world. . . .

'Interesting facts'
Peter Cook *Pop Goes Mrs Jessop* 1960

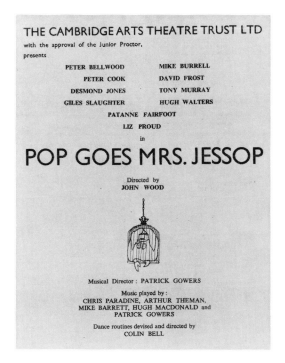

THE CAMBRIDGE ARTS THEATRE TRUST LTD
with the approval of the Junior Proctor,
presents

PETER BELLWOOD   MIKE BURRELL
PETER COOK   DAVID FROST
DESMOND JONES   TONY MURRAY
GILES SLAUGHTER   HUGH WALTERS
PATANNE FAIRFOOT
LIZ PROUD
in

POP GOES MRS. JESSOP

Directed by
JOHN WOOD

Musical Director : PATRICK GOWERS

Music played by :
CHRIS PARADINE, ARTHUR THEMAN,
MIKE BARRETT, HUGH MACDONALD and
PATRICK GOWERS
Dance routines devised and directed by
COLIN BELL

1960

JOHN WOOD is the Secretary of the Marlowe, plays the trombone and generally refers to himself as Cambridge's best actor. Slightly obsessed by Bristol.

PETER COOK has already made Shaftesbury Avenue, and is bound for the Edinburgh Festival soon. President of the Footlights and survivor of " Last Laugh.

PETER BELLWOOD is a trouper in the old tradition, unfortunately. Does most of the harder dance routines. Sings. Plays several instruments of the Ukelele family, such as the Ukelele.

DAVID FROST is the first Caius-man to edit Granta under a pseudonym. A brilliant mimic, freeman of Beccles, and intimate of the great.

PATANNE FAIRFOOT is unemployed. Most would have chosen National Assistance rather than Jessop every time, but she has the spirit that built the Empire.

HUGH WALTERS is the least indolent of an idle lot. Acts all over Cambridge in anything from Brecht to Congreve.

MIKE BURRELL is the one most likely to walk into the pit without his glasses. Has the rangy build of a song-and-dance man, but doesn't eat enough.

DESMOND JONES, fresh-faced and manly, is Christ's own jester. Can be observed counting under his breath during musical numbers.

GILES SLAUGHTER was chosen for his resemblance to his grandfather. They're his own teeth.

LIZ PROUD has played Ondine in her time. Also Mrs. Arthur, a role she created, and an Ionescu maid, created for her.

TONY MURRAY sings without any provocation at all. With the University Jazz Band, in operetta, now with the Footlights. Has a rugged charm, they say.

EWAN MACLEOD designed " Springs to Mind." President of the True Blue, no-one calls him the Aubrey Beardsley of Trinity.

PATRICK GOWERS has done it all before : to alleviate boredom, proposes to coax Basie-sized sound from five polyglot pit-dwellers.

COLIN BELL, quiet and scholarly, is sometimes called a Trotskyite wrecker. By Trotskyites.

Cast credits, 1960

opener and closer, a rather Crankish ensemble number about persuading a Brittania-like Mrs Jessop to emit a tiny 'pop'). The director was John Wood, now better known as the actor John Fortune. The second number, 'Ducks', a manic dialogue for a duck trainer, has the authentic Cook

John Wood (John Fortune), 1960

voice. 'It's quite a triumph, not like winning the war, but quite a triumph, I mean these ducks are completely under my control, eating's second nature to them now!' 'Interesting Facts' brought together codfish, eagles, Chinamen and grasshoppers. There was no doom-laden theme, as in 1959, but the bomb still lurked. A Civil Defence team plans to frighten off the Russians with notices; a pilot drops a hydrogen bomb on Manchester instead of Murmansk to save government money. The similarity of Welsh and Anglo-Indian accents sparked off a sketch in a coalmine with four miners trying to discover which one of them is the suspected alien.

> D: Now now now now, aren't we in danger of losing our sense of proportion? Let us extend a little toleration; I mean what does it matter if one of us is an Indian, I mean we're all the same beneath the skin.
> A: Ah, now we know.
> B: We know who the dirty Hindu is.
> C: Now we know who planted the birayani.
> A: Why did you come here in the first place, throwing good honest Welshmen out of the pit?
> C, B & A: Eh, eh, eh? Give us an answer, why, why?
> A: Why did you have to come to Llangrythly, why couldn't you stay back home where you belong in Cardiff?
> D: What, and live with all those filthy negroes?

The revue also featured two monologues by David Frost. In view of his later career as a television entrepreneur, his speech as Head of Adulterated Rediffusion has a certain resonance:

> We at Adulteration House are making three great new British series . . . *Texas Ranger* . . . *Son of Texas Ranger* . . . and *Hurried Marriage of Texas Ranger* . . . Now there have been those who've said that we at Adulteration House cater only for entertainment, and not for serious music, talks, poets and that . . . well, we admit we don't have them on all the while . . . I don't think we'd want them on all the while . . . but we certainly do not ignore them . . . and at 11.46 every night, we shall have *Culture Dip*, with Hughie Green as your compère, and until Hughie Green takes the slip out of the hat . . . provided by the British Hat Association . . . no one will know what sort of culture we're going to get tonight . . . not even the studio audience – they'll be blindfolded of course . . . you may get anything from Mantovani to Nancy Spain . . . .

It was as an entrepreneur that Frost was able to help the careers of a slightly later generation of Footlights writers and performers, but the efforts he made on his own behalf while at Cambridge did not make him many friends. His determination to succeed was off-putting. He has said of his arrival in Cambridge in 1958, 'I got there at five o'clock, and I felt perfectly at home at six.' Frost had two ambitions, to edit *Granta*, and run the Footlights. His official biographer Willi Frischauer takes up the story:

> To some of the younger students the university's literary and theatrical cliques seemed a bit snobbish and remote. Not to David. He did not have to knock at their doors too long. The pieces he wrote for *Varsity* and *Granta* were amusing and readily accepted, including a well-written interview with a voguish publisher which he brought back from a trip to London. He was also interested in the production of *Granta*, raring to get his hands on it.

Frost did indeed become editor of *Granta*; he also very nearly achieved his other ambition:

> His tell-tale grammar school accent became polished – but not affected – producing the classless voice that now appeals to many listeners. It easily earned him a place among the Footlights . . . he was at his best doing monologues.

Frost only managed to become Secretary, not President of the Footlights. (The President, Peter Bellwood is now a screen writer in America.) He entered office in October 1960, at an important moment in the club's history.

For the first time since 1939, the Footlights once more had a home. The idea of a new club room had been around for some time; it would attract more members and lead to better productions; it was also something of a financial necessity. Ever since the Arts Theatre had been managing the club's revue finances a sizable sum had been building up in their account. If the Trust paid this money to the Footlights it would be impossible to avoid paying tax on the revue profit. In October 1958 the club and the Trust agreed that the Arts would spend the money on their behalf, by leasing a club room. The Trust opened a Rehearsal Room reserve fund for such a purpose. In May 1960 the lease was signed on the premises in Falcon Yard, off Petty Cury, not far from the Arts Theatre. Falcon Yard was to be the Footlights' home for the next twelve years.

David Frost

Falcon Yard. The entrance to the club is on the left,
the windows of the clubroom are on the first floor above

CHAPTER V

'Cambridge Circus'

'Hardly any other activity in the University arouses so much ambition, excitement, hatred, jealousy and bitterness as the Theatre.'
Varsity Handbook 1960

The move into the new club rooms came at a time when the public's awareness of University revue was changing. On 22 August 1960 two Footlights performers, Jonathan Miller and Peter Cook, with two graduates of Oxford revue, Alan Bennett and Dudley Moore, gave the first performance of *Beyond the Fringe*. This was not an amateur revue, but an official production for the Edinburgh Festival. It is not the purpose here to follow the professional careers of Footlights members during the comedy boom of the 1960s – that has been done very well by Roger Wilmut in his book, *From Fringe to Flying Circus* – yet those professional circumstances were in part the creation of the Footlights, and in turn new members were influenced by what their predecessors were doing.

Beyond the Fringe was a hit at Edinburgh and, in spite of being bankrupt as a result of his investment in *The Last Laugh*, William Donaldson secured the rights to put it on in London. The transfer was not immediate; the show had a try out before an uncomprehending audience in Brighton, and a very warm reception at the Arts in Cambridge, before it opened at the Fortune Theatre in May 1961. The revue was to run at the Fortune, and then at the Mayfair, until the Autumn of 1966. The original cast went to New York in October 1962 and ran for a year there. (There was an echo of Footlights tensions when Peter Cook vetoed David Frost as his replacement after he had auditioned for the new London cast).

The success of *Beyond the Fringe* was phenomenal. Yet the London revue that ran the longest was also virtually the last. The old fashioned revues were killed off by comparisons with the wit of *Beyond the Fringe*, while the unique circumstances of its creation meant that it would produce no successor. At the same time, *Beyond the Fringe* opened up all sorts of possibilities for University talent. The 'satire-boom' of 1960 to 1963 has several strands, but they all pass through the circle of contacts made in the Footlights and the less formalised revue school at Oxford. Peter Cook was a key figure: *The Last Laugh* and *Pop Goes Mrs Jessop* anticipate *Beyond the Fringe*; with the money from revue writing Cook was able to go into partnership with Nick Luard, the Footlights Junior Treasurer 1959/60, and open the Establishment Club in October 1961; Cook and Luard became major shareholders in the magazine *Private Eye* in April 1962 (the first trial issue was in October 1961). John Bird (who must take the credit for having 'discovered' Peter Cook) was involved in the early stages of the BBC's *That Was The Week That Was*, first broadcast in November 1962, the programme that laid the foundation of David Frost's career. David Frost, in turn, became a major employer of script-writing talent and encouraged University writers.

The journalists' phrase 'satire-boom' is of course a misnomer. Michael Frayn described satire as a 'poor, broken-winded' idea as early as 1963 when he wrote an introduction to the published script of *Beyond the Fringe*:

> The humour which bred like mould in the damp
> Fenland air of Cambridge was predominantly
> fantastical, veering with Jonathan Miller towards the
> zany, with Peter Cook towards the absurdity of Ionesco
> and the eccentricity of Pinter. Alan Bennett and I did
> our National Service together (in that seminal
> institution, the Joint Services Russian Course – also at
> Cambridge) and we put on a series of cabarets and
> revues in which we sent up the army and the church and
> so forth but not, as far as I can remember, in any way
> which put the continued existence of the army or church
> in any peril.

There was a certain frustration with the protracted complacency of Tory rule; the term 'the Establishment' had been coined to explain the interlocking political, social and cultural institutions (of which Cambridge was one and the BBC another) that seemed to conspire to prevent change, while assuring people that they had never had it so good. *Private Eye* was scurrilous, and as Cook has said, '...extremely bad taste flourished at *The Establishment*', but there was no true subversion. When the possibility of real political controversy arrived with the imminence of a General Election in 1964, *That Was The Week That Was* was taken off the air.

The boom in intelligent comedy however – which is what really took place – had a profound effect. Michael Frayn, who was at the second night of *Beyond the Fringe*, noted:

> ... the sheer surprise of going to a revue and finding
> oneself addressed not by hired spokesmen, zombies with

neatly squared-off, bulled-up theatrical faces, repeating someone else's jokes, but directly, by recognisable human beings, who talked about things that human beings talk about outside the theatre, and not special demonstration topics brought out of formaldehyde only for revues. It was also, after all the years of being nervously nursed back to sobriety after each joke with torch-songs and *pas-de-trois* representing jealousy, the grateful shock of finding that the management trusted one not to dislocate one's jaw or be sick over the furnishings if one was allowed to laugh continuously for the whole evening.

John Wood (or, if you like, John Fortune) had already noticed something else about the cast of *Beyond the Fringe* when they visited Cambridge in April 1961. He commented in the *Cambridge Reveiw:* 'They also wrote all the material; so they had that intuitive feel for it which inspires confidence and ultimately laughter.'

Intelligent material demands intelligent performance. The writer-performer is the natural product of the Footlights system, where the emphasis is on original material, and the most original material is that which one writes for oneself. There is no dead space between the writer's intention and what the actor presents, for they are the same person. (Later on, in the 1970s, the tighter control enforced by Equity on entry into the profession gave additional significance to the writer-performer principle: the writer could insist that only he used his material and so acquired rights and experience as a performer.)

Above all, the example of *Beyond the Fringe* showed what fooling about at Cambridge could lead to. As we have seen, the Footlights had been the training ground for professional actors, writers, journalists and broadcasters since the 1890s; *Beyond the Fringe*, as Graham Chapman of *Monty Python* says, '. . . opened all the doors for us. It made it possible for undergraduates to be seen as funny by a large number of people – it made a career like that seem possible.' And for Graham Chapman, and several others, so it has proved.

The title of the 1961 Footlights revue, *I Thought I Saw It Move*, was a more or less conscious tribute to Peter Cook, since it was one of his Wisty-ish catch phrases. John Cleese came up to Cambridge in October 1960: 'Cook's influence was so thick in the air for two or three years you could cut it with a knife. The way Cook uses words is really quite original – the way he can make a perfectly blunt and banal statement sound terribly funny, just by the choice of certain words. I remember Trevor Nunn . . . used to sit around and convulse us merely by recounting sketches Peter had done.'

Peter Bellwood,
I Thought I Saw It Move, 1961

Some of the mantle, indeed possibly some of the material, of Peter Cook fell on the shoulders of David Frost, one of the stars of *I Thought I Saw It Move*. The show was watched by Richard Armitage, the son of Noel Gay and head of the Noel Gay Agency. The Footlights were familiar to him, for he had written the title song to *La Vie Cambridgienne* in 1948. 'I went to Cambridge at the invitation of two other members of the Footlights cast — never mind their names .... After a quarter of an hour I knew that I did not want either' (Armitage explained to Frost's biographer Willi Frischauer). Then Frost reeled off a string of jokes in a monologue: 'They were not very good . . . but this man had his own atmosphere.' Armitage got Frost an engagement at *The Blue Angel* club in London (during the day he worked as a trainee for Rediffusion) and it was from there that he moved to *That Was The Week That Was*.

Frost had helped to see the club into its new premises. The rooms, which had once housed the Cambridge University Labour Club, were on the first floor in Falcon Yard, above the back of MacFisheries, and so there was a smell about the place, not so much of grease-paint, as of fish. The club spent £1,300 on refitting the room, built a stage across one end and installed a small bar. Harold Fuller, a waiter at Trinity, was the first Steward. The rent was £160, plus rates of £75, and for purposes of taxation and the liquor licence it was the Rehearsal Room of the Arts Theatre, just around the corner. The rent was modest, because the whole area was scheduled for redevelopment.

The rooms were open from 12.30 until 2.30 on weekdays; usually the evenings began at about nine and ended when the Steward went home. Membership of the Footlights was therefore the key to two essential requirements in undergraduate life: a central place to have lunch and somewhere where you could get a drink after the cinema, after the theatre, or after the pubs were shut. The late licence, sometimes very late licence, was the chief attraction. Performers at the Arts came round after the show, so there was a constant mingling of amateurs and professionals. It was, of course, a place to hold smokers and private parties, and the rooms were also used for jazz sessions and poetry readings. The poet Michael Horovitz has fond memories of performances there — 'it was always very full and happy', as full as the enormous brandy glasses that were a feature of the bar.

The club rooms became very much the centre of Cambridge theatrical life, for after 1962 the ADC ceased to do any catering in its club room in Park Street. For people like Eric Idle and Graham Chapman the club became their college. Russell Davies, who joined in October 1964, at the same time as Germaine Greer and Clive James, remembers the room chiefly for its 'conspiratorial' atmosphere. 'You

Felicity Hough performs

John Cameron, Eric Idle
and Graeme Garden play

President Graeme
Garden entertains

went down this dark alley, and up this creepy little stair-case. . . .' By the end of the decade a lot of the glamour had been knocked off the furniture and fittings, but Graham Chapman remembers it in the early days. 'It felt very smart and swish to me, I mean the committee wearing dinner jackets and sashes at smokers and so on. It seemed like an exclusive club – which I suppose it was.'

Falcon Yard changed the nature of the club – it made it a much more exciting institution to belong to – but the financial responsibilities were heavier. The club began the year in the red on its current account every year until 1970. Previously, there had been an unofficial ceiling of about sixty on membership. As in the 1930s, the need to finance the rooms required an expansion to eighty or more. Subscriptions went up to three guineas and in 1964 Associate Membership was created for drinking rather than performing members. The club revised its constitution in 1960, but the President remained a powerful figure, with the right to suggest his successor. In concert with the committee

Trevor Nunn, 1962

John Cleese, 1963

he chose the director of the May Week revue – in the 1960s he was usually found from among the most successful Cambridge directors, for instance, Trevor Nunn, the future Artistic Director of the Royal Shakespeare Company, was chosen to direct the 1962 revue. The President and committee had a large say in who performed in the revue, which is why committee and cast are often so similar. A 'script committee' was introduced to edit material produced by the smokers.

To ease the duties of the Junior Treasurer, a Registrar was made responsible for membership and the club catering called for the service of officials variously known as Major Domo and Victualler. The location suggested the purely honorific post of Falconer, which continued in being after Falcon Yard was demolished. The steady expansion of demand for cabaret performances, which could earn a great deal of money in undergraduate terms, obliged the club to assert control over the use of its name and material. The first Master of Cabaret had been John Drummond (now Director of the Edinbrugh International Festival) in 1958. The President had sole choice of the membership of the Footlights Cabaret Team. Inevitably there were squabbles over money. In 1961 the committee agreed that 75% of the fee should go to the performers, 25% to the club Sinking Fund; in 1965 a 'royalty' of 7/6d was agreed for script-writers.

Not every cabaret engagement was a success. Graham Chapman and John Cleese were part of a team sent to the Cambridge Allotment Society Annual Dinner. Chapman found that '. . . the audience could not understand us at all, even though it was the sort of stuff that went down very well in prisons. John Cleese went right over the top, when he started emphasising the jokes in order to explain them. It was about a bald man who had a rabbit tattooed on the top of his head . . . . Yet afterwards one of the Allotment people came up and said, 'We do wish we'd had your education'. Having an education still did not guarantee success. The minutes for 15 January 1965 read: 'The Club was warned by the Cabaret Team never to accept a Varsity Rugger Match Ball cabaret again.'

'Unofficial' cabarets were discouraged and so was the selling off of useful material. Under the heading 'That Was

The Week That Was' the committee minutes for 17 January 1963 read, 'The President [Tim Brooke-Taylor] was of the opinion that the strongest possible obligation should be placed on members not to sell to the programme any material that might be accepted for the May Week revue until after that was over (i.e., to keep back everything except what is of purely topical interest).' Great care had to be taken in the May Week programmes that the script credits went to the right people in the event of sketches being bought piecemeal.

Neither Graham Chapman nor John Cleese found it particularly easy to get into the club. Graham Chapman had seen a television excerpt from a Footlights show and thought 'that's *good*'. Indeed, he seems to have chosen to do medicine at Cambridge rather than elsewhere on the strength of it. For freshmen, the social year begins with a visit to the University Societies Fair and in October 1960 he presented himself in front of the Footlights stall, at which sat David Frost. Chapman explained that he wished to join the Footlights. 'Frost told me that I couldn't join.' Then how did he get to be a member? 'I had to be invited to audition. I asked what was the point of having a stall then. He said, "None whatsoever."' John Cleese had a similarly humiliating experience. 'They said, "Well, what do you do? Do you sing? . . . Do you dance?" – well of course, if there's anything I'm worse at than singing, it's dancing. So I said, "No," and they said, "Well, what do you do?", and I said, "I make people laugh" – and I blushed the colour of beetroot and ran – literally.'

Chapman solved the problem by organising a smoker in his own college at the end of his first year. He invited the Footlights committee and gave them lots of claret, and after that everything went smoothly. Neither Chapman nor Cleese got into the 1961 revue, though they auditioned in the traditional manner. 'After that it became a mission of John Cleese and myself to oust all singing and dancing, which we largely achieved. By 1963 the main musical content was Bill Oddie.' Chapman and Cleese met after they had both auditioned for a smoker. 'We went off and had a cup of coffee in the Kenco Coffee House, and decided to try writing together.'

Smokers were the ritual festivals in the annual cycle from October to June. Usually there were three in the Michaelmas and Lent Terms (at least one would be a Ladies' Night); the Summer Terms were mainly given over to exams and preparations for the revue. For each smoker a chairman (often, two chairmen; one to supervise the acts, the other to operate the curtain) was appointed, who in turn would hold auditions for performers a day or two before. Some twenty-five might audition, of whom about a dozen would be chosen. Until late in the 1960s dinner jackets were *de rigueur*, with sashes for the committee and a special jacket for the President. Smokers were a hard school. The actor Simon Jones, who was a member at the beginning of the 1970s, recalls, '. . . people could be very cruel. Some smokers could be accounted failures and fiascos. A lot of people who came to smokers were rather like opera fans. They were immensely critical, but they contributed nothing. Mind you, auditioning for smokers was far worse.' The potential humiliation of a smoker concentrated the mind. Eric Idle describes the attitude of a Cambridge audience: 'Make sure it's funny – get on with it.'

The smokers threw up a pile of material for inclusion in the revue. Because of the intervention of exams (and the fact that Footlights members were busy in many other productions) there was always a frantic rush to get the May Week revue ready in time. The Arts has a crowded schedule, so there was a general panic on the weekend before the show opened, with the staff having to work through most of Sunday night. (The budget for the revue – £1,144 in 1961; £1,831 in 1965; £2,573 in 1970 – precluded a Tuesday night opening, even with a two-week run). Revues being what they are, designs would arrive late, there would be last-minute script changes, props would be hired and then eliminated, scenery built and rejected. Until theatrical censorship was abolished in 1968 the last straw for the management was a mad dash to London on the morning of the opening to get the Lord Chamberlain's approval for the final script.

One of the negative effects of *Beyond the Fringe* was that it blocked off whole areas of comedy by occupying them so well. The drab, bunker-like set and the downbeat suits and pullovers of the cast successfully put the coffin lid on glamorous revues; the problem now was how not to look or sound like *Beyond the Fringe*.

The cast of the 1962 revue was helped in a number of ways. For one thing the set was also being used for Trevor Nunn's production of *Much Ado About Nothing*, so they had to work round Nunn's Gothic arches. They were also a much younger generation, for the end of National Service in 1959 meant that by now most undergraduates arrived straight from school. 'Youth' was becoming a cult word and the example of the Beatles made its impact on Cambridge as elsewhere. While the majority of undergraduates carried on in tweed jackets and flannels, the *avant-garde* wore jeans and black rollneck sweaters or striped shirts with square-ended knitted ties. A jacket in black leather with a scarlet silk lining was the height of fashion. The clothes gradually

Double Take, 1962

became more decorative and exotic, and the hair longer, as
the Sixties got into their swing. Satire was out; frivolous-
ness, later silliness, was in the air.

According to Tim Brooke-Taylor, *Double Take* in 1962
'. . . was the first complete runaway from satire.' There was
a self-conscious reference in the punchline to an interview
sketch with the Colonial Secretary: 'Bleed the black man
white. Hm, that's very good you know. (*Picks up telephone*)
Oh Smithers, get me that Peter Cook fellow would you . . .?'
There is a brilliant parody of Restoration Comedy, as good
as the mock Shakespeare in *Beyond the Fringe*, which
exploits the joke about 's' being printed as 'f' – as in the
title, 'Virtue Foil'd'.

HUFBAND: Gad's curfe! Here is Jack Worthless, the
Poetafter, as loofe in pocket as in tongue. He's playing

New readers begin here:—

ROBERT ATKINS

22-year-old, blue-eyed, mink-haired President of the Footlights, he reads Fine Arts in Corpus. He has a deep-seated admiration for Groucho Marx, and he wants to write poetry on a Greek island when he grows up. He is also President of the Cambridge University Theatre Company, which will be on the Edinburgh Fringe for the first time this year. Unspoiled by success he is still unmarried.

NIGEL BROWN

Husky ex-President of the A.D.C. from sunny Kenya, 'Theatre World' has called him a clever character actor. He reads History in his third year at John's, and has produced 'Maria Marten' and 'Epitaph For George Dillon' at the A.D.C. Never without a chuckle his voice has been compared with Bud Flanagan's. He intends to return to East Africa, no doubt to impart some of that old white magic to the natives.

MIRIAM MARGOLYES

Lusty, raven-haired wench ("Call me Midget"), from Newnham, she reads English in her second year. One of Cambridge's most successful dramatic actresses, this is her first appearance in Revue. An eccentric cyclist, she is usually to be seen in a blue woollen top hat and a black cloak. Her voice ranges from dulcet to raucous, and she has a priceless vocabulary collection.

HUMPHREY BARCLAY

21-year-old flesh-coloured secretary from Trinity (Trinity Street, Cambridge), he reads Classics. Beneath his urbane exterior he conceals the caricaturist's pen : a specialist in clerical parts on the A.D.C. stage, he has no aspirations to the Cloth. First ex-Head of Harrow to be in the Revue two years running since 1571, he is a fully paid-up member of the Pitt.

TIM BROOKE-TAYLOR

Master of double-takes, he is short, fair and handsome. Now in his second year at Pembroke, he reads law. In his time he has played Pantomime Dames and Chekhov; so the finances of the club are in good hands, despite his head for figures. Centre forward for Pembroke's 2nd XI, he says he is 21 : he shares with the President a dwarf-fixation. He is nearly 22.

GRAHAM CHAPMAN

Lanky, and mobile of face, he is a third year Medic in Emmanuel. World famous for his grotesque mimic ability, and Bristol-acclaimed star of the Footlights visit, he refuses to let it affect his confidence. He smokes a cool pipe, and will not admit that he sleeps in a cupboard : understandably he is non-commital about the Common Market.

TONY HENDRA

Hispanophilic, flaxen-haired, pre-Celtic under-the-counter-tenor from Lower Hendra in Cornwall, he reads Literature in John's, and speaks Middle-English like a Middle-Briton. He has inherited a range of six octaves from his mother and father. Hoping to be the second English Pope, he went to Nicholas Breakspeare's school : besides the guitar he plays the lute, flute, mandolin, sackbut and psaltery.

TREVOR NUNN

Smokes in his sleep and is the first man ever to produce both the Marlowe (this year's 'Macbeth') and the Footlights. " My duffle coat is a decade old, and is a decayed old duffle coat," he said. He has no sense of humour. He is in Downing and is President of the University Actors, and intends to make the Theatre his profession. He is taking the Marlowe to the Sarah Bernhardt Theatre in Paris in July with 'Much Ado About Nothing' which with the Stratford "Hollow Crown," will form the British contribution to the Theatre des Nations.

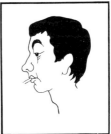

JOHN CLEESE

Bluff, slate-faced, 22-year-old Registrar, he reads Law and plays soccer for Downing. He grew his beard to avoid being mistaken for Pete Murray : an enthusiast for verbal humour, he is nevertheless always prepared to stoop to slapstick, where he rates the custard pie above the banana skin. He has a laugh which is coarse and ingenuous to boot : he says he cannot sing, and keeps a locked piano in his room to prove it.

HUGH MacDONALD

Laughing tune-monger from Pembroke, he is Vice-President of the Club and Musical Director. This is the fourth Revue for which he has been in the Pit : ' I've seen it all before ' he mumbled. Born on January 31st, he is writing the score for a musical, and drives a multi-punctured van between band engagements. He has graduated with a first in music, and hopes to spend his life in the company of the Muse. For further information see programme notes for the last three years.

ALAN GEORGE

A gaunt and raven-beaked antick reading English in his third year at Corpus. He has a way with a violin. His female impersonations, a new departure for him, make Joyce Grenfell look like an afternoon tea-party. He is engaged to be married, and has given up smoking. During spells of acute depression he fancies himself to be a bird, and his sole ambition is to become a busker.

drawings by Barclay

Cast credits, 1962. Drawings by Humphrey Barclay

the fol-le-la with thofe rights which made me fole pofsefsor of me Agapema's chaftity. Like a fcurvy privateer he ftorms the fafe harbour where rides at anchor that worthy floop, me marriage-bed. I will force him to the ifsue. I truft he has no blade.

LADY (*afide*): Pox on't! I know he has no blade.

There are even harbingers of *Monty Python's Flying Circus*: a list of euphemisms for death that reappears, much extended, in John Cleese's parrot sketch, and a Python-style link: 'I think we've seen all there is to see in here, and we'll go straight into the next number . . .' The critics noticed the sadistic element in Chapman and Cleese's mountaineering sketch. The ruling tone, though, was set by the physical clowning – a karate sketch, Chapman's impersonation of a carrot – and an exuberant sense of music hall. Bill Oddie contributed an Adam Faith number, catching the shift from modern jazz to rock and roll, just as jazz had supplanted the tinkling pianos. The cast included Miriam Margolyes, who has become a professional actress, and Tony Hendra, who moved to America and edited *National Lampoon* magazine.

Although Footlights revues had previously visited Oxford, and of course London, *Double Take* was the first to appear on the fringe of the Edinburgh Festival. (The Festival opens in late August and runs for three weeks.) The Footlights President, Robert Atkins, was a founder member of the Cambridge University Theatre Company, set up in 1962 to run a play and a late night revue for three weeks in a converted church hall. (The Oxford Theatre Group was established with the same idea.) The revue always subsidised the straight production at Edinburgh and the Footlights steadily lost money in backing the Theatre Company, though Edinburgh has since become as important a date in the club's calendar as May Week. Eric Idle emphasises the value of Edinburgh: 'May Week was a guaranteed sell-out. Edinburgh was real show business, you had to go out and pull in the punters.' (In 1962, in order to avoid appearing in Ibsen's *Brand*, Chapman and Cleese booked themselves to do an early evening show at a coffee-club which was about to evolve into the Traverse Theatre: the first night there were only two in the audience, and they couldn't leave, because they were there to serve the coffee.)

In 1963 the May Week title painfully arrived at was *A Clump of Plinths* – a rejected title was 'You Can't Call A Show "Cornflakes" ', which shows the difficulties they had had. At least the title described the set. Graham Chapman had gone off to medical school, but Tim Brooke-Taylor and John Cleese were still in the cast, while Bill Oddie joined them and Humphrey Barclay, who had performed in 1962, directed. The new recruits were Chris Stuart-Clark, Jo

Miriam Margolyes, 1962

1963

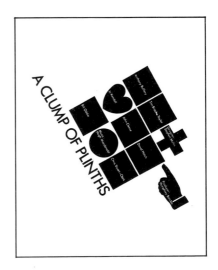

'Swap a Jest', 1963. Tim Brooke-Taylor
behind Chris Stuart-Clark

Kendall, David Hatch and Anthony Buffery. The music hall
flavour of *Double Take* became more concentrated. In the
Cambridge Review Rose Vaddim tried to respond to the
show's surrealist qualities:

> Tailor's clerk, J. Briefdragger Cleese, Gobbling Hatch,
> digs gardens, jelly Beatles, W. Oddie, digs birds. The
> bird in the case was No Jo King, self-confessed oldest
> female and mantamer. But of the whole thugogmagog
> the spickspookspokesman seemed huffery puffery
> Buffery, a sadfellow, simple pieman inspires slingslang
> spieman . . .

The impresario Michael White, who was making a number
of investments in revue at the time, booked the show into the
tiny Arts Theatre in London. The dreadful title was changed
to *Cambridge Circus*, which caused all sorts of confusions
about the location and nature of the show, but was exactly
right.

The London critics were tepid: The *Financial Times*
found it 'not as good as the '54'. Bernard Levin found the
material 'pretty thin'. *The Times* said it '. . . was not a land-

mark in the history of revue', and Philip Hope-Wallace in the *Guardian* called it a 'minor unpretentious affair' that was unlikely to face the ultimate punishment faced by *Beyond the Fringe*, 'playing before totally uncomprehending audiences.' Though at the cost of later facing some audiences who wondered where the animals were, *Cambridge Circus* proved to be the Footlight's most successful production.

The show transferred to the Lyric Theatre, Shaftesbury Avenue, and ran in London until November. The American rights had been bought by the TV personality Ed Sullivan and, with the posssibility of an appearance on Broadway in the offing, the cast temporarily dispersed. At first nothing happened and Ed Sullivan sold his interest to the promoter Sol Hurok. Still with an American production in mind, in May 1964 Michael White arranged a six-week tour of New Zealand. Here there were some uncomprehending audiences, but while they were in New Zealand confirmation came that they were indeed to appear in New York. In October 1964, eleven months after they had closed in London, *Cambridge Circus* opened at the Plymouth Theatre on Broadway. They ran for only twenty-three performances, but then transferred to a café theatre in Greenwich Village until the end of the year. Ed Sullivan invited the cast to make an appearance on his television show – they shared the bill with The Animals and Joan Sutherland, while President Johnson made a nationwide broadcast the same night. At the end of 1964 an American cast took over, but the show folded almost immediately.

Cambridge Circus could be counted a professional success even without the glamour (and toughening experience) of playing New York. The London run coincided with a new recruitment drive by the BBC's Light Entertainment Department. The immediate post-war generation of radio comedy writers was beginning to tire. Peter Titheridge, an old hand who had written for the Crazy Gang, was given the job of finding new blood. He arranged for writer/producer contracts to be offered to Humphrey Barclay, John Cleese and David Hatch. Tim Brooke-Taylor meanwhile had got a job with ATV. A broadcast of *Cambridge Circus*, followed by three radio shows under the title *I'm Sorry I'll Read That Again*, pointed the whole cast in the direction of professional performance.

David Hatch has said that at the revue's inception probably only Bill Oddie and Jo Kendall had ideas of turning professional. In the end, the entire cast of the New York version of *Cambridge Circus* began careers in comedy. Of the originals, Chris Stuart-Clark left towards the end of the London run and went into teaching; Tony Buffery left at the transfer from the Arts to the Lyric and has become an

Graham Chapman, David Hatch, 1963

Jo Kendall, 1964

Cambridge Circus on Broadway, 1964.
Jonathan Lynn, Bill Oddie, David Hatch.
Kneeling: John Cleese, Tim Brooke-Taylor, Graham Chapman

Tony Buffery, 1963

experimental psychologist, though he did appear in the television series *Twice a Fortnight*. (He remained an active member of the club until he moved to Oxford in 1968). Their places were taken by Jonathan Lynn, who had been playing in the band, and Graham Chapman, who managed to qualify as a doctor before devoting himself wholeheartedly to humour. Both Humphrey Barclay and David Hatch returned to the BBC after *Cambridge Circus*. Barclay is now Head of Comedy at London Weekend Television, Hatch Controller of BBC Radio 2.

In terms of comedy, *Cambridge Circus* succeeded not because it was *clever*, in the *Beyond the Fringe* mould, but simply because it was *funny*. Revue, under pressure from the snappy timing of television, was getting faster and faster. Point numbers and torch songs were out, so was most singing and dancing. The aim was gags, rather than good lines, and there was no room for sentiment. There was one moment when pathos threatened, as Bill Oddie appeared as an ancient stage-door keeper and began to reminisce about the stars of music hall .... 'They were rotten' saw that off. Music hall, even though in a sent up, surrealistic form, filtered by the cast's childhood memories of *Variety Bandbox* and *The Goon Show*, supplied the energy for the show. It is no accident that the final, climactic sketch 'Judge Not' features – along with such silly names as Arnold Fitch (Tony Buffery) and Sidney Bottle (Bill Oddie) – Tim Brooke-Taylor as Percy Molar, 'music hall comedian and company director of no fixed abode.' (In that description variety and *Goon Show* are synthesised.) The energy of *Cambridge Circus* spun off into *I'm Sorry I'll Read That Again*, which ran for eight series between 1965 and 1973 after the cast returned from America. *I'm Sorry I'll Read That Again* preserves the innocent and amateur appeal that made *Cambridge Circus* a hit (hence the important part played by the audience), though it is highly professional in its own terms.

Indirectly, *Cambridge Circus* made a break for Eric Idle, who had only been elected to the Footlights in March 1963, after impressing Bill Oddie and Tim Brooke-Taylor in a Pembroke smoker. The London run diverted *Cambridge Circus* from its scheduled tour to Edinburgh via the Robin Hood Theatre, Averham, and the York Festival, and it was necessary to fill the commitment to the Cambridge University Theatre Company. Humphrey Barclay summoned Idle by telegram back from a holiday in Germany, and Idle, Barclay, David Gooderson and Richard Eyre (now an Associate Director of the National Theatre) stood in as *Footlights '63* – 'We were very suave, we performed in dinner jackets.'

John Cleese, 1964

Bill Oddie, 1963

'Judge Not', 1963.
John Cleese, David Hatch, Tim Brooke-Taylor, Chris Stuart-Clark

CLEESE: You are Arnold Fitch, alias Arnold Fitch?
BUFFERY: Yes.
CLEESE: Why is your alias the same as your real name?
BUFFERY: Because, when I do use my alias, no-one would expect it to be the same as my real name.
CLEESE: You are a company director?
BUFFERY: Of course.
CLEESE: Did you throw the watering can?
BUFFERY: No.
CLEESE: I suggest that you threw the watering can.
BUFFERY: I did not.
CLEESE: I put it to you that you threw the watering can.
BUFFERY: I didn't!
CLEESE: I submit that you threw the watering can!
BUFFERY: No!
CLEESE: *Did you or did you not throw the watering can!*
BUFFERY: I did not!
CLEESE: YES OR NO? DID YOU THROW THE WATERING CAN?
BUFFERY: No!
CLEESE: *ANSWER THE QUESTION!!*
BUFFERY: I – I didn't throw it!
CLEESE: So – he *denies* it! Very well – would you be surprised to hear that you'd thrown the watering can?
 (pause)

BUFFERY: Yes.
CLEESE: And do you deny *not* throwing the watering can?
BUFFERY: Yes.
CLEESE: HAH!
BUFFERY: No!
CLEESE: Very well, Mr Fitch – would it be true to say that you were lying if you denied that it was false to affirm that it belied you to deny that it was untrue that you were lying?
BUFFERY: Ulp . . . Er . . .
CLEESE: You hesitate, Mr Fitch! An answer please, the court is waiting!
 Ah ha ha hah! Ahahha hah! . . . .
BUFFERY: Yes!
CLEESE: What?
BUFFERY: Yes!
 (CLEESE desperately tries to work out if it is the right answer or not)
CLEESE: No further questions, m'lud.

'Judge Not'
John Cleese *Cambridge Circus* 1963

Footlights, 1964

Yet the success of *Cambridge Circus* rebounded on the club. It was a hard act to follow and the two succeeding revues, *Stuff What Dreams Are Made Of* in 1964 and *My Girl Herbert* in 1965, were treated by the critics as auditions for television. The cast of *Stuff* . . . in part encouraged this, by presenting a very television-based entertainment, at least in terms of targets, from the Beatles to Arman and Micheala Denis. Cambridge references were abandoned and the director Mark Lushington talked in terms of a 'class-less' revue.

Eric Idle describes it as 'a bit like a very poor light entertainment show'. But then he wasn't in it. 'I was really destroyed when I didn't get into *Stuff* . . . I had worked so hard to get Mark Lushington made director. Those things are good for you though, they make you think about whether you want to carry on.' That, too, was part of the professional experience and, with the enormous expansion of opportunities in television, the undergraduate of the mid-1960s saw the advantages Cambridge theatre offered. The actor and playwright John Grillo, a member of the 1965 May Week cast, told a journalist that university theatre was '. . . a full time job for which students do not get any money.' Eric Idle exaggerates only slightly when he says, 'Certainly in your last year you were nobody if you didn't have at least three agents coming to look at you in a smoker. . . .'

The attention which the success of *Cambridge Circus* and its antecedents drew to the commercial possibilities of under-graduate humour caused some strain with the management of the Arts Theatre Trust. In 1962 there was a furious row

GOLCHAS *and* FAFNIR, *sitting at a table*, PRANSKL,*the commentator, stands behind them.*
PRANSKL: 'Smurtot yach Proxl?' This week Golchas and Fafnir are in a restaurant. They are deciding what to eat. 'Smurton kaplooey dabogtrifnis eat'. Yes 'eat' is the same word in Proxl as it is in English. See if you can follow what they are saying.
GOLCHAS: 'Schmurtot eat helg, garod schmurtot eat pflastishlbog?'
FAFNIR: 'Pflastishbogl.'
PRANSKL: Did you notice how Golchas said 'garod' instead of 'quodmrt' when he was asking Fafnir to decide? That is because Golchas and Fafnir come from different villages in Proxl. If they came from the same village he would have said 'Quodmrt'. If they come from the same family, Fafnir would be asking Golchas to decide, and she would have said:
FAFNIR: 'Schmurtotl eatl helgl, quodmrtl schmurtotl eatl pflastishbogl?'
PRANSKL: Are you noticing how Fafnir adds an 'l' sound to each world she says? That is because she has a speech impediment. Let's listen, they are deciding on dessert. . . .

My Girl Herbert 1965

Dr H. C. Porter

when the cast agreed to appear on Anglia Television (the local commercial station) without consulting the Arts, who were alarmed at the prospect of 'their' props and costumes being carried away from the theatre without permission. The rights of the Arts in the exploitation of what the Trust had made possible were uncertain. In 1963 the new Senior Treasurer of the Footlights, Dr Harry Porter (a member in the mid 1950s, who on his return from teaching in the United States and Canada took over the post in 1962), negotiated a new agreement to clarify the situation. It was also an opportunity for the Footlights to assert control over its members. For 'the period of the May Week revue' (which could be taken to extend as far as the Edinburgh Festival) all rights to the show were to be handled by the club; for the same period the Arts were to have an interest in any 'deals' with television, and, as the Arts were technically the original presenters (as financiers) of the show, their rights in any subsequent production were protected. The club, however, was responsible for financing the summer vacation tour, which usually began at Oxford and ended at Edinburgh.

The administrator of the Arts, Commander Andrew Blackwood, who succeeded Norman Higgins in the late 1950s, had the added responsibility of overseeing the accounts of the 'Arts Rehearsal Room' – in other words, the Footlights club room. The staff wages were paid through his office and at first the club bought its drink from the Arts. By the end of 1963 the club owed the Arts £500 and it became necessary to rearrange financial affairs between them. The introduction of Associate Membership increased the club's non-revue revenue, but undergraduates of the 1960s proved no better at settling their bar bills than previous generations had been. In 1966 over £500 was owed to the club by past and current members.

None of this hampered the business of putting on revues. In 1964 there was an invitation to appear at a Festival in Padua; the possibility was discussed of exchanging revues with the Harvard Hasty Pudding Club; and there was even a vague invitation to do something in Bermuda. Such were the expansive ideas of the Sixties. In 1965, the club appeared at the Nuffield Theatre in Southampton in March and following May Week *My Girl Herbert* was presented at Oxford, Bury St Edmunds, Newark, the Lyric Hammersmith, Worcester and Edinburgh. The appearance at the Lyric did not come up to the expectations raised by *Cambridge Circus* and the club lost £600 on the tour.

Eric Idle was President of the Footlights in his last year, 1964 to 1965. His predecessor, Graeme Garden, went on to qualify as a doctor while working on *I'm Sorry I'll Read That Again*, but like Graham Chapman he then chose comedy in preference to medicine. David Gooderson, also in

the cast of *Stuff What Dreams Are Made Of,* resisted the
lure of the stage for two years as a teacher before going to
Salisbury Rep in 1966.

Idle freely admits that '. . . our last two years were not as
funny as the Cleese years', which formed the immediate
models for the club. But the Idle years seem to have been
more fun. The pop music explosion, and the attitudes that
went with it, changed social fashions in the University. 'It
was no longer all right to have gone to a public school, or to
belong to the Pitt Club, as John had done. The year before
no one at Cambridge would have discussed who was your
favourite Beatle or whether George really played that solo.'
Musicians rather than actors were beginning to set the style
and Eric Idle's Vice-President and Musical Director, John
Cameron (who has had a successful career as a film music
writer), was a strong presence, both on stage, with his jazz-
rock for *My Girl Herbert,* and off.

Eric Idle was intrigued to read the old programmes and
other memorabilia of the club that were handed on from
President to President. But the Sixties attitude to tradition
was to send it up. He and John Cameron produced this
Cambridge farewell:

Clive James, John Grillo,
Eric Idle, John Cameron, 1965

> We're going down from Cambridge
> Where the streets are paved with gold,
> And we've had three years of happiness
> And now we're getting old.
> The Progs have chased and chased us
> Up and down and round the town,
> But they can't catch us anymore
> Because we are going down.
>
> Cheer oh Cambridge, we must say goodbye,
> Dear old Cambridge, won't leave without a sigh,
> No more breakfasts in the Copper Dive,
> Cheer oh Cambridge in 1965.
> The girls they will all miss us
> As the train it pulls away.
> They'll blow a kiss and say 'Come back
> To Cambridge town some day.'
> We'll throw a rose neglectfully and turn and sigh
>   farewell
> Because we know the chance they've got
> Is a snowball's chance in hell.
>
> Cheer oh, Cambridge, cuppers, bumps and Mays
> Trinners, Fenners, cricket, tennis
> Footlights shows and plays.
> We'll take a final, farewell stroll

Along dear old K.P.,
And a final punt up old man Cam
To Grantchester for tea.

In tune with the 'classless' times, Idle strove to open up the club. Associate membership brought in 'all the naughty boys', which improved the atmosphere in the club room, but he was anxious also to simplify the system for recruiting performers. This had reached a point of considerable elaboration. Firstly names were taken at the Societies Fair, followed by a 'squash' in the club rooms, where would-be members were introduced to the facilities and some of the club's past successes. Following that a recruit would be invited to audition, possibly with a script supplied by the club, in front of the whole committee. 'It was a terrifying performance, enough to frighten anyone away from Falcon Yard for the whole of their Cambridge career.' Instead, Idle suggested an 'audition smoker', which then could lead to election.

Idle's far more revolutionary proposal, however, was the admission of women. It was an idea that deeply upset some of the members who remembered the bright days of the 1950s. Women had been accepted as revue performers since 1957, but were not members. The first woman to perform in a smoker was Eleanor Bron, in a sketch by Bamber Gascoigne, although this seems to have been an aberration. The actress Miriam Margolyes, who played in *Double Take* in 1962, was deeply hurt when she was not allowed to attend the cast party because she was not a member. Moves to change the situation were afoot during Tim Brooke-Taylor's Presidency in 1963, but he opposed this: '. . . it wasn't a sexist thing – the actresses at Cambridge were *actresses* – they took over the ADC, and they were suddenly going to make the Footlights a very theatrical club.' The same objections were raised in 1964 when a former committee member, Hugh Macdonald (who had directed the music for *Cambridge Circus* with Bill Oddie and is now Professor of Music at the University of Glasgow), asserted that the club would be open '. . . to the worst type of careerist feminocrat, a genre that is mercifully not too common here though it has a stranglehold over all types of institution in many other universities.' In March 1964 the committee decided that '. . . there was no reason to bar women from the club' and Felicity Hough and Sue Heber-Percy, the girls picked for the May Week revue, were given the special status of 'revue members' (and were not charged subscriptions).

Eric Idle was determined to mark his Presidency by securing the full admission of women. He pointed out that the argument that women 'weren't funny' was false, because they weren't allowed or encouraged to do revue. He pointed out that at the Edinburgh Festival in 1964 'Oxford had the advantage of a very attractive and talented girl in the cast.' (This was Annabel Leventon, now an actress.) He wrote to the Senior Treasurer, 'I think it is degrading and fantastically backward looking that women should not have the same opportunities at University as men, and it is rather sad that the Footlights lag even behind the Union in this.'

These arguments carried the day and on 20 October 1964 the first four women were elected members of the club, among them the future author of *The Female Eunuch*, Germaine Greer, then doing research at Newnham. The victory was not complete: women were not allowed to be members of the committee nor could they be Associate Members, for fear that male members of the club would swamp the place with their girl friends. The bar on committee membership was lifted in November 1965, when Germaine Greer became 'Registrice'. The bar on Associate Membership went in October 1966, but it was another thirteen years before a woman became President. The 'drag' tradition began to die out (though it has never disappeared completely.) Eric Idle: '... there was no need for drag – Germaine did all that.'

Germaine Greer, 1965

The end of the Footlights' all-male tradition is another sign of the passing of the old order in Cambridge institutions. The Footlights, the ADC and the Marlowe faced competition from new groups who rejected the hierarchies of elections and committee structures in favour of 'doing your own thing'. The 'theatre' was no less important to the rising generation than to its predecessors. The number of productions at the ADC increased from twenty a year in 1960 to over forty in 1974. But in line with developments elsewhere, Cambridge grew its own 'fringe' which challenged the traditional structures of the clubs, just as fringe productions challenged their formal procedures of presentation. Complaints of 'fragmentation' in Cambridge Theatre begin to surface in 1964. Meanwhile the University, paralleling the role of the government through the Arts Council, began to subsidise the ADC. In October 1965 the ADC received £300 from the University and a further £250 from King's. The ADC's Senior Treasurer, John Tanfield, wrote in the *Cambridge Review* on 25 October: 'Fragmentation is excessive in Cambridge. Apart from the College Societies, we have half a dozen ambitious groups, against two in Oxford. The multiplicity is sometimes only apparent – the leading figures are often a stage army, and the committees interlock. But talent is spread much too thinly.'

The new view is represented by Richard Eyre, who graduated in 1964. 'The first year I was in a coma of awe and the second year I exploited the opportunities. . . . Then the third year I regurgitated it all and I felt very uncomfortable. I became aware it was like being in a film set, and of the sense of privilege and gift being there, and then I suddenly recanted. . . .' Such feelings inspired David Hare (a Footlights member) to set up the Independent Theatre Group and put on plays by contemporaries like John Grillo and Howard Brenton. Cambridge, it will be remembered, has no *formal* role for the theatre in its curriculum. The nearest thing to a drama course was at the drama department of Homerton College, a women's teacher-training college which supplied much of Cambridge's female acting talent. Homerton became 'an approved society of the University' in 1976.

Revue, as a more than fifty-year-old genre, was beginning to be affected by the change of fashion, as David Frost pointed out in *Punch* when he reviewed *My Girl Herbert* as kindly as possible at the Lyric Hammersmith in July 1965:

> . . . it is at this moment in time virtually impossible to present a successful stage revue. The old 'topical' revue is dead. It was always more contemporary than topical anyway, but now television can beat the most topical of stage revues to the draw. Equally, the determinedly non-topical revue is invariably seized upon as old old-hat, out of date and generally an abdication of responsibility.

From 1966 until 1970 there were no commercially successful revues in the West End. In July 1970 Kenneth Tynan's exploitation of the end of censorship, the erotic revue *Oh Calcutta!*, opened at the Roundhouse and transferred to the Royalty in September. This, however, was the exception that proved the rule. (Stage nudity did not reach Cambridge until 1971.)

In Cambridge, the rock and roll revolution continued. The *Varsity Handbook* (which was of course promoting the idea) told freshmen in 1967:

> Once it was champagne and white tie, London Debs and effete young men. Once the bands were kept in the background, and a man had to amuse his partner with sparkling conversation as he whirled her around the floor. But the beat groups have taken over the Cambridge social scene. They provide the music, the amusement and the figureheads.

Within their magic circle, the Footlights were not much concerned by the general shift in taste. Their relationship was as much with Cambridge Town as Gown; and there were

Supernatural Gas, 1967

still audiences big enough to fill the Arts Theatre, to make an appearance at Edinburgh a sell-out, and to justify increasingly elaborate tours in-between. A television or radio broadcast usually occurred along the way. In 1966 *This Way Out*, something of a change of tack in that it had a cast of nine, with elaborate sets, props and costumes, went to Oxford, York, Newark and Bury St Edmunds. The following year *Supernatural Gas* had a cast of nine, appearing in Edinburgh in a scaled down version as *The Complete Works*, in which form it returned to the Arts in the Michaelmas Term.

The reputation of the Footlights extended well beyond Cambridge and the question of who should represent them in cabaret appearances became a vexed one. In October 1966 a cabaret 'workshop' (the new fashionable term) was instituted by Germaine Greer to improve the quality of performances. The standard fee for a Footlights cabaret was set at twenty guineas; by 1968 this had risen to forty guineas for a four-person team. In November 1967 a notice posted in the club room reminding members of the ground rules for cabarets caused considerable resentment, but the committee stuck to the view that '. . . cabarets had always been a committee perk.' The minutes also reveal that Cambridge itself was no longer the main area for such activity: '. . . when Footlights cabarets had been rife in Cambridge there were

NEWSVENDOR: Good evening and welcome to the Great War, the first in a new series.
ANNOUNCER: Food is short, and the government has instituted a new system of praying for meals. Never mind, festive crowds still throng the West End, and at the Adelphi, queues have been thronging to see the Salvation Army ensemble, who are doling out soup in the Foyer to the music of the Baden-Powell Lovelies, now playing before packed lunches. The spirit of raw endeavour abounds. After centuries of drudgery, women are on the march and at last becoming militant.
NEWSVENDOR: Enraged mother of five slays renegade Bishop.
ANNOUNCER: Thousands of young men have received white feathers.
NEWSVENDOR: RSPCA appeal for denuded pigeons.
GIRL ANNOUNCER: This year's fashions, as seen at the War Office's Spring Collection suggest khaki, off-the-shoulder trousers, with metal accessories (*Girl model on*), and everyone else is exchanging witty trench jokes. (*Enter man and girl*)
GIRL (*handing man a white feather*): If you know of a better hole, go to it.

Barry Brown *Supernatural Gas* 1967

Jane Barry, Germaine Greer, Chris Mohr, *This Way Out*, 1966

always complaints about the constant repetition of well-worn sketches.' In 1968/9 the Cabaret Team appeared at St Mary's Medical School, Reading University, Merton College Oxford, The London School of Estate Management Ball, Birmingham Law Students Society Ball, Downing Boat Club Ball, Somerville College Oxford and the Hurlingham Club.

The Footlights revues of the latter half of the 1960s bore the distinctive mark of Clive James. He arrived in Cambridge in 1964, having come to England with a degree from the University of Sydney in 1962. He remained at Cambridge (and still lives there) until he gave up his work for a research degree at the beginning of 1969, since when, of course, he has made a reputation as a television critic and man of letters. He was made Registrar in 1965 and became President in 1966. James evidently took his duties seriously. The minutes for 6 February 1967 record his views:

1967

> ... smut was to be stamped on; no jokes were to be passed for performance at a smoker which had the appearance of being dirty purely for the sake of being dirty. The club had a duty to educate the taste of its members, and to encourage them to go for the fine, subtle and difficult laugh rather than the easy and cheap one. Mr James's words were heeded.

It was during James's Presidency that the news broke that Prince Charles was to study at Cambridge. The club secretary posted a notice in the club banning jokes about him: 'Prince Charles, hampered as he is by disadvantages of birth, will have enough to cope with in the coming months without bad jokes and worse manners from members.' When Prince Charles came up he proved to have a taste for comedy and he performed in a Trinity College revue. The Footlights made him an Honorary Member in May 1968 and invited him to their smokers – but he did not perform with the club.

Clive James directed every revue, either for May Week or in the Edinburgh adaptation, from *Supernatural Gas* in 1967 to the *Footlights Festival Commonwealth Games*

Clive James, 1969

With just a word
A single sign of care
With just a touch
I could have been beguiled
But circumstances never smiled
Because the magic wasn't there.

Who was it then?
The poet who once said
How beautiful they are
The trains you miss
So time can't put an end to this.
I have the memory instead.

These nothing scenes are still experience,
You even weep for what did not take place.
Events that don't occur are still events.
Some people vanish with a trace, with just a word.
A single sign of care
With just a touch
I could have been beguiled
But circumstances never smiled.
And now what never happens drives me wild,
Because the magic wasn't there.

Clive James *Fools Rush In* 1969

Drama! The game has been stopped by the Hanoi
players, who are refusing to go on unless Saigon confine
their play to their own half. Saigon are showing their
own determination by executing various minority
groups in this goal-mouth. It's nice to see these quaint
old legacies of French colonial rule still lingering on.
But will the game go on? Yes, the players have swapped
shirts, released a thousand sacred doves and three
political prisoners, to mark the outbreak of the Chinese
New Year, this year called the Year of the Stoat in
honour of Richard Nixon.

Turns of the Century 1968

We've seen all the turns of the century
We've been at it it since 1899
Things may not seem quite what they're meant to be
But everything will turn out fine.

Opening chorus *Turns of the Century* 1968

Tattoo Revue in 1970. His song writing partnership with the
musician Pete Atkin began at Cambridge and Julie Covington's first commercial record, 'The Magic Wasn't There' was
a James/Atkin Footlights song. (Julie Covington was a
student at Homerton and played in the 1967 and 1968
revues.) James's revues were always directed with pace and
style, but the musical element reverted to 'point' numbers
and sentiment. (The choice of his friend Joyce Grenfell as
guest of honour at the 1967 Footlights Dinner suggests an
admiration for the pre-*Fringe* genre.) In 1981 Harold
Hobson called him '. . . the Vera Lynn of university revue.
. . . His absorption with young girls who had tearfully lost
their sweethearts used to make audiences sob, and it is not
sufficient consolation that since he left Cambridge revues
their satire has enormously improved.'

Russell Davies, a close friend of Clive James, who gave up
research at St John's at the same time (and has since also
become a television critic) agrees that their style of revue
'. . . wasn't political, really, but it wasn't about television
shows either.' Apart from a number on Vietnam, the 1968
revue *Turns of the Century* (directed in Cambridge by
Kerry Crabbe) appears almost a throw-back, with its boaters
and long dresses, though the Edwardian atmosphere is
exploited in the same way that the Beatles were dressing up
in military uniforms and playing at circuses in *Sgt Pepper's
Lonely Hearts Club Band.*

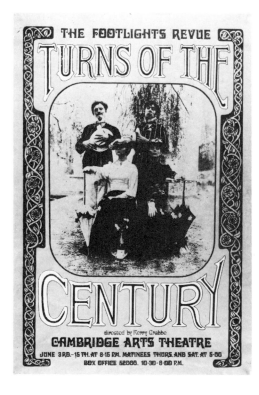

1968

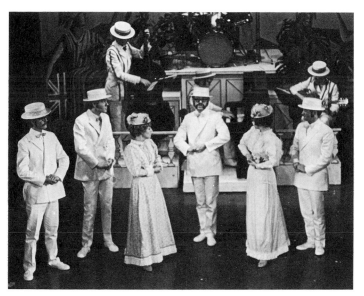

Pete Atkin, Russell Davies

Turns of the Century, 1968   Finale

Julie Covington, Maggie Scott

According to Russell Davies, the change in style was partly fortuitous. 'We had two good girl singers, Maggie Scott and Julie Covington, and Peter Atkin was very interested in becoming a singer. A lot of the verbal energy went into the songs, which by definition is a lot gentler.' Russell Davies was himself a jazz trombone player; with Chapman and Cleese no longer there to express their contempt, dancing as well as singing came back into fashion. Russell Davies: 'We did feel competitive with the shows that had preceded us, but we didn't feel overshadowed by them – the hour of the Monty Python lot was yet to come. If we did feel overshadowed at all it was by *Beyond the Fringe* – not that we knew the actual material that well. I think we felt that we couldn't surprise people in the way they had. You could say that our style of revue was conservative – but it was also pure.'

There is no doubt about the popularity of these shows, or the polish of their performance, but as a genre revue was on the defensive, as Clive James's programme note to *An Hour Late* in Edinburgh in 1969 shows:

> The critics have no way of approaching [the revue artist] except in terms of the latest fashion, and if [the revue artist's] *methods* antecede those of the latest fashion he is automatically out of the running for significance. He can say until he is blue in the face that non-thematic, variegated revue with black-outs between

numbers and spotlights on the songs is a perfectly valid format ultimately vindicated by the audience's applause, attentive silence or laughter. He can say that there is a poetry of humour and that the test of social relevance . . . is necessary but *insufficient*. He can say these elementary things until he is tired under the eyes and balding at the crown and he will still be in the situation we have been in for the last two years – playing to a packed, delighted house *every night of the run*, forming *every night of the run* the kind of rapport with an intelligent audience that the Living Participatory Open Space Inner Sanctum On Your Lap and Up Your Nose theatre of fashion can only *talk* about forming.

By the end of its tour *An Hour Late*, featuring Russell Davies, Robert Buckman and Maggie Scott, had been seen by 10,000 people and had also been seen on television. In October 1969 it returned to the Arts (with Julie Covington in the cast) and then ran as a late-night revue at the Hampstead Theatre Club in London. The possibility arose of a transfer to the West End, but these were no longer the generous days of *Cambridge Circus* and Equity would not agree to the use of these 'amateurs'. Maggie Scott, however, has since had a career as an actress and television presenter (as Maggie Henderson) and Robert Buckman has successfully combined the professions of doctor and comic.

Hampstead featured two further Clive James devised shows, *Late Again* and *Songs From the Footlights*, first performed at matinées in Edinburgh in 1968. Clive James also had a hand in the first and only Oxford and Cambridge

Russell Davies

DAVIES: Soho
BUCKMAN: This is
DAVIES: Solly Hull
BUCKMAN: with a recipe guaranteed to
DAVIES: Brighton
BUCKMAN: every
DAVIES: Hove. – Swiss Cottage
BUCKMAN: Pie. First take a
DAVIES: Hull, John O'Groats, Stornaway
BUCKMAN: in a warm
DAVIES: Kilburn
BUCKMAN: at gas mark 13, baste liberally with
DAVIES: Slough,
BUCKMAN: add a couple of
DAVIES: Cleethorpes
BUCKMAN: if you like that sort of
DAVIES: Tring.
BUCKMAN: Now take a large greased
DAVIES: Basingstoke
BUCKMAN: the kind you use for
DAVIES: Melton Mowbray. . . .

Russell Davies and Robert Buckman *Fools Rush In*
1969

Robert Buckman

1969

collaboration, *Without the Lord Chamberlain's Permission*, a revue at the Arts in October 1968 mounted and filmed at the Arts to raise money for the Oxford and Cambridge Shakespeare Company. (Diana Quick was in the Oxford contingent.) The Footlights President of 1968, Jonathan James-Moore (who also happened to be President of the ADC) was a partner in the company's foundation and for ten years the company was to take an Oxbridge Shakespeare production on a tour of American East Coast campuses during the Christmas vacation. Its start was rocky, to say the least, since it depended on a film deal for the revue that failed to materialise. The revue was filmed, but only because the judicious application of plasticine to telephone receivers prevented a call coming through to the Arts telling the technicians to stop work. (The film exists, but has never been seen.)

Artistic differences also spoiled the collaboration between the Oxford and Cambridge revue artistes and between Clive James and the Shakespeare Company's professional director, Richard Cottrell. As a result the Oxford actors withdrew from the revue and a Footlights-only team performed late-night on the tour. In view of the uproar the first tour had caused, the next Footlights Committee prudently decided to disassociate themselves from the Oxford and Cambridge Shakespeare Company, although individual Footlights members and their material continued to contribute to the Company's late-night shows.

An Hour Late, Edinburgh 1969.
Bill Gutteridge, Ian Taylor, Russell Davies

Edinburgh, 1971

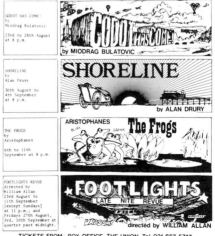

Oxford, 1969

Pantomime, 1971

Clive James and Kerry Crabbe (who directed the May Week shows of 1968 and 1970) appear to have extended the life of traditional Cambridge revue further than the shifts in student fashion would normally allow. The majority of undergraduates, of course, continued to wear grey flannels and work for their degrees, but there is a sense of political aggression in the air after 1968. The Students' Representative Assembly was formed to agitate for increased student participation in University affairs. In February 1970 left-wing students led a demonstration against a Greek government tourist promotion at the Garden House Hotel in Cambridge; windows were broken and seven undergraduates received sentences ranging from six months borstal to eighteen months in prison. The Proctors were criticised for the use of their powers in indentifying left-wingers to the Police. A series of sit-ins were held to advertise student grievances.

The upheavals of the early 1970s were a distraction from the traditional theatre clubs, just as a new wave of politically committed journalism was causing traditional publications like *Granta* to flounder. (The National Union of Journalists, like Equity, had made it harder for graduates to make a smooth transition from student to national journalism.) The Footlights committee evidently felt that they were failing in some way, as a meeting of 1 December 1970 shows:

> There followed a long discussion on why the Footlights were not encouraging the talent that exists in Cambridge. Dr Porter wondered where the Jonathan Millers and Julian Slades were? J.N. Thomas suggested that they might be writing for the *Shilling Paper* and playing in *Henry IV*. He then pointed to the Footlights' camp and frivolous reputation, which was ever being revived, as a cause of its limited appeal to worthwhile talent. This was answered by the jumbled – 'look at *Oh! Its A Lovely War on Want!*', 'You can't say Biafra on stage and expect people to laugh.' Steve Thorn tried to explain the difference between humour and jokes, but a select few failed to see this.

There was another difficulty facing the club, the sheer success of their former members, be they *The Goodies* or *Monty Python's Flying Circus*. The actor Simon Jones recalls, 'We were always being accused of not coming up to the standard of people who came before, which meant the Pythons or *I'm Sorry I'll Read That Again*.' Inflation was also making life difficult: it is noticeable that while the cost of mounting the revue was rising steadily, the profit fell as a proportion of the budget – £301 in 1971, £560 in 1972.

The club did make some innovations that have stood them in good stead. At Christmas 1970 they joined forces with the ADC to mount a pantomime (the ADC had revived their pantomime performances in 1968) and in the following March they took over the ADC theatre for three nights to present a Late Night Revue. This took the process of evolving the May Week show a stage further, by acting as a pilot for the eventual show. But the club's fascination with the media it parodied made a revue like *Gone With The Clappers* in 1971 appear a derivative of show business rather than a witty comment on its pretensions. (The fascination with the film theme extended to the inclusion of an actual film sequence, directed by Richard Brown, parodying cinematic styles.) For the first time since the war the club called on an 'outside' director, Bert Parnaby, a former BBC radio producer who was working as H.M. Inspector of Schools in Cambridgeshire. (He has since returned to the stage as a member of the Royal Shakespeare Company.) The experiment was not a total success.

While the reputation of the Footlights appeared to be slipping with both the critics and the general public (Edinburgh was also less of a success in 1971) the club now faced

Simon Jones, 1971

Last days at Falcon Yard.
Steward John Cant at the bar

Douglas Adams, film sequence
for *Norman Ruins*, 1972

eviction and the demolition of the club room. The long postponed and much argued-over redevelopment of the Lion
Yard area was going ahead. The ploy of making the
developer an Honorary Member of the club had failed to
produce new premises or a stay of execution and a compulsory purchase order was served on the landlords. The
imminence of demolition discouraged repairs and the club
room, last renovated in 1966, had become decidedly tatty;
the carpet was full of holes and the stage curtains no longer
worked. No one thought it worthwhile to mend them. The
last year of the club's occupation of Falcon Yard was made
even more unpleasant by the subletting of the Cruising
Club's rooms above to Snoopy's Discotheque. The club was
broken into and there were fights on the stairs. John Cant,
who replaced Falcon Yard's second Steward, Edgar Orriss,
following Orriss's dismissal by Commander Blackwood in
1968 (Russell Davies served as Steward during the inter-
regnum), reflects the loss of morale in his letter of resigna-
tion on 18 May 1972. 'After two years (during which I have
enjoyed working here) the support for the club by its committee and members seems to have dwindled to almost non-
existence and I now feel that my job is not worth doing.'

Falcon Yard was demolished on 19 June 1972, two days
after the May Week revue closed at the Arts Theatre prior to
a visit to the Oxford Playhouse and the Roundhouse in
London. There was perhaps an unintentional message in the
title, *Norman Ruins*. 'Norman Ruins' proved to be an
elderly impresario whose reminiscences of past glories of the
theatre supplied a linking theme. The critics found the idea
old-fashioned rather than ironic.

The last smoker had been held on Friday 5 May, under
the title, 'Prepare to Drop them Now'. Simon Jones, in the
cast of *Norman Ruins*, was there: 'That last smoker was a
good one, though there was an apocalyptic note about the
sketches. It was a fairly drunken night. People were worried
that it might really be the end of an era. I felt saddest when I
went to Falcon Yard the day before the place was pulled
down. Everything had gone, all the photographs and posters
and so on. The only thing that was left was an engraving of
a portrait of 'The Honourable George Germaine'. The
legend was that it had been put up by Germaine Greer.
Nobody seemed to want it, so I've got it now.'

> This is the bulldozer closer
> We've done what we could with patter-killer-actors
> We're handing over now to caterpillar tractors
> And the roof is caving in.
> But not because of Snoopy's.
> They're putting on a roadshow,
> But strictly not for groupies.

This'll bring the house down,
This is one more rending ending.
We've died so many deaths on this stage that we feel
It's only right to put up the scaffolding for real.
We've gone through all the drill
And now the drill is going through the show.

If you're glad it's all demolished
Then there's one thing you should know:
One old Lion Yard is worth a lot of new Lion parking,
Point nine meters – end of show.

Norman Ruins, 1972

Chox, 1974

CHAPTER VI

'Tag!'

'I see the Footlights have
won the fizzy water award –
how appropriate.'
Oxford revue actor on the
Perrier 'Pick of the Fringe' award

Undergraduate memory is, on average, no more than two years long. With the exception of the occasional research student, or the senior member whose recollections of his undergraduate days are usually listened to politely and then ignored, consciousness of a history that goes back further than those gigantic figures who dominated one's first year at University is little more than folk-memory and mythology. Quite rightly, the current members of a club are interested in what is happening next; the mistakes they avoid are those of their immediate predecessors. Since, very broadly, there is only a limited number of funny situations, and a finite range of targets, it is not surprising that variations on the same theme recur in Footlights revues in three- or four-yearly cycles. The most recent events in the private life of the Footlights have also repeated in miniature the history of the previous ninety years.

The demolition of Falcon Yard was undoubtedly a severe blow to the club and it was struck at a time when the reputation of the Footlights appeared to be working against them. An undergraduate journalist commented in one of the new 'alternative' Cambridge newspapers, *Stop Press*:

> What other University Society would discover that
> people were glad its clubroom had been destroyed to
> make way for the Lion Yard development? The truth, as
> usual, is more complicated. Footlights only worked
> because of élitism; it managed to create a mystique, a
> Thespian life-style, stars if you like, that at once
> parodied and surpassed anything that any other group
> of people had to offer.

The new President in October 1972, Robert Benton, was well aware of the difficulties he faced. He sent out a circular positively pleading for new contributors and inviting them to an informal meeting, in order '. . . to give some idea of the sort of thing which was done in the past. This session is not intended to lay down the limits of what Footlights considers to be good taste, or even good humour, but is intended to remove one of the main barriers which prevents people writing for the Footlights, namely the problem of not knowing what the club does . . . .'

Both the ADC and the Footlights, Cambridge's senior dramatic societies, were in financial difficulties. Following the demolition of Falcon Yard the possibility of the Footlights occupying a warehouse (the 'seed store') next to the ADC's Theatre in Park Street was discussed, but a conversion was estimated to cost a minimum of £12,000. In the meantime, the University took over the administration of the Park Street Theatre from the ADC; in January 1974 the committee of management turned the seed store proposal down. The hopes of a room in the arts centre projected as part of the Lion Yard redevelopment came to nothing and the Fire Brigade vetoed a tentative proposal for a club room as part of the Cambridge Arts and Leisure Association's buildings in Warkworth Street.

Without a club room the Footlights had less to offer and membership declined, although smokers continued in Trinity College Theatre, and in December 1972 the Footlights and the ADC again jointly put on a pantomime, *Dick Whittington*. (The script was partly written by Robert Benton, who combined Presidency of the Footlights with Secretaryship of the ADC.) In the Easter Term of 1974 the club took a room at *The Rose* in Rose Crescent on two nights a week, but the experiment failed. The difficulties of the club are reflected by the cancellation of smokers, in February 1974 '. . . owing to national crises and a dearth of good material', and in February 1975 '. . . due to pressure of events, disease among the chairmen, and a sudden world shortage of things to laugh at.' The status of Associate Member was abandoned and in October 1974 subscriptions were reduced to £1, though even that seems to have been rarely paid.

On the other hand, the change in the club's circumstances removed the taint of exclusivity. And it did not affect the quality of the product. In 1973, *Every Packet Carries A Government Health Warning*, with a large cast and a strong musical contribution from Nigel Hess and Nic Rowley, was considered superior to its immediate predecessors. The drama critic of the *Cambridge Evening News*, Deryck Harvey, went so far as to say that it restored 'the club's failing reputation in recent years.' The director, Stephen Wyatt, was a research student who had appeared in the 1968 and 1970 revues and he followed the successful Clive James/Kerry Crabbe formula of openers, closers, semi-

Footlights at the Roundhouse, 1973

Every Packet Carries A
Government Health Warning, 1973

serious songs and numbers about such 'non-satirical' subjects as Agatha Christie, folk singers, May Balls and J. S.
Bach.

The decline in club membership forced the committee to
widen its net at auditions. Griff Rhys Jones (later of *Not*
The Nine O'Clock News) performed in *Every Packet . . .*
without being a member of the club, although he was elected
shortly afterwards. He was spotted when a Mummers
production of Heathcote William's *AC/DC*, which had been
playing to tiny audiences in the Christ's College Theatre,
gave a benefit performance to the students staging the last
great Cambridge sit-in, on the Sidgwick Avenue development site. (The difference between their reception at
Christ's Theatre and the sit-in shows the shift in student
taste.) Rhys Jones also happened to have been at Brent-
wood Grammar School with two Footlights members, the
President, Robert Benton, and the scriptwriter Douglas
Adams. He recalls that when he came up in October 1972
'Both the ADC and the Footlights had a camp, glittering
image – the leading club in those days was the Mummers,

Griff Rhys Jones

who wanted to put on shows anywhere but the ADC Theatre. In my second year, though, the Footlights changed. It became much more a writers' club, and it got a lot less cliquey because it would cast from anywhere. The auditions were really open. The use of outside directors – outside the committee, that is – helped as well.'

In the Footlights calendar, the Christmas pantomime was beginning to assume an importance equal to that of the May Week revue. But the collaboration with the ADC was coming under strain. Both clubs saw the pantomime (apart from the sheer pleasure involved) as a means of raising money, but there was an imbalance between the financial and creative contributions of each side. The ADC supplied the theatre, but by 1973 most of the ideas came from the Footlights.

Cinderella, in 1973, proved a controversial production. The Footlights committee found it necessary to reprimand the director, Crispin Thomas, who was President of the ADC, for failing to conduct sufficient rehearsals. At the same time the Footlights' half of the budget was overspent by £600, so that when the receipts came to be divided, the ADC made a profit and the Footlights made a loss. This led to a long wrangle between the Senior Treasurers, with the Footlights Senior Treasurer, Dr Porter, asking, 'as a mere historian', the ADC's Dr Mellor, who was a member of the Philosophy Faculty, whether it was 'fair, moral, legal, just, equitable, etc' that the Footlights should lose money and the ADC gain. The philosopher's ethical judgment was: yes. The following year the Christmas pantomime was an entirely Footlights production. (In 1975 the ADC came back on a 60/40 split to the Footlights.)

In 1974 the previous year's President Robert Benton was chosen to direct the May Week revue, *Chox*. The invitations to audition reminded potential members of the cast that there was always the possibility of a London transfer – which to everyone's surprise did indeed materialise, with a four-week run at the Comedy Theatre, the first time the club was back in the West End (as opposed to the Roundhouse and the Hampstead Theatre Club) for ten years. Griff Rhys Jones says that '. . . no-one was more surprised than the cast.' *Chox* was considered not very good in Cambridge and at the Comedy Theatre Michael Billington of the *Guardian* found it 'dismal . . . amateur vaudeville and etiolated whimsy.' In the *Financial Times* B. A. Young called it 'astonishingly nostalgic'. With its concentration on pop singers, television and advertising *Chox* seems to have been a throw-back even further than *Every Packet* . . . .

Crispin Thomas (forgiven after the row over *Cinderella* in 1973) was in the cast and redirected the show for Edinburgh. This time, however, the Cambridge Footlights

In association with Michael White, Richard Jackson & Antony Root present the Cambridge Arts Theatre Trust Production of

The 1974 Footlights Revue

Directed by Robert Benton

Chox

Comedy Theatre
Panton Street W1

**July 15 for
4 weeks only**
Mon-Thurs 8pm
Fri, Sat 6pm & 9pm
Box Office
930 2578

Designed by Charles Maude

Footlights at the Comedy, 1974

Chox, 1974.
Jane Ellison, Griff Rhys Jones,
Sue Aldred, Jon Canter.
(Behind:) Crispin Thomas, Geoff
McGivern

had the embarrassment of being presented by the Oxford
Theatre Group, for the Cambridge University Theatre
Company had been unable to raise sufficient funds. The
company was another victim of the general cash crisis in the
theatre and it was finally wound up in the following year.
Since 1974 Oxford and Cambridge revues have shared the
same Edinburgh venue, St Mary's Hall. The arrangement
makes financial sense, but from time to time university
rivalries have come to the surface.

While striving to maintain a regular programme of
smokers, the Christmas pantomime, a late Night revue in
the Lent Term, the May Week revue and then a summer
tour to such places as Oxford, Southampton, Newark, York
and then the Edinburgh Festival, the club began to
encounter difficulties with the Arts. Although the dis-
appearance of the club room removed one area of admini-
strative friction, the Directors of the Arts Theatre
apparently felt that the Footlights were not sufficiently
responsive to their wishes. (In 1974 there was an unpleasant
dispute when the members of the Footlights band insisted on
being paid full Musicians' Union rates, rather than the sub-
sistence allowance, during their second week at the Arts.)

In November 1974 the Footlights committee were faced
with a suggestion from the Arts that in future the Trust
would take over the responsibility for the May Week production, that it would appoint a director and that auditions
would be open to all-comers – though the Footlights would
be welcome as individuals, of course. Such a proposal, if it
had gone through, would have removed the Footlights
raison d'être. Fortunately the club was able to point to its
1960 constitution, which gave it the right to appoint a May
Week director. At the same time the club let it be known
that it would put on the 1975 May Week revue at the ADC.

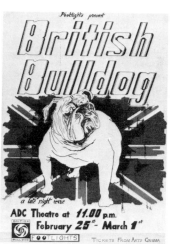

Late night
revue, 1975

Late night
revue, 1979

John Lloyd, 1975

1975

Programme Notes, *Paradise Mislaid*, 1975

May Week is a guaranteed sell-out for the Arts and the Trust did not press their point. The 1975 revue ran at the Arts for two weeks, as usual.

The director in 1975 was John Lloyd, a member of the 1973 cast who had given up his attempts to become a barrister and joined the BBC's Radio Light Entertainment Department. He was one of a group of new writer/producers recruited by David Hatch, then Head of Light Entertainment, in order to bring new blood to the department (just as he, a member of the *Cambridge Circus* generation, had been brought in in the mid-1960s). Hatch and the Head of Television Light Entertainment, Jimmy Gilbert, set up a scheme that enabled them to place up to three young comedy writers a year on a non-renewable twelve-month contract. Writing and performing for radio programmes like *Week Ending* has remained a steady source of early professional experience for ex-members of the club. In 1978 John Lloyd moved to BBC Television and set up *Not the Nine O'Clock News*, first broadcast in October 1979.

With *Paradise Mislaid* (or, *The Touring Inferno*) John Lloyd tried a different (though not new) tack with a theme

Paradise Mislaid, 1975 Griff Rhys Jones, Simon Levene, Chris Keightley, Hilary Cobb

revue, set in Hell. Griff Rhys Jones, who was in the cast, believes this was the most successful revue of those he was associated with, even though, echoing its illustrious forebear *The Last Laugh*, the first night ran for two hours and forty-five minutes. The show picked such suitably apocalyptic targets as *Jesus Christ Superstar*, Ken Russell, Hitler, Milton and Enoch Powell. The long shadow of *Monty Python's Flying Circus* seems to lie across Cambridge humour at this time, notably in the writing of the 'Adams Smith Adams' team – Will Adams, Martin Smith and Douglas Adams, future author of *The Hitch-Hiker's Guide to the Galaxy*. The 1974/75 committee had gone so far as to consider asking the Pythons' producer Ian MacNaughton to direct the revue. A recast and shortened version ran for a week at Edinburgh, where the Footlights faced competition from the Cambridge Light Entertainment Society, appearing as 'The Automatic Punchline Company'.

In 1976 the Footlights again attempted a theme revue, *A Kick in the Stalls*, loosely constructed on the Russian takeover of Bogoffia. The President, Chris Keightley, announced that they were making a '. . . definite move back into the satirical (undergraduate humour has taken a frothy turn recently).' But although the director, Douglas Adams, produced an elaborate construction with numerous props and scene changes, the *Cambridge Evening News* critic found the result 'crushingly unfunny and woefully overlong' *A Kick in the Stalls* lost money in Cambridge and at Edinburgh. (In Edinburgh Griff Rhys Jones used the same dressing room as Rowan Atkinson, who was appearing in the Oxford revue, but apparently they did not meet.)

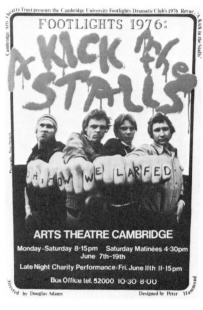

1976

A Kick in the Stalls, 1976

The critical reception of *A Kick in the Stalls* produced a reaction against the *Monty Python* brand of humour. Television, with its facility for great speed and dazzling special effects, is technically too advanced to be a good model for stage revue – yet there was no other model available. Chris Keightley told the *Cambridge Evening News*: 'We are getting past the overlap of people who used to know the club room. You have to go round asking people to write things. They might have a good idea for a sketch but they don't know anything about the mechanics of getting a script down.' His successor as President, Jimmy Mulville, announced that the 1977 revue '. . . will be as far away from *Monty Python* as we can get – even if it means going back to the days of *Beyond the Fringe.*'

Tag!, directed by Griff Rhys Jones, began the move back, if not to *Beyond the Fringe*, then to a more literate, or at least verbal, form of revue. The jokes were still cast in familiar formats – 'Dixon of Dock Green' in franglais, an Ancient Roman Bingo Caller. Cast member Martin Bergman said in an interview later in the year: 'We've consciously said to ourselves no more silliness, after all that *Monty Python* stuff which has become tedious. We've had to ignore the influence of television and get back to the stage revues of the 1950s. If the show is satire, then we've satirised attitudes more than anything else. The Seventies have been hopeless for political satire; there are no sacred cows left to lampoon.'

1977

LE GENDARME: Soir, all. Vous savez, un gendarme's lot n'est pas une heureuse une. Cette semaine, par exemple, j'étais sur le frappe quand nous avions un petit spot de trouble. C'était la même vielle histoire de la femme infidèle et le husband jaloux. La femme dans la question était une certaine Frou-Frou La Gorge, une jolie piece de crackling, avec des bons frappeurs et une vrai cul de sac. Son husband était un professeur and a boring old bugger to boot.
LE HUSBAND: Au revoir, chérie, je vais au travail.
LE GENDARME: Mais avant que tu puisse dire 'Jack Robinson', entre l'autre homme.
L'AUTRE HOMME *(entering):* Frou-Frou!
FROU-FROU: Ooooh! *(they embrace)*
LE GENDARME: Pendant cette hors d'oeuvre, cette petite piece de cordon bleu, this little bit of how's you père, oui, vous avez guessed it.
LE HUSBAND *(entering):* J'arrive!. . . .

Rory McGrath and Jimmy Mulville *Tag!* 1977

Tag!, 1977. Robert Bathurst, Nicholas Hytner.

Electric Voodoo, 1980

The Footlights have made one excursion outside what has become the current style of their revues with *Electric Voodoo* in 1980. Crispin Thomas, who had become an assistant director at the Northcott Theatre in Exeter, was brought back to direct. He promised '. . . a return to the good old days of "spectacular" theatre,' and chose a cast of four men and four women. (Of the women Anne McLaughlin was American, Sheila Hyde Sierra Leonian, Sandi Toksvig Danish and Jan Ravens English.) Thomas's answer to the problem of competition with television was '. . . to try to provide as near as possible the same conditions on the stage', not in terms of *Monty Python*, but colourful costumes and lots of singing and dancing. In spite of the withdrawal under pressure from their Colleges of two of his four men, he produced a polished revue, though amiable rather than original. He did not however seem to have a very high opinion of the material he was given to work with. He later described his experience in the *Arts Theatre Club News*:

> . . . the bemused Footlights producer is confronted on his first visit to Cambridge by a group of young things who are attractive and reasonably amusing but fundamentally devoid of any real sense of direction at all, who present him with a heap of sketches written

over the past twelve months which follow a multitude of
recent and not so recent trends in Television and Radio
Humour, but possess no real style of their own at all.
(Indeed the bulk of this heap is totally without
amusement, having survived on paper at all only
because of its mild success at some smoker where
Corrida and Pernod gilded its charms.)

Thomas's high theatrical style did not sit well with the main-
stream of Footlights taste. Jan Ravens replied to Crispin
Thomas in the next issue of the *Arts Theatre Club News*.
Had he '. . . opined to the committee that revue was dead
before his services were engaged, the cast would have conducted the wake in their own style rather than his.'

Since then, the Footlights have been busy proving that revue
is not dead, in spite of all reports to the contrary. They have
also shown – as was the case between 1947 and 1960 – that
the possession of a club room, though useful, is not essential
to the steady production of smokers, pantomime and revue.
In October 1977 Martin Bergman succeeded Jimmy
Mulville as President. He was determined that the Footlights should be restored to its former position in Cambridge
and that it should once more have a club room. He had to
overcome a great many difficulties to do this and, like an
eminent secretary before him, he did not always make
friends in the process. There were money worries. The revue
had again lost money at Edinburgh and there had been
considerable tension with the Oxford Theatre Group. There
were wrangles within the committee over who should direct
the 1978 revue, in which Bergman was defeated, and there
was renewed pressure from the Arts, who complained that
the revues were becoming predictable and stereotyped. In an
echo of 1974, they suggested that the revue should run for
only one week.

In spite of these difficulties, on 25 February 1978 Martin
Bergman was able to welcome past and present members to
a Gala Smoker featuring Jonathan Lynn, Robert Buckman
(with his University College Hospital colleague Chris
Beetles), Pete Atkin, Clive James and Griff Rhys Jones. The
club was inaugurating its new rooms, but there was something ominous about the affair. Griff Rhys Jones remembers
it as '. . . a strange night, all these famous Footlights people,
standing around affecting not to know each other. It was the
coolest audience I've ever played to.'

The new rooms were in the cellars of the Cambridge
Union Society, in Round Church Street, a stone's throw
from the ADC Theatre. The location should have been ideal,
but there were awkward restrictions: entrance was through

1978

the Union, so the club could not keep its own hours; the Union insisted on supplying the bar and the personnel to run it, thus removing the potentially most profitable side of the club's operations. Because of the shared premises, club members either had to belong to the Union or pay an extra fee, and there were difficulties over advertising events. The rent was £600 a year; estimated running costs were £1,800 annually.

No expense was spared in making the long, low-ceilinged room look attractive; some £7,800 was spent on furniture and fittings, which accounted for most of the Footlights reserve fund with the Arts. Jan Ravens recalls that when new 'the place looked like a New York speakeasy, all bar stools and tubular steel glass topped tables. Unfortunately the chairs fell apart and the tables kept getting broken, so we ended up with a pile of frames and no glass. It would have been lovely to have had somewhere to go, but even when we got the new club room, it didn't work.'

In the Lent Term of 1979 Martin Bergman organised an enterprising programme of events to bring the place alive. He arranged visits by revue groups from Bristol University, East Anglia and Durham. But the rooms proved uninviting. Even the comedienne Victoria Wood played to an audience of only twenty. No event made money. The experiment was repeated in the Lent Term of 1980, but by December of that year it was evident that the room was not going to function with the independent ease of the Masonic Hall or Falcon

Yard. The secrets of success are a late license and your own key. In the meantime, it was easier to have a drink in the *Baron of Beef*.

Clubroom opening Gala, 1978.
Martin Bergman, Jonathan Lynn,
Chris Beetles, Robert Buckman

It may be that the style of student life in the 1980s is not suited to the exclusive atmosphere created by smart rooms and secret elections. There is also the sheer expense of maintaining premises. The Cambridge Pitt Club now survives only by subletting part of its property to a restaurant; the Cambridge Union has had to be rescued by the university and is now administered by the Societies Syndicate, which similarly manages the ADC Theatre. It is a measure of the continued success of the Footlights that it is the only club in Cambridge that has to worry about Corporation Tax.

The Footlights still have their club room in the Union cellars, though it does not operate on a day-to-day basis. It is used for smokers and rehearsals, and to that extent the tradition continues from the early days in Sidney Street. But the room, when it was first occupied, proved something of a liability, for the club once more began to acquire a reputation for exclusivity and cliqueishness. The glossy, entrepreneurial style put people off.

As if to make amends, the club has not only tried to make itself accessible once more, but given proper recognition to women. Jan Ravens has said, 'When I joined the Footlights, no woman would dream of writing anything. You have to have confidence to write something down and know that it is funny. Men are more confident than women – the confidence isn't just to do with writing. The way the world is seen is as though it is run by men.' In recent years Footlights performers like Emma Thompson, Sandy Toksvig and

1979

Jan Ravens herself have been as successful as their male counterparts, Hugh Laurie, Stephen Fry or Tony Slattery, not only in performance, but in writing material and climbing the first steps of the professional ladder.

Jan Ravens, *Cinderella*, 1979

1981

In October 1979 Jan Ravens became the first woman President of the club. She co-wrote and directed, with Sean Cranitch, the 1979 pantomime *Cinderella* and then made an independent gesture, by directing Cambridge's first ever all female revue, *Woman's Hour*, in Lent Term 1980. In 1981 the Footlights broke the taboo altogether and invited Jan Ravens back to Cambridge to direct the 1981 revue, *The Cellar Tapes*. Both in Cambridge, Edinburgh and on television this has proved the most successful of recent revues. In Edinburgh the Footlights won the first £1000 Perrier 'Pick of the Fringe' award and – this being the narrow

'Shakespeare Masterclass', 1981.
Hugh Laurie, Stephen Fry, Tony Slattery

STEPHEN: Good evening. Welcome to 'Shakespeare Masterclass', the third in our series 'An Actor Prepares'. Last week if you remember, we were working with the body and later Tony will be showing what he's been doing with his body over the week. This week, however, we're turning our attention to vocal work, and I've got Hugh here with me in the studio who's going to work with me on a speech. What speech have you got for us, Hugh?
HUGH: It's from *Troilus and Cressida* Act II, scene three, the Ulysses speech.
STEPHEN: T & C II 3, Ulysses. If you'd like to follow in your Ardens at home it's on page 149. First of all, Hugh, I'd like you just to read it through. Imagine a racing car with a camera inside, driving round the track to give us a picture of the whole. Later on we'll

Eighties rather than the expansive Sixties – the revue had a short season at the tiny New End Theatre in Hampstead. The cast have found work in television, radio, the theatre and screenwriting, and Jan Ravens has followed other ex-members of the Footlights into the Radio Light Entertainment Department of the BBC before returning to performance. She calls herself, tongue in cheek, 'the first female BBC producer officially credited with a sense of humour.'

When the cast of *The Cellar Tapes* was presented with their award by Perrier, a Perrier Public Relations girl told *The Tatler*: 'We would have loved to have discovered a totally

The first Perrier Award, 1981.
Hugh Laurie, Rowan Atkinson, Tony Slattery,
Stephen Fry, Penny Dwyer, Emma Thompson, Paul Shearer

unknown struggling company who were absolutely brilliant. Unfortunately that didn't happen.' Over the past hundred years the Footlights have become a finely tuned machine for the production of stage revue. The style and circumstances of revue have changed since its evolution before the First World War and it is true that it is no longer a successful genre in the commercial theatre. (Though who is to say that commercial theatre is itself a successful genre any more?) It is still, however, an attractive form of live entertainment, as the queues outside St Mary's Hall demonstrate each year, while the number of revue groups at Edinburgh multiply annually.

The Footlights revue at Edinburgh is the product of an almost year-long process that begins in October with the auditions for the Christmas pantomime. The pantomime gives an opportunity for freshman talent to show its paces and creates a working atmosphere for the Michaelmas Term smokers. In the Lent Term the cast and material for May Week begin to assemble and a Late Night revue at the ADC

be taking the engine apart, of course, oiling it and putting it back together again. So, T & C II 3.
HUGH: Time hath, my lord, a wallet at his back
Wherein he keeps his alms for oblivion
A great-sized monster of ingratitude.
Erm, that was a bit, er, you know . . .
STEPHEN: Well obviously there are a lot of things to be done there. Let's start shall we with the first word. What's the first word that Shakespeare starts his sentence with, Hugh?
HUGH: Erm, Time.
STEPHEN: Time. Now, how has Shakespeare decided to spell that, Hugh?
HUGH: T-I-M-E.
STEPHEN: T-I-*M*-E! What sort of spelling of 'Time' is that?
HUGH: It's the conventional spelling.
STEPHEN: The *conventional* spelling! And why do you think Shakespeare chose the conventional spelling, Hugh? . . . Think. Was it a mistake? Or did he do it deliberately, Hugh?
HUGH: Deliberately – to get a conven—
STEPHEN: To get a conventional sense of the word 'Time', exactly! Time in its conventional sense. But not just time in its conventional sense, there's something else, isn't there? Think of its placing in the sentence, Hugh? Where does the word come?
HUGH: It's the fir— the first word in the sentence.
STEPHEN: It's the first word in the sentence. And what does that mean?
HUGH: Shakespeare attached a lot of importance to it?
STEPHEN: Yes, I think he did that. But there's something else isn't there. What about the typography, Hugh?
HUGH: It starts off with a capital letter!
STEPHEN: The first letter there, very much upper-case, isn't it, Hugh? And it's the only letter in the word which is. So we have a word in its conventional sense, but also with a capital letter to give us an abstract, what I like to call an abstract conceptual sense. So, Hugh, bearing that in mind – getting that sense of conventional time and abstract conceptual time – would you like to try saying it now?
HUGH: Just the one word, Steve?
STEPHEN: Just the one word, Hugh.
HUGH: *(breath)*
STEPHEN: Wo wo wo. Where do we gather from, Hugh?
HUGH: Oh, from the buttocks.
STEPHEN: Gather from the buttocks, always from the buttocks. So. . . .
HUGH: *(gathering)* Time—
STEPHEN: Well, there are a number of things I liked about that, Hugh, there was . . . there was . . . there was a number of things I liked about that. All right, try it again, keeping the sense of time conventionally, the sense of time as a conceptual abstract, and this time try and bring in a sense of Troy falling, a sense of ruin, of folly, of anger, of decay, of hopelessness and despair, a sense of greed—
HUGH: Ambition?
STEPHEN: No, leave ambition out for the moment if you would, Hugh, of greed, of mortality and of transience. All right? And try to suffuse the whole with a red colour. . . .

'Shakespeare Masterclass'
Hugh Laurie and Stephen Fry *The Cellar Tapes* 1981

1982

Tony Slattery, 1982

takes the creative process a stage further. The May Week director is chosen, and writers and performers come up at the end of the Easter vacation for a 'writing week' before the distraction of working for exams. Fresh material can be tested in a summer smoker and with exams out of the way the rush to get the show for May Week is on.

The two-week run at the Arts is only the beginning of a further process of polishing and refinement for the subsequent three- or four-week tour or longer to regular dates at Southampton, Newark, Bury St Edmunds, York and elsewhere. Finally, honed down to a performance of little more than an hour, and without an inconveniencing interval, it has a two- or three-week run at the Edinburgh Festival. After that, all sorts of possibilities exist, but a television or radio recording is almost a certainty. The cast disperse, some to the round of theatre jobs that will enable them to get an Equity card, others to work that has nothing to do with the theatre, content with their Cambridge careers. Those who have yet to graduate return to Cambridge and use their experience to begin the cycle once more.

These are the mechanics of production, and the machinery alone cannot manufacture talent. But the concentration of intelligence in one of the country's leading universities guarantees that a fresh supply of potential talent is available every year, and the Footlights have the means to focus it. The Cambridge years are crowded with harmless opportunities to test and develop that talent, often in people with the most unlikely exteriors and the humblest ambitions. They have a chance to discover their comic selves alongside those who always knew that Cambridge was the route to a career in the theatre or television.

It might be argued that the Cambridge Footlights have too easy a connection with the wider network of professional entertainment and that the seemingly natural progression from the Arts Theatre to the BBC or commercial television is a cultural conspiracy, built on the privilege of a Cambridge degree. David Hatch, who has seen this conspiracy from both sides, as employee and employer, agrees that '... there is a danger that any group can tend towards self-generation', but says that is not the reason why so many Footlights members have (since the start of the Corporation) gone to work for the BBC. 'It used to be my job to go round the universities, and up to the Edinburgh Festival and so forth, on the look out for talent. I went to Edinburgh each year and normally the most professional show on the Fringe happened to be the Footlights one, because of the Footlights tradition, and you can't go against that. One deliberately went to look for writers and performers, and there was always a fair percentage of the Footlights who want to get in and get on. I was looking for that kind of commitment.' Jan Ravens takes a different view of the conspiracy: 'I *can't* employ all my friends – they're all too busy working.'

The last ten years have not seen as many spectacular successes in professional comedy as the Footlights generations of the mid-1950s to mid-1960s have enjoyed, but that is because the opportunities have not been the same – and most of them have been seized by those earlier generations, who have not yet reached middle age. There has always been a close relationship between the Footlights shows and professional entertainment: at times the Footlights have merely aped the London stage, at others they have given it a lead. And since 1896 they have been quite at home with the idea of appearing on it.

This, however, has been the history of a club at Cambridge and, like any other undergraduate club, the Footlights have produced their crop of academics, barristers, bishops, scientists, civil servants, politicians and bankrupts, besides the writers, directors, musicians and administrators that have been singled out for attention here – and it has not been possible to mention them all, except in the Appendix.

The club has changed and developed, as has the University, and it has been sustained by its tradition, to the extent of surviving suspension during two wars and at least two moments of near financial collapse. It is now the only major undergraduate club in Cambridge that is self-sufficient, a position it has achieved by at once being expert in the ephemeral art of revue and quietly remaining the same beneath the turns of fashion. The present style of

1982

Simon Levene as the Dame,
Babes in the Wood, 1974

Premises, Premises, 1982.
Tony Slattery, Robert Harley, Morwenna Banks,
Neil Mullarkey, Kate Duchene, Will Osborne

revue exploits the vein of intelligent, literate comedy that has persisted since the 1930s, while the knock-about humour, the topical songs and the transvestism of the panto-mimes of today would not have seemed unfamiliar to the Victorian cast of *Uncle Joe at Oxbridge*. The smokers continue as they have always done, and there are still jokes about Cambridge.

Besides the efficient system the club has developed for creating revue, the Footlights have maintained themselves through their social rituals, the rites of election, the holding of office and the struggles for power that mimic those of the wider world. In 1976 the committee decided that '. . . the days of the Swinging Sixties are truly over' and now once more the officials appear at smokers dressed in dinner jackets. The President in 1980 may have been a woman, but her successor was an Old Etonian who rowed for the University.

The summer revue has its own special position in the festival of May Week. The senior members of the University and the townspeople of Cambridge witness the conclusion of another academic year, the gathering of another harvest.

But for many in the audience, and for a good many of its performers, this is the last Cambridge event they will take part in — hence that note of anticipatory nostalgia that can creep into the celebration. The Footlights have become mediators between the private world of the Cambridge undergraduate and the world he or she is about to enter. They interpret that world, and challenge it, by imposing their own style and humour upon it. The performers thus have a double glamour, as stars within Cambridge society, and as its messengers.

The entertainers may appear in different masks, they may mimic different figures of authority and parody changing styles, but the essential carnival continues. As the Footlights prepare for their second century, we can still hear the laughter of that cheerful band of amateurs who set out for Fulbourn Asylum in 1883.

So let's take a last look round
If it's going down well, it always will,
It was Cambridge then, and it's Cambridge still
It will always be the same.

GORDON: Roger!

ROGER: Gordon!

GORDON: Christ, when did you get back from Ceylon?

ROGER: Oh, just a couple of weeks ago.

GORDON: Your tan's still brown.

ROGER: It was unbelievable.

GORDON: I can believe it.

R. & G. *(together):* Ya.

GORDON: Actually, I spent the vacation working in a factory.

ROGER: Was that the stud-pressing factory?

GORDON: Yeah, and I spent the whole summer, y'know, like. . . .

R. & G. *(together)*: Pressing studs. Yeah. Yeah.

GORDON: And it was amazing, 'cos there was a couple of black people there.

R. & G. *(together):* Oh, they're great, yeah.

GORDON: And in the evening, y'know, we used to go drinking. And then one of them said . . . 'What d'you do?'

R. & G. *(together):* Oh, no!

GORDON: So, like, really low-key, really low-key, I said, 'Actually, I'm at er. . . . university.' And they said . . . .

R. & G. *(together):* 'Which one?' yeah, yeah.

ROGER: Oh, that is awful. Look, that is so embarrassing. I can *not* bear to tell them I'm at Cambridge. You know, 'cos they immediately think you are really clever. So, I mean, you know, I just chicken out. I just say I'm at Oxford.

GORDON: Well, no, actually, I said Cambridge, and they said 'Really' and I said 'Really,' and we just talked all evening.

ROGER: I can imagine, 'cos it was exactly like that in Ceylon.

GORDON: Amazing.

ROGER: Amazing, ya.

GORDON: Sure.

ROGER: Because, like the conditions out there are just—

R. & G. *(together):* Unreal.

GORDON: Ya.

ROGER: Whereas, y'know, *here* . . .

R. & G. *(together):* Cambridge

ROGER: Well, they're . . .

GORDON: They're *not* real.

ROGER: They're *not* real, no. . . .

Will Osborne and Richard Turner
Premises, Premises 1982

A Note on the Sources

The principal sources for this book, besides the recollections of members, have been the club archives, that is to say the minute-books, correspondence, programmes, photographs and files of press cuttings and other memorabilia, now in the care of the Archivist, Dr H. C. Porter. Until 1968 it was obligatory to submit the proposed script of a public performance to the Lord Chamberlain's Office, so with certain exceptions it is possible to read the scripts of Footlights revues in the Manuscript Room of the British Library, where the Lord Chamberlain's archive is now deposited.

In addition to the newpapers, magazines and other material referred to in the text, I have quoted from the following published sources: Michael Baker, *The Rise of the Victorian Actor*, Croom Helm, 1978: Michael Frayn, introduction to *Beyond the Fringe* (Bennett, Cook, Miller, Moore), Souvenir Press, 1963; T. W. Craik and Clifford Leach (editors), *The Revels, A History of Drama in English* Volume VII, Methuen, 1978; Willi Frischauer, *David Frost*, Michael Joseph, 1972; Norman Hartnell, *Silver and Gold*, Evans Bros, 1955; Ronald Hayman (editor), *My Cambridge*, Robson Books, 1977; Jack Hulbert, *The Little Woman's Always Right*, W. H. Allen, 1975; Eric Maschwitz, *No Chip on My Shoulder*, Herbert Jenkins, 1957; H. E. Wortham, *Victorian Eton and Cambridge: The Life and Times of Oscar Browning*, Arthur Barker, 1956; Roger Wilmut, *From Fringe to Flying Circus*, Methuen, 1980. I have been greatly assisted also by three articles by Dr H. C. Porter: 'Corpus Christi College and the Footlights Club', *The Letter of the Corpus Association*, Michaelmas, 1982; 'Footlights Dramatic Club, The Early Years, 1883-1913', *Cambridge*, No 10, 1982; 'The Professional Theatre in Victorian Cambridge', *The Cambridge Review*, 28 January 1983.

Glossary

ACADEMICALS: academic dress, consisting of cap (mortar board) and gown. It was compulsory to wear a gown after dark until the late 1960s. In the nineteenth and early twentieth century undergraduates were forbidden to smoke in academic dress, an endless source of jokes. Undergraduates were also required to keep their cap and gown in good order.

THE BACKS: the walks, college courts and gardens behind the colleges of King's Parade and Trinity Street and beside the river that provides the City with its most familiar views.

BEDDER, BEDMAKER: female college servant responsible for cleaning undergraduates' rooms.

BLUE: A member of the University who has represented the University in one of a number of recognised sports, for instance rowing.

BULLDOG, BULLER: Escort to the Proctor (q.v.) in his role as University policeman. Usually a senior college porter, his duty is to chase and restrain recalcitrant undergraduates. In the nineteenth century his uniform included a top hat.

BUMPS: Rowing Races on the Cam, which is too narrow to permit boats to compete side by side. Accordingly, each boat tries to 'bump', that is touch, the one in front, and avoid being 'bumped' by the one behind.

COURTS: college quadrangles.

CUPPERS: inter-college sporting contests.

FENNERS: the University cricket ground.

GATE PENCE: until recently, undergraduates were obliged to be in their colleges by a certain time at night. Those who arrived late paid a fine to the Porter at the College Gate. Other preferred to climb in over the walls and hoped not to be caught.

GYP: male college servants, responsible for Fellows' and undergraduates' rooms, and for waiting in Hall.

HALL: Colloquialism for dinner in the College hall.

K.P.: a colloquialism for King's Parade, also for the defunct 'King's Parade Restaurant.'

LITTLE GO: a 'previous' examination, which had to be passed before beginning courses leading to the B.A.

MAYS: bumping races held during May Week.

OAK: the outer of two doors to an undergradutate's or Fellow's room. When the door was closed, that is to say 'sported', it was understood that the occupant was not to be disturbed.

PITT CLUB: founded in 1835 in celebration of the prime ministership of William Pitt. A Conservative club, which retains those overtones, though by the 1850s it had already become a largely social and sporting institution. It moved to its present premises in Bridge Street in 1866.

PROCTOR, PRO-PROCTOR: a College Fellow (usually one of two) chosen to serve as a University official for one year. Besides manifold ceremonial duties, the Proctors are responsible for enforcing University discipline. They have the power to demand the name and college of any undergraduate, they may levy fines and if necessary bar an undergraduate from the University. Accompanied by Bulldogs (q.v.) they patrolled Cambridge at night in academic dress, and on occasion, still do. PRO-PROCTOR, an assistant proctor.

PROG: slang for Proctor. To be progged: caught or fined by Proctors.

THE REX: a cinema which in the fifties specialised in continental films.

SENATE, GRACE OF THE SENATE: the Senate consists of all MAs of the University; a Grace of the Senate is a formal decision taken by it.

SIX-AND-EIGHTPENCE: by custom, the fines imposed by the Proctors were based on multiples of a third of a pound sterling, in old money, six shillings and eightpence.

STATU PUPILLARI, IN: the term applied to junior members of the University, that is, undergraduates who are pupils.

STROKE: the oarsman who faces the cox and is responsible for setting the time for his fellow oarsmen.

TRIPOS: the Cambridge honours examination, usually taken in two parts during a three-year course.

UNIVERSITY TERMS: the Cambridge year is divided into three-terms with intervening vacations. Undergraduates are usually in residence for eight weeks each term. These are the Michaelmas Term, between mid-October and early December, the Lent Term, between late January and March, and the Easter Term, between April and the beginning of June.

VICE-CHANCELLOR: the most senior resident member of the University, responsible for its government. The Chancellor is a largely ceremonial figure.

The following is a list of all the committees and contributors to May Week productions, as they appear in the May Week programmes, or can be reconstructed from other sources. The committees are listed only as they stood in May Week; changes of office took place from time to time during the period of service, which ran from October to the following June. The Footlights have also performed at other times of the year, but except where they are of special interest, only the May Week productions are listed here. While we may assume that the committee lists are reasonably accurate, beware of pseudonyms and little jokes in the cast lists.

Appendix

1883   No committee listed.

(June) THE LOTTERY TICKET   **Author:** Samuel Beazley;
   BOMBASTES FURIOSO   **Author:** William Barnes Rhodes; **Director and Designer:** W. B. Redfern (Theatre Manager,
New Theatre Royal); **Musical Director:** S. F. H. Dicker (Christ's); **Company:** M. H. Cotton (Christ's), L. H. Outram
(Christ's), F. T. Dobson (Trinity Hall), C. E. M. Hey (Caius), S. F. H. Dicker (Christ's), H. A. Hickin (Corpus), J. H. Murphy
(Trinity Hall).
(November) ALADDIN   **Author:** H. J. Byron; **Director:** S. F. H. Dicker (Christ's); **Musical Director and Conductor:**
H. A. Hickin (Corpus); **Company:** F. T. S. Dobson (Trinity Hall), L. H. Outram (Sidney Sussex), C. E. M. Hey (Caius),
M. H. Cotton (Christ's), A. Y. Baxter (St. John's), P. S. G. Propert (Trinity Hall), J. H. Murphy (Trinity Hall), R. L. Allwork
(Corpus), W. B. Hamilton (Trinity), A. G. W. Bowen (King's), H. H. M. Beddington (Trinity), W. E. Cornell (Caius),
A. S. Hicks (Christ's), E. W. Beach-Hicks (Corpus), I. Roper (King's), A. P. Theobald (Caius), C. M. Ware (Trinity Hall).

1884   No committee listed.

THE BELLS   **Author:** Leopold Lewis.
   THE TRIAL SCENE FROM PICKWICK   **Company:** L. H. Outram (Sidney), J. R. Orford (King's), A. G. W. Bowen
(King's), A. Y. Baxter (St. John's), A. F. Glover (St. John's), F. T. S. Dobson (Trinity Hall), J. H. Murphy (Trinity Hall).

1885   No committee listed.

THE CHIMNEY CORNER   **Author:** H. T. Craven.
   UNCLE JOE AT OXBRIDGE – *A new and original comic operetta in one act.* **Author:** L. H. Outram; **Conductor:**
S. Duffield, New Theatre Royal; **Decor supervised:** W. B. Redfern, New Theatre Royal; **Company:** L. H. Outram (Sidney),
A. Y. Baxter (St. John's), W. Campbell (Trinity), F. A. E. Leake (St. John's), A. M. Ware (Trinity Hall), R. D. Jones
(St. John's), H. F. Mosenthal (Caius), J. H. Murphy (Trinity Hall), A. F. Glover (St. John's), C. H. Taylor (Downing),
H. W. Bathurst (Clare), A. P. Burton (Trinity Hall), A. B. Featherstone (St. John's), W. Dunn (Trinity), J. A. Leon (St. John's),
F. W. R. Dewdney (Jesus).

1886   **President:** F. W. Mortimer. (Corpus Christi); **Vice-President:** H. Clabburn. (Corpus Christi); **Hon. Secretary:**
A. E. Nathan (Trinity Hall); **Treasurer:** G. E. Hale (King's); **Committee:** H. W. Bathurst (Clare), F. A. E. Leake (St. John's),
A. Clark (Jesus), G. Howard (King's).

DISESTABLISHMENT   *A new and original farce in one act.* **Author:** J. J. Withers; **Company:** C. Cargill, E. H. Wynne,
F. Lloyd.
   TOM COBB   *A comedy.* **Author:** W. S. Gilbert; **Company:** E. F. Mayeur, J. J. Withers, F. A. E. Leake, H. W. Bathurst,
G. Howard, J. Valerie, F. Lloyd, A. E. Nathan, G. Beddington; **Stage Manager:** J. J. Withers; **Leader of Orchestra:**
S. Duffield, New Theatre Royal.

1887 **President:** J. J. Withers (King's).
No other committee members listed.

THE BLIND BEGGARS **Author:** Offenbach, in an English version by H. B. Farnie.
 TOM COBB **Author:** W. S. Gilbert.
 UNCLE **Author:** H. J. Byron; **Company:** J. J. Withers, T. F. Lloyd, A. J. Evans, W. F. Massey Berry, E. F. Mayeur, H. W. Bathurst, G. Howard, W. M. Wilcock, E. J. Hainsworth, A. E. Duxford, T. A. Carlyon, A. E. Nathan, C. L. M. Fenn, J. O. Adams.

1888 No committee listed.

THE BLIND BEGGARS **Author:** Offenbach, in an English version by H. B. Farnie.
 ON BAIL **Author:** W. S. Gilbert; **Company:** E. F. Mayeur, A. J. Evans, T. F. Lloyd, E. J. Hainsworth, E. Johnson, R. Lawson, S. F. Beevor, M. C. Berkeley, H. Crofton Atkins, R. Harrison, H. W. Edwards, A. L. Thomas, G. MacNeile, W. Walker, J. Binney, P. Langdon Down, W. E. Norris.

1889 No committee listed.

COX AND BOX **Author:** Sullivan and F. C. Burnand.
 BETSY **Author:** F. C. Burnand; **Company:** C. E. F. Copeman, M. C. Berkeley, J. Carrington, R. Harrison, T. F. Lloyd, R. W. H. M. Palk, H. J. Chart, W. H. Tingey, A. E. Nathan, R. P. Jackson, A. E. Matthew, S. Wilkinson, E. J. Hainsworth, A. L. Thomas, R. W. Wilberforce, E. Hall.

1890 **President and Hon. Treasurer:** Oscar Browning MA (King's); **Vice-President:** R. Harrison (Trinity Hall); **Hon. Secretary and Assistant Treasurer:** G. W. Hardy (Caius); **Committee:** R. Lachlan (Trinity), W. G. Bruty (Jesus), W. G. A'Beckett (Jesus), A. P. Shaw (Trinity).

TO OBLIGE BENSON **Author:** Tom Taylor.
 BRAGANZIO THE BRIGAND **Author:** R. W. H. M. Palk; **Director:** H. J. Chart; **Company:** A. H. Spender, C. T. Goode, G. W. A'Beckett, W. W. Phelps, G. J. Bland, H. G. Chart, R. Harrison, R. W. H. M. Palk, M. C. Berkeley.

1891 No committee listed.

BILLY DOO **Author:** C. M. Rae.
 ALONZO THE BRAVE: OR FAUST AND THE FAIR IMOGEN **Author:** F. C. Burnand; **Music Supervised:** E. A. Philpots; **Company:** M. N. Phelps, A. P. Shaw, A. V. Johnson, S. G. Wilkinson, G. J. Whitehead, J. Hobday.

1892 **President and Hon. Treasurer:** Oscar Browning (King's); **Vice-President:** A. P. Shaw (Trinity); **Hon. Secretary and Assistant Treasurer:** J. B. Pearman (Trinity); **Committee:** G. R. Stansfeld, R. A. F. Phillips, H. C. Pollitt, A. M. Smith.

ALMA MATER *A comedy Burlesque.* **Author:** A. P. Shaw; **Composer:** E. A. Philpots; **Stage Manager:** J. R. Cobbing (Sidney); **Musical Director:** E. A. Philpots (Trinity); **Company:** R. C. Pearman, J. B. Pearman, S. H. Bell, J. R. Cobbing, C. F. Wedemeyer, A. S. Field, G. R. Stansfeld, R. Sweny, A. M. Smith, R. A. F. Phillips, W. Edmonds, H. C. Pollitt, H. L. Darley, A. C. Hobson, A. G. P. Littleton, C. W. Stickland, R. T. E. Gilbert, J. L. Kirk, R. E. Brundrit, L. Cranmer-Byng, G. H. Joshua, F. H. Russell.

1893 No committee listed.

THE MIXTURE   **Author:** A. P. Shaw; **Composed by:** E. A. Philpots; **Company:** C. F. Wedemeyer, C. T. Mathew, J. Hobday, C. O. Gregory, H. C. Pollitt, (no others listed).

1894 **President and Hon. Treasurer:** Oscar Browning (King's); **Vice-President:** C. O. Gregory (Trinity Hall); **Hon. Secretary and Assistant Treasurer:** D. Mappin (Trinity); **Committee:** J. F. Beale, H. L. Darley, C. E. Few, L. A. Pile.

THE MIXTURE REMIXED   *A second edition of the extravaganza.*   **Author:** A. P. Shaw; **Composer:** E. A. Philpots; **New Songs:** J. C. Burlison; **Choreography:** H. C. Pollitt, C. O. Gregory; **Musical Director:** A. C. Hobson (Trinity); **Stage Manager:** M. G. Donahoo (Clare); **Company:** C. J. Mathew, G. T. Elder, A. C. Hobson, M. G. Donahoo, C. E. Few, W. B. Pike, D. Mappin, G. R. Stansfled, M. Longridge, H. C. Pollitt, H. W. Moore, G. R. Barton, W. F. Lanchester, C. A. Newman, C. O. Gregory, C. F. S. Crofton, P. H. Waistell, A. Parry, R. B. Lucas, H. Harrison, W. R. Wyldbore Smith, F. H. Russell, J. P. Pearman.

1895 **President:** Oscar Browning, MA; **Vice-President:** H. C. Pollitt; **Hon. Secretary:** G. S. King; **Committee:** G. H. Rittner, M. V. Leveaux, W. F. Lanchester, G. T. Elder.

(December) CHISELLING *A farce.*   **Authors:** Joseph Dilley, James Allen; **Company:** Frank Towle, Percy Soper, C. A. Knapp, G. S. King, H. W. Brodie.
    A SERPENTINE   **Author:** H. C. Pollitt.
    A HUMOROUS MUSICAL SKETCH   **Author:** C. A. Knapp.
    MEM VII *A comedietta*   **Author:** Walter Ellis; **Company:** S. G. Anderson, M. V. Leveaux, G. H. Rittner, H. W. Brodie; **Stage Managers:** F. P. P. Soper, S. G. Anderson.

1896 **President:** H. C. Pollitt (Trinity); **Vice-President:** G. H. Rittner (Trinity); **Secretary:** M. V. Leveaux (St. John's); **Stage Manager:** S. G. Anderson (Trinity Hall); **Assistant Stage Manager:** F. W. Towle (Trinity); **Junior Treasurer:** R. F. Graham (Trinity); **Musical Director:** J. L. A. Cock (Trinity); **Also:** F. P. P. Soper (Jesus), H. W. Brodie (Clare), C. E. Muggeridge (Trinity); A. J. Moorless (Trinity).

THE SHAM DUKE   **Words:** H. T. Whitaker, H. Lennard, Adrian Ross; **Music:** J. C. Burlison, V. H. Pennell; **Director:** Charles Terry; **Cast:** F. W. Towle, V. H. Pennell, C. E. Muggeridge, H. W. Brodie, F. P. P. Soper, A. C. Lawrence, R. F. Graham, W. B. Langmore, J. H. Beith (Ian Hay), H. S. B. Johnson, S. G. Anderson, G. B. Smythe, H. C. Pollitt, H. Rottenburg, G. H. Rittner, O. J. Kuhn, C. A. Anderson, P. D. Bailey, A. G. Bate, C. A. Ealand, D. Hanbury, W. W. Jones. E. L. R. Kelsey, A. L. R. Goldie, E. B. T. Lee, C. M. Mackenzie, W. E. Mather, B. S. Maxwell, N. P. Norris, R. K. Orlebar, A. F. Part, A. C. Wild.

1897 **President:** H. C. Pollitt (Trinity); **Vice-President:** M. V. Leveaux (St. John's); **Treasurer:** R. H. Adie (Trinity); **Secretary:** A. J. Moorlees (Trinity); **Stage Manager:** G. B. Smythe; **Assistant Stage Manager:** H. W. Brodie (Christ's); **Junior Treasurer:** A. Kirke-Smith (Trinity); **Musical Director:** J. L. A. Cock (Trinity); **Assistant Musical Director:** C. O. Toone (Clare).

THE NEW DEAN   **Libretto:** Harold Ellis; **Music:** J. W. Ivimey, Walter Rubens, Paul Rubens, H. W. Brodie; **Director:** Lawrence Grossmith; **Cast:** F. P. Soper, G. H. Rittner, A. Kirke-Smith, H. C. Pollitt, H. W. Brodie, H. Wacher, A. J. Moorlees, S. G. Anderson, E. Ledgard, E. L. R. Kelsey, L. E. Faber, C. S. Bell, J. T. McGaw, A. H. Stocker, H. Rottenburg, B. S. Maxwell, W. B. Langmore, B. Smythe, H. F. Severn, R. H. Adie, T. A. Cock, G. A. Crane, B. F. Graham, G. H. Cripps, E. Fitzpatrick, C. E. Muggeridge, G. F. Walker, E. T. Tomlinson.

1898 **President:** M. V. Leveaux (St. John's); **Hon. Vice-Presidents:** S. W. Burgess (Jesus), H. Higgins (King's); **Vice-President:** A. J. Moorlees (Trinity); **Treasurer:** R. H. Adie (Trinity); **Secretary:** O. J. Goedecker (Trinity); **Stage Manager:** H. W. Brodie (Clare); **Assistant Stage Manager:** A. C. Lawrence (Trinity Hall); **Junior Treasurer:** C. H. Cripps (Trinity); **Musical Director:** H. V. Rubens (King's); **Auditors:** T. W. Freshfield (Trinity), T. B. Wood (Caius).

A CLASSICAL TRIP   **Libretto:** Harold Ellis, Paul Rubens; **Music:** Paul, Herbert and Walter Rubens, H. W. Brodie; **Director:** Lawrence Grossmith; **Cast:** S. W. Burgess, A. J. Moorlees, G. B. Smythe, R. W. J. Heale, H. W. Brodie, S. G. Anderson, A. C. Lawrence, H. H. Bennett, H. C. Lafone, G. C. Garrick. J. M. Henderson, J. L. A. Cock, G. F. Bird, C. L. Toone, H. Rottenburg, J. O. M. Clark, R. F. G. Scott, H. C. Jerome, E. S. Baker, N. F. Barwell, J. C. Brundritt, T. A. Cock, H. C. Cripps, F. Drake, R. H. Geoghegan, A. L. Clover, W. H. Hastings, B. Hudson, H. M. Maitland, J. F. Neale, R. W. B. Scholefield, G. W. Sharpe, F. P. P. Soper, C. A. Wanton, C. S. Wasbrough, J. M. Yates.

1899 **President:** S. W. Burgess (Jesus); **Hon. Vice-Presidents:** H. Higgins (King's), G. I. Bland (Caius); **Vice-President:** C. H. Cripps (Trinity); **Treasurer:** R. H. Adie (Trinity); **Secretary:** G. C. Garrick (Trinity); **Stage Manager:** H. Rottenburg (King's); **Assistant Stage Manager:** H. L. Lafone (Trinity); **Assistant Treasurer:** O. J. Goedecker (Trinity); **Musical Director:** C. L. Toone (Clare); **Auditors:** T. B. Wood (Clare), A. L. Clover (Pembroke).

THE FRESHMAN   *A fantastic musical absurdity in two acts.* **Author:** Harold Ellis; **Music:** Walter Rubens; **Additional Music and Lyrics:** P. A. Rubens; **Company:** H. W. Brodie, H. Gaskell, J. M. Henderson, R. J. White, R. H. Geoghegan, A. L. Clover, R. H. Robson, G. C. Garrick, S. G. Anderson, H. E. Monro, J. G. G. Gardner Brown, A. H. Bennett, H. C. Lafone, H. Rottenburg, C. B. Scott, O. J. Goedecker, E. S. S. Baker, A. E. Beeton, C. W. Bowle, J. S. Griffith Jones, W. H. Hastings, E. S. Hervey, S. M. Mackenzie, M. Muirhead, T. A. Levett-Prinsep, C. H. Radcliffe, J. E. Stanning, E. Stobart, A. D. B. Scott, A. W. E. Smith, C. L. Toone.

1900 **President:** O. J. Goedecker (Trinity); **Hon. Vice-President:** H. Higgins (King's), H. G. Comber, H. C. Lafone; **Vice-President:** G. C. Garrick (Trinity); **Hon. Treasurer:** R. H. Adie (Trinity); **Secretary:** H. E. Monro (Caius); **Stage Manager:** H. Rottenburg (King's); **Assistant Stage Manager:** C. B. Scott; **Junior Treasurer:** R. H. Geoghegan; **Musical Director:** R. J. White.

THE NEW DEAN   *A musical absurdity in two acts.* **Author:** Harold Ellis; **Music:** J. W. Ivimey; **Additional Numbers:** Paul Rubens, J. F. Marshall, H. W. Brodie; **Producer:** Ernest Lambart; **Conductor:** Herbert V. Rubens; **Company:** H. Rottenburg, W. H. Hastings, E. W. Thornely, C. B. Scott, H. W. Brodie, H. E. Monro, R. J. White, H. C. Lafone, O. J. Goedecker, W. H. Hoggan, A. W. E. Smith, H. R. Robson, T. R. Blake, S. M. Mackenzie, A. D. B. Scott, A. A. Harris, H. H. Bennett, E. K. Fordham, R. H. Adie, I. G. Back, F. H. C. Day, A. Bolden, H. E. Duberly, Hon. T. Heneage, R. W. Ironside, P. D. Knight, R. B. Sanderson, A. McCosh, W. A. Smith, R. H. Geoghegan.

1901 **President:** R. J. White; **Hon. Vice-President:** H. Higgins; **Vice-President:** H. E. Monro; **Treasurer:** R. H. Adie; **Secretary:** Hon. T. R. Heneage; **Stage Manager:** A. A. Harris; **Assistant Stage Manager:** E. K. Fordham; **Junior Treasurer:** W. H. Hastings; **Musical Director:** T. R. Blake.

THE ORIENTAL TRIP or AT HOME AND ABROAD   *A musical farce in two acts.* **Author:** Eric Burke; **Music:** M. Percivale; **Musical Director:** E. A. Martell; **Producer:** Lawrence Grossmith, H. W. Brodie; **Company:** A. D. B. Scott, A. A. Harris, C. B. Scott, T. R. Blake, G. D. Burnaby, E. V. Sassoon, H. R. Robson, R. Muir Mackenzie, R. J. White, R. B. Sanderson, E. W. Thornely, F. H. C. Day, W. F. Bilson, E. K. Fordham, W. C. Falcon, T. P Searight, J. Heard, G. S. Holden, C. W. Bowle, L. C. G. Clarke, W. D. Clements, R. B. Corbin, W. B. Gourlay, Hon. T. R. Heneage, F. W. Morley, W. A. K. Redfern, F. L. Tabor, G. L. Webb, H. Westbrook, G. B. Wordsell, N. Zambra.

1902 **President:** E. K. Fordham; **Hon Vice-Presidents:** H. Higgins, T. B. Wood; **Vice-President:** Hon. T. R. Heneage; **Treasurer:** R. H. Adie; **Secretary:** Hon. T. R. Heneage; **Stage Manager:** T. R. H. Blake; **Assistant Stage Manager:** W. C. Falcon Steward; **Junior Treasurer:** C. W. Bowle; **Musical Director:** E. A. Martell; **Auditors:** G. L. Welsh, W. C. Falcon-Steward.

THE FRESHMAN **Author:** Harold Ellis; **Music:** Walter Rubens; **Extra numbers:** Paul Rubens, F. H. Shera; **Director:** Lawrence Grossmith; **Cast:** R. J. White, Hon. T. R. Heneage, F. H. Shera, G. F. Thomas Peter, H. R. L. Sheppard, D. H. Cox, V. T. A. Shaen-Carter, F. Emrys Jones, E. K. Fordham, F. B. Wilson, G. B. Worsdell, J. Heard, T. R. H. Blake, R. B. Sanderson, W. C. Falcon-Steward, H. B. leD. Tree, F. L. Tabor, H. M. Eisdell, A. T. Isaac, C. Mackenzie, A. M. Milligan, A. H. Habgood, K. D. Wheatcroft, L. C. G. Clarke, C. W. Bowle, G. L. Webb, P. L. Davy.

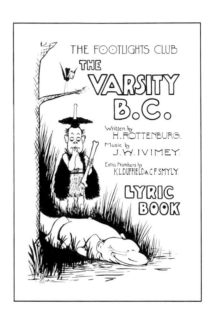

1903 No committee listed.

THE AGRICULTURAL TRIP **Author:** J. Heard; **Music:** F. H. Shera, Percy Harmon, E. A. Martell; **Director:** H. W. Brodie; **Cast:** R. J. White, C. Mackenzie, W. C. Falcon-Steward, T. R. Blake, F. H. Shera, E. V. Sassoon, G. S. Heathcote, R. Spencer.

1904 **President:** G. S. Heathcote; **Hon. Vice-Presidents:** Gordon Campbell, H. W. L. McCall; **Vice-President:** C. MacKenzie; **Treasurer:** R. H. Adie; **Secretary:** N. F. Norman; **Stage Manager:** H. Rottenburg; **Assistant Stage Manager:** J. E. H. Terry; **Auditors:** P. L. Dary, M. Lea; **Junior Treasurer:** W. H. Charlesworth; **Musical Director:** C. B. Hawthorne.

THE NEW DEAN **By:** Harold Ellis; **Music:** J. W. Ivimey; **Extra Numbers:** Paul Rubens, Walter Rubens; **Producer:** Hugh W. Brodie; **Cast:** W. F. McQuade, J. Dearbergh, A. C. N. Bourner, D. L. Ingpen, H. Rottenburg, H. Sawyer, N. Heard, J. E. H. Terry, C. B. Hawthorne, T. F. Burdett, L. R. Fergusson, H. P. Butler, K. L. Duffield, W. R. Haines, E. H. Hincks, H. N. Coleman, G. S. Heathcote, F. C. Newnum, C. MacKenzie, Barry Cook, O. Dixon, H. R. Peel, E. G. Martin, G. Dickinson, H. V. Anderson, F. J. Richardson, A. G. Fergusson, G. K. Sawday.

1905 **President:** G. S. Heathcote; **Hon. Vice-Presidents:** Gordon Campbell, W. L. H. Duckworth; **Vice-President:** H. Rottenburg; **Treasurer:** R. H. Adie; **Secretary:** N. F. Normad; **Stage Manager:** T. F. Burdett; **Assistant Stage Manager:** E. H. Hinkes, **Auditors:** W. R. Haines, D. L. Ingpen; **Junior Treasurer:** C. F. Smyly; **Musical Director:** C. B. Hawthorne.

PAYING THE PIPER or A TALE OF OLD CAMBRIDGE   *A musical absurdity in two acts.* **Authors:** Hugh Brodie,
James Heard; **Lyrics:** James Heard; **Music:** J.W. Ivimey; **Additional numbers:** Paul A. Rubens, Herbert E. Haines;
Musical Director: J.W. Ivimey; **Producer:** Hugh W. Brodie; **Company:** H. Rottenburg, C.B. Hawthorne, W.R. Haines,
T.F. Burdett, N.F. Norman, T.L. De Mesa, E.H. Hincks, F.C. Newnum, C.F. Smyly, W.R. Burrill, H.N. Coleman,
F.I. Richardson, K.L. Duffield, E.H. Sawyer, W.F. McQuade, D.L. Ingpen, N. Heard, E.H. Brandt, H.P. Butler,
W.E. Carter, H.S. Crace, A.D. Craig, R.V. Crake, G.F. Dickinson, H.A. Lucas, A.F. Marsham, H.R. Overbury,
C.W.B. Richardson, P.M. Sanger, H.G. Weber.

1906   **President:** H. Rottenburg; **Hon. Vice-Presidents:** P.L. Gaul, T. Hall, **Vice-President:** D.L. Ingpen; **Treasurer:**
R.H. Adie; **Secretary:** H.P. Butler; **Stage Manager:** W.R. Haines; **Business Manager:** A.D.E. Craig; **Junior Treasurer:**
H.N. Coleman; **Musical Director:** C.F. Smyly.

A CLASSICAL TRIP   **By:** Harold Ellis; **Music:** Paul, Walter and Herbert Rubens; **Additional Material:** Constance
Tippett; **Musical Director:** J.W. Ivimey; **Producer:** Hugh W. Brodie; **Cast:** W.R. Haines, H.N. Coleman, H.P. Butler,
H.E. White, H. Rottenburg, D.L. Ingpen, R.L. Pyman, A.D.E. Craig, J. Sterndale Bennett, G.F. Dickinson, C.G. Sharpe,
V. Chapman, E.A. Lloyd, J.S. Murray, K.L. Duffield, N. Heard, A.F. Marsham, W.F. McQuade, A.C.N. Bourner,
C. Brierley, N.L. Cappel, G.E. Clark, C.W. Foster, B.C. Glen, L.B. Gullick, W.P. Hulton, S.A. Meller, F.I. Richardson,
C.F. Smyly, L.W. Thynne.

1907   **President:** H. Rottenburg; **Hon. Vice-Presidents:** R.H. Adie, Rev. G.A. Weekes; **Vice-President:** H.E. White; **Treasurer:**
H. Rottenburg; **Secretary:** A.F. Marsham; **Stage Manager:** K.L. Duffield; **Business Manager:** J.S. Murray; **Junior
Treasurer:** G.E. Clarke; **Musical Director:** H.R. Overbury.

THE HONORARY DEGREE   **Author:** H. Rottenburg; **Music:** J.W. Ivimey; **Extra Numbers:** Paul Rubens, H.E. Haines,
K.L. Duffield; **Musical Director:** J.W. Ivimey; **Producer:** E.H. Kelly; **Cast:** D.L. Ingpen, J.S. Murray, C.K. Allen,
N.L. Cappel, C.G. MacAndrew, J.G. Robinson, G.H.D. Ascoli, G.E. Clarke, E.L. Adeney, F.M. Mosely, S.A. Meller,
H.K. Baynes, H. Rottenburg, W.F. MacQuade, H.R. Overbury, P.M. Sanger, L.B. Tillard, K.R. Gordon, W.B. Brierley,
R.V.J.S. Hogan, C.V. Hogan, R.B. Horsfield, F.W. Hicks, F. Lacey, G.M.M. Robinson, J.W. Stoddard, A. Warden,
G. Beresford.

1908   **President:** J.S. Murray (Trinity); **Hon. Vice-Presidents:** R.H. Adie, MA (St. John's); J. Stanley Gardiner, MA (Caius);
Vice-President and Hon. Treasurer: H. Rottenburg, MA (King's); **Hon. Secretary:** L.B. Tillard (St. John's); **Hon.
Assistant Treasurer;** J.G. Robinson (Trinity); **Business Manager:** W. Dunkels (Trinity).

THE VARSITY (B.C.)   *A new and prehistoric musical absurdity in prologue, three acts and epilogue.* **Author:**
H. Rottenburg; **Music:** J.W. Ivimey; **Additional Numbers:** C.F. Smyly, K.L. Duffield; **Choreography:** N. van Raalte;
Musical Director: J.W. Ivimey; **Producer:** Ernest Lambart; **Company:** W.F. McQuade, G.A. Beresford,
G.F. Melson-Smith, J.S. Murray, O. Fordham, W. Dunkels, J.G. Robinson, W.B. Brierley, J.G. Annan, G.H.D. Ascoli,
A.S. Warden, G.R. Mitchin, A.T. Miller, H. Rottenburg, L.B. Tillard, R.L. Jump, H.R. Plowden, R.G. Soper, J.B. Hales,
N. Gordon Lennox, C.A. Douglas Hamilton, E.L. Adeney, H.O. Crowther, J.S. Harrowing, S.A. Meller, N. van Raalte,
L.F. Schuster, S.H. Greville-Smith, F.H. Wright.

1909   **President:** L.B. Tillard; **Hon. Vice-Presidents:** J.H. Widdecombe, W. deL. Winter; **Vice-President:** A.T. Miller;
Treasurer: H. Rottenburg; **Secretary:** O. Fordham; **Stage Manager:** J.G. Robinson; **Business Manager:** J.B. Hales;
Junior Treasurer: F.M. Moseley; **Musical Director:** W.A.L. Midgley.

A READING PARTY   **Author:** H. Rottenburg; **Music:** J.W. Ivimey; **Lyrics:** C.S. Rewcastle; **Extra Numbers:**
C.F. Smyly, E.M. Besly, G. Melson Smith; **Musical Director:** J.W. Ivimey; **Producer:** Mervyn Dene; **Cast:** J.W. Stoddard,
J.B. Hales, A.T. Miller, O. Fordham, L.B. Tillard, J.G. Robinson, A.R. Inglis, G.H.D. Ascoli, R.G. Soper, C.A. Douglas-
Hamilton, G. Melson Smith, S. Greville Smith, C.G. Beard, G. Arnfield, H.O. Crowther, J.S. Harrowing, R.A. Lloyd-Barrow,
A.R. Lovelock, C.L. Meer, G.R. Minchin, J.S. Pooley, P.D. Ravenscroft, W. Roskill, L. Schuster, C.M. Sing, J. Stackhouse,
E.A. Sternberg, G.W. Syme, R. Whitehead.

1910   **President:** A.R. Inglis (Trinity); **Vice-President:** R.A. Lloyd-Barrow (Jesus); **Hon. Treasurer:** H. Rottenburg
MA (King's); **Hon. Secretary:** W.G. Roskill (Trinity Hall); **Hon. Assistant Treasurer:** C.M. Stuart (Trinity Hall);
Business Manager: P.D. Ravenscroft (Jesus); **Stage Manager:** G.W. Syme (Caius); **Musical Director:** E.W.B. Vaughan
(Trinity).

1910 (November) THE SOCIALIST *A musical satire in two acts.* **Author:** H. Rottenburg; **Music:** J. W. Ivimey; **Lyrics:** J. L. Crommelin-Brown; **Additional Numbers:** E. M. Besly, C. F. Smyly; **Musical Director:** J. W. Ivimey; **Producer:** Walter Pearce; **Company:** A. K. O. Cochrane, G. W. Prince, C. A. A. Douglas-Hamilton, R. A. Lloyd-Barrow, G. Hutchinson, P. D. Ravenscroft, W. G. Roskill, P. J. Richardson, J. G. Robinson, C. J. W. Miller, C. L. Marburg, J. B. Neale, N. Gordon-Lennox, E. W. Sharp, G. W. Syme, A. R. Inglis, L. F. Cole, H. V. Tennant, O. C. Hawkins, W. E. Harris, J. B. Hales, R. G. Soper, W. G. D. Batten, T. G. G. Bolitho, G. L. Brown, F. W. Card, G. L. Cazalet, M. Clark, P. Holman, E. R. Langley, J. Stackhouse.

1911 **President:** A. R. Inglis (Trinity); **Hon. Vice-Presidents:** R. H. Adie MA (Trinity), Gordon-Campbell LLD (Trinity); **Vice-President:** R. A. Lloyd-Barrow (Jesus); **Hon. Treasurer:** H. Rottenburg, MA (King's); **Hon. Secretary:** W. G. Roskill (Trinity Hall); **Stage Manager:** G. W. Syme (Caius); **Assistant Stage Manager:** C. J. W. Miller (Trinity); **Business Manager:** P. D. Ravenscroft (Jesus); **Hon. Assistant Treasurer:** C. M. Stuart (Trinity Hall); **Musical Director:** E. W. B. Vaughan, BA (Trinity); **Assistant Musical Director:** J. E. Dexter (Jesus).

PAYING THE PIPER, or A TALE OF OLD CAMBRIDGE *A musical absurdity in two acts.* **Authors:** Hugh Brodie, James Heard; **Lyrics:** James Heard; **Music:** J. W. Ivimey; **Additional Numbers:** Paul A. Rubens, Herbert E. Haines; **Musical Director:** J. W. Ivimey; **Scenery:** B. & H. Drury, Brighton; **Producer:** Lawrence Grossmith; **Company:** W. E. Harris, G. L. Cazalet, A. R. Inglis, P. J. Richardson, P. Holman, W. S. Watkins, A. F. M. Greig, P. D. Ravenscroft, G. Hutchinson, L. S. Straker, R. A. Lloyd-Barrow, R. M. Dexter, C. J. W. Miller, H. V. Tennant, J. B. Neale, R. G. Soper, O. C. Hawkins, W. D. Batten, G. F. V. Anson, S. H. Batty-Smith, G. L. Brown, J. F. Forbes, T. N. C. Garfit, G. A. C. Moore, O. W. Nicholson, A. Portago, J. H. Stackhouse, G. W. Syme, E. F. N. Taylor, O. D. Winterbottom.

1912 **President:** P. D. Ravenscroft (Jesus); **Vice-President:** O. D. Winterbottom (Trinity Hall); **Hon. Treasurer:** H. Rottenburg, MA (King's); **Hon. Secretary:** C. J. W. Miller (Trinity); **Stage Manager:** W. E. Harris (Pembroke); **Business Manager:** G. A. C. Moore (Trinity); **Hon. Assistant Treasurer:** W. S. Watkins (Trinity Hall); **Musical Director:** J. E. Dexter (Jesus); **Assistant Musical Director:** Alan Murray (Pembroke).

THE VEGETARIANS *A dietetic absurdity in two acts.* **Author:** H. Rottenburg; **Music:** J. W. Ivimey; **Additional Numbers:** C. F. Smyly, Alan Murray; **Additional Lyrics:** James Heard, R. F. Patterson; **Musical Director:** J. W. Ivimey; **Producer:** Walter McEwen; **Company:** R. M. Dexter, G. A. C. Moore, P. D. Ravenscroft, C. J. W. Miller, O. D. Winterbottom, H. Cuthbertson, H. C. M. Farmer, E. F. H. Taylor, O. W. Nicholson, W. S. Watkins, L. S. Straker, S. d'A. Luard, J. B. Neale, W. E. Harris, R. W. Gosse, S. H. Greville-Smith, R. A. Evans, M. Cuthbertson, D. Carmichael, H. V. Tennant, G. L. Cazalet, B. P. Ayre, T. S. Bowen, P. R. Hollins, A. A. Kingsland, A. F. de. Ledesma, F. Ollerenshaw, N. M. Penzer, V. F. J. Sanfuentes, E. G. Snaith, K. R. Mason.

1913 **President:** C. A. A. Douglas Hamilton, BA (Trinity); **Hon. Vice-Presidents:** R. H. Adie, MA (St. John's), J. C. Lawson, MA (Pembroke); **Vice-President:** O. D. Winterbottom (Trinity Hall); **Hon. Treasurer:** H. Rottenburg, MA (King's); **Hon. Secretary:** E. G. Snaith (Magdalene); **Stage Manager:** M. Cuthbertson (Pembroke); **Business Manager:** D. Carmichael (Jesus); **Assistant Treasurer:** R. M. Dexter (Jesus); **Musical Director:** Alan Murray (Pembroke).

CHEER-OH CAMBRIDGE!   *A musical comedy in three acts.* **Author:** Jack Hulbert (Caius); **Music:** Alan Murray (Pembroke); **Additional Numbers:** J. W. Ivimey, C. F. Smyly (Trinity Hall); **Additional Lyrics:** H. Rottenburg, J. L. Crommelin-Brown; **Musical Director:** J. W. Ivimey; **Producer:** A. E. Dodson; **Company:** Jack Hulbert, E. G. Snaith, R. M. Dexter, A. Portago, N. M. Penzer, F. Ollerenshaw, H. C. M. Farmer, P. L. Barrow, T. P. Ellis, L. S. Straker, M. Cuthbertson, D. Carmichael, H. V. Tennant, C. W. Long, T. S. Bowen, H. Patterson, R. W. Barnett, J. R. Eden, L. H. James, G. A. Mayer, F. R. Orme, C. H. W. Tollemache, F. E. P. Barrington, S. E. H. Orde, C. Temperley, D. H. H. Grayson, W. H. A. Heald, L. Hewitt.

1914 **President:** M. Cuthbertson (Pembroke); **Vice-President:** F. Ollerenshaw (Magdalene); **Hon. Treasurer:** H. Rottenburg, MA (King's); **Hon. Secretary:** P. L. Barrow (Pembroke); **Stage Manager:** D. Carmichael (Jesus); **Business Manager:** E. G. Snaith (Magdalene); **Assistant Treasurer:** T. P. Ellis (Pembroke).

WAS IT THE LOBSTER?   *A plotless musical satire in three acts.* **Author:** H. Rottenburg; **Music:** J. W. Ivimey; **Additional Lyrics:** J. Heard, J. L. Crommelin Brown, P. L. Barrow; **Additional Numbers:** C. F. Smyly, P. L. Barrow, H. Garstin; **Producer:** Walter McEwen; **Company:** D. Carmichael, A. R. Rawlinson, R. R. Glen, G. M. Mayer, C. E. Temperley, W. J. Barnato, M. Cuthbertson, L. B. Felton, L. C. Mandleberg, B. M. Greenberg, C. F. D. Perrins, T. P. Ellis, P. L. Barrow, C. V. Miles, F. Ollerenshaw, W. K. Innes, D. H. Gratson, J. Ransom, T. W. Greenhill, R. D. Tonge, C. J. M. Riley, E. G. Snaith, R. E. Atkinson, F. Barrington, E. W. Carr Forster, W. D. Holland, A. V. Insole, M. H. Jupe, K. S. Kelway, J. F. Mills, B. D. Nicholson, A. Parke, L. W. Woodroffe.

1919 **President:** B. D. Nicholson; **Vice-President:** C. N. Hulbert; **Hon. Vice-Presidents:** R. H. Adie, Com. G. Coleridge RN; **Treasurer:** H. Rottenburg; **Sectretary:** E. A. R. Ennion; **Stage Manager:** P. J. H. Tildsley; **Business Manager:** Sub. Lt. C. G. W. Penn Curzon RN; **Junior Treasurer:** G. G. Tomlin; **Musical Director:** K. L. Spooner. RECONSTRUCTION *An original topical revue.* **Author:** H. Rottenburg; **Music:** J. W. Ivimey; **Extra Material:** J. Heard, C. F. Smyly, P. J. H. Tildsley, C. N. Hulbert, K. L. Spooner; **Musical Director:** J. W. Ivimey; **Producer:** Commander Guy Coleridge, RN; **Cast:** H. Rottenburg, Sub-Lt. G. L. Romme, RN, Comdr. Guy Coleridge, RN, Lieut. N. A. C. Hardy, RN, M. De. H. Watts, W. G. D. H. Nicol, M. C. H. Kingdom, T. G. Bird, W. E. M. Mackay, B. D. Nicholson, Sub-Lieut. T. L. Bulteel, RN, Sub-Lieut. C. G. W. Penn-Curzon, RN, W. H. Gervis, C. N. Hulbert, H. Shaw, Lieut. R. S. Ollerhead, RN, C. G. Tomlin, A. G. Batterham, C. G. Vernon, P. J. H. Tildsley, O. E. Simmonds, Sub-Lieut E. S. Felton, RN, Lieut. N. A. C. Hardy, RN, Sub-Lieut. H. C. Skinner, RN, P. H. Cox, E. A. R. Ennion, C. G. Vernon, J. P. Marsden, H. M. Burrows, L. C. R. Cornford, W. H. Gervis, J. E. Hobson, M. C. H. Kingdon, E. J. M. Milner, A. G. Rodger, A. R. R. Thomas, R. R. Thomson.

1920 **President:** B. D. Nicholson; **Vice-President:** K. S. Kelway; **Hon. Vice-Presidents:** R. H. Adie, Com. G. L. Coleridge RN; Treasurer: H. Rottenburg; **Secretary:** E. A. R. Ennion; **Stage Manager:** C. N. Hulbert; **Business Manager:** P. T. H. Tildsley; **Musical Director:** N. A. Williams; **Junior Treasurer:** F. R. J. Peel; **Property Master:** R. Noel Hill.

HIS LITTLE TRIP **Authors:** R. Noel Hill, L. J. Culverwell; **Lyrics:** L. J. Culverwell, M. D. Lyon, C. N. Hulbert, Com. G. Coleridge RN, M. H. Watts, R. Noel Hill, P. J. H. Tildsley, J. Heard; **Music:** N. A. Williams, M. D. Lyon; **Extra Music:** F. St. J. Brougham, M. H. Watts; **Producer:** Com. Guy Coleridge, RN; Company not listed.

1921 **President:** M. D. Lyon (Trinity); **Vice-President:** F. S. Bates (Jesus); **Hon. Vice-President:** B. D. Nicholson (Trinity); **Hon. Treasurer:** H. Rottenburg, MA (King's); **Stage Manager:** F. F. Gorell-Barnes (Pembroke); **Musical Director:** K. M. Leslie Smith (King's); **Hon Secretary:** H. Malcolm Smith (Pembroke); **Business Manager:** E. A. R. Ennion (Caius); **Assistant Hon. Treasurer:** A. S. F. Reeves (Christ's); **Property Master:** F. J. Buckland (Pembroke).

WHAT A PIC-NIC *A caricaturistical farce.* **Author:** H. Rottenburg: **Music:** M. D. Lyon, Leslie Smith; **Additional Numbers:** C. F. Smyly; **Lyrics:** Leslie Halsey, C. N. Hulbert; **Additional Lyrics:** J. Heard; **Musical Director:** T. Gilby Briggs; **Producer:** E. Hay-Plumb; **Company:** F. J. Buckland, B. H. Grayson, E. I. Nathan, F. E. Powell, J. A. C. Hudson, M. D. Lyon, M. L. H. Watts, F. F. Gorell-Barnes, N. B. Hartnell, R. B. Brown, F. S. Bates, D. B. Aitken, C. N. Hulbert, Petersen, H. Shaw, H. S. Williams-White, A. G. Sharpe, J. C. Ambrose, W. C. Brown, A. Brunner, J. H. Douglas, M. H. Drake, J. F. T. Fenwick, A. J. A. Hollins, R. W. L. Heppard, C. Howard, J. C. Hogg, B. L. Henson, T. C. Lowrie, A. B. S. Laidlaw, E. B. McBain, H. L. A. May, St. J. T. Plevins, W. G. Riley, R. Williamson.

1922 **President:** M. D. Lyon (Trinity); **Vice-President:** C. H. Prowse (Trinity); **Hon. Vice-President:** C. W. Long (Caius); **Hon. Treasurer:** H. Rottenburg, MA (King's); **Stage Manager:** W. C. Brown (Jesus); **Musical Directors:** A. C. Ferguson (Christ's), M. D. Lyon (Trinity); **Hon. Secretary:** John Boyce (Pembroke); **Business Manager:** R. W. l'E. Heppard (St. Catharine's); **Assistant Hon. Treasurer:** F. E. Powell (Jesus); **Property Master:** J. C. Ambrose (Clare); **Assistant Property Masters:** G. R. D. Shaw, W. E. B. Bateman (Jesus); **Assistant Stage Manager:** L. L. S. Thole (St. Catharine's).

THE BEDDER'S OPERA **Authors:** H. Cecil Leon, Brian Davies, N. B. Hartnell; **Music:** M. D. Lyon, A. C. Ferguson, Brian Davies; **Lyrics:** H. Cecil Leon, Leslie Halsey; **Musical Director:** A. C. Ferguson; **Producer:** Gordon Sherry; **Company:** W. G. Riley, M. D. Lyon, J. C. Ambrose, P. Bathurst, John Boyce, W. A. Leon, R. W. l'E. Heppard, F. E. Powell, R. B. Brown, N. B. Hartnell, W. C. Brown, C. G. Pilgrim, J. F. T. Fenwick, R. E. Watson, C. H. Prowse, G. R. D. Shaw, A. H. B. Schofield.
  THE LIVING DEAD **Author:** H. Rottenburg; **Company:** J. C. Ambrose, T. S. Webster, H. Rottenburg, T. H. Grayson.
  THE WARMTH THAT KILLS *A Turkish drama in one act.* **Authors:** M. D. Lyon, E. Maschwitz, H. Rottenburg; **Company:** R. B. Brown, R. W. l'E. Heppard, M. D. Lyon, Messers R. J. Sayres, Allen, W. E. B. Bateman, Hawkes, Harvie, Curtis, Griebe, Howard, Maclellan.

1923   **President:** F. E. Powell (Jesus); **Vice-President:** L. L. S. Thole (St. Catharine's); **Hon. Vice-Presidents:** C. W. Long (Caius), C. H. Budd, MA, H. Rottenburg, MA; **Hon. Secretary:** T. S. Webster (Pembroke); **Hon. Treasurer:** H. F. Shaw (Christ's); **Assistant Hon. Treasurer:** J. B. R. Davies (King's); **Business Manager:** L. H. Savill (Jesus); **Musical Director:** R. J. Sayers (Sidney Sussex); **Stage Manager:** W. E. B. Bateman (Jesus); **Property Master:** J. A. C. Barradale (King's); **Assistant Business Manager:** F. A. Rice (Sidney Sussex); **Assistant Stage Manager:** R. H. B. Longland (King's); **Assistant Musical Director:** A. Barkby (Christ's); **Assistant Property Master:** N. K. Chapman (Trinity).

FOLLY   *A farcical foolishness in three acts.* **Author:** F. A. Rice; **Music:** J. A. C. Barradale, R. J. Sayres; **Lyrics:** J. A. C. Barradale, J. D. Miller, F. A. Rice; **Additional Numbers:** J. B. R. Davies, C. G. Pilgrim; **Musical Directors:** C. F. Smyly, A. Barkby; **Producer:** A. E. Dodson; **Company:** C. G. Pilgrim, N. B. Hartnell, J. A. C. Barradale, A. H. B. Schofield, E. S. Webster, H. J. Warrender, R. J. Sayres, F. E. Powell, C. Hildyard, R. B. Brown, L. L. S. Thole, W. E. B. Bateman, D. G. W. Acworth, N. K. Chapman, C. F. Halford, S. M. Dewey, E. A. Lane, J. Wrench, Messers, Bathurst, Barclay, Carver, Gill, Macfarlane, Miller, Orford-Smith, Skerrett-Rogers, Van Milligen.

1924   **President:** J. A. C. Barradale (King's); **Vice-President:** F. A. Rice (Sidney Sussex); **Hon. Vice-Presidents:** C. W. Long, C. H. Budd, H. Rottenburg; **Hon. Secretary:** J. W. Webster (Pembroke); **Hon. Treasurer:** H. F. Shaw, BA (Christ's); **Stage Manager:** H. H. B. Gill (Trinity Hall); **Musical Director:** F. T. Corbett (Jesus); **Business Manager:** H. J. Warrender (Magdalene); **Property Master:** J. H. Carver (Magdalene); **Assistant Hon. Treasurer:** P. Bathurst (Clare); **Assistant Musical Director:** G. E. Paul (Pembroke); **Assistant Stage Manager:** E. H. Huntington Whitely (Trinity).

BUMPS   *A revue.* **Authors:** F. F. Ogilvy, D. K. H. Roberts; **Music:** Gerald E. Paul, F. T. Corbett, J. A. C. Barradale, H. Rubens; **Lyrics:** Gerald E. Paul, F. T. Corbett, J. A. C. Barradale, H. Warrender, H. Rottenburg, D. Curtis Bennett; **Additional Sketches:** F. A. Rice, G. Addis, H. Rottenburg, D. Curtis-Bennett; **Orchestration:** C. F. Smyly, W. Mayerl; **Orchestra Director:** Gerald E. Paul; **Producer:** Gordon Sherry; **Company:** F. F. Ogilvy, J. Gunning, J. A. C. Barradale, P. Bathurst, D. Gulland, N. K. Chapman, J. Tetley, L. S. N. Hoare, J. D. Burrows, G. L. Alcock, L. Bentall, Hon. J. Bethell, Hon. W. Bethell, T. Larkworthy, A. N. J. Grossman, G. H. Lunge, M. P. Griffiths Jones, D. Cary, H. J. Warrender, P. Edmunds, T. S. Robson, J. St. F. B. Barclay, H. Rottenburg.

1925   **President:** H. J. Warrender (Magdalene); **Vice-President:** E. P. Shaw (Caius); **Hon. Vice-Presidents:** C. W. Long, C. H. Budd, H. Rottenburg; **Hon. Secretary:** T. C. Larkworthy (Emmanuel); **Hon. Treasurer:** H. F. Shaw, BA (Christ's); **Stage Manager:** E. A. Huntington-Whiteley (Trinity); **Musical Director:** F. T. Corbett (Jesus); **Business Manager:** L. G. Bentall (Trinity Hall); **Property Master:** R. S. Muttlebury (Trinity); **Assistant Hon. Treasurer:** F. H. Curtis-Bennett (Trinity); **Assistant Mucical Director:** T. V. Anson (Trinity); **Assistant Manager:** H. C. Martineau (Trinity).

ALL THE VOGUE   *A revue.* **Authors:** F. F. Ogilvy, D. K. H. Roberts, Noel Scott, H. J. Warrender; **Music:** F. T. Corbett, T. V. Anson; **Lyrics:** F. T. Corbett, D. K. H. Roberts, G. Addis, F. R. Wells; **Orchestration:** C. F. Smyly; **Orchestra Director:** F. T. Corbett; **Producer:** Gordon Sherry; **Scenery:** André Charlot; **Company:** R. A. Hignett, T. C. Larkworthy, J. D. Houison-Craufurd, N. S. Ehrlich, L. S. N. Hoare, A. D. Ross, E. D. Vaux, R. M. Pearson, A. C. G. Thesiger, G. W. Albu, A. D. S. Pasley, D. Maclennon, G. L. Alcock, H. J. Warrender, M. P. Griffiths-Jones, D. J. Kinnard, F. R. Wells, Cecil Beaton, E. P. Shaw, E. A. Huntington-Whiteley, J. W. Strickland, F. T. Corbett, T. V. Anson; **Musicians:** R. M. Pearson, D. Moonan, C. M. D. Gooch, H. Leetham, W. K. Faulkner, H. C. Martineau; **Musical Sketch:** Denys Roberts, Francis Ogilvy, H. J. Warrender; **Lyrics:** D. Roberts, F. T. Corbett; **Music:** F. T. Corbett.

1926   **President:** J. D. Houison Craufurd (Trinity); **Vice-President:** R. W. Le. R. de. Koven (Pembroke); **Hon. Vice-Presidents:** C. W. Long, C. H. Budd, H. Rottenburg, Howard Curtis; **Hon. Secretary:** Norbert Ehrlich (Caius); **Hon. Treasurer:** H. F. Shaw, MA, LLB (Christ's); **Stage Manager:** H. C. Martineau (Trinity); **Musical Director:** Howard Curtis (Emmanuel); **Business Manager:** C. A. C. Birkin (Jesus); **Property Master:** J. M. Taylor (Trinity Hall); **Assistant Hon. Treasurer:** G. Albu (Trinity Hall); **Assistant Stage Manager:** M. F. V. Phillipps (Caius); **Assistant Director:** J. H. Tylee (King's).

MAY FEVER   *A revue.* **Authors:** Noel Scott, Norbert Ehrlich, H. Rottenburg; **Music:** Howard Curtis, M. F. V. Phillipps; **Additional Numbers:** Hon. A. Thesiger, J. H. Tylee; **Lyrics:** Noel Scott, M. F. V. Phillipps, D. K. H. Roberts; **Additional Sketches:** P. H. Bellew, D. K. H. Roberts; **Orchestration:** C. F. Smyly; **Orchestra Director:** Howard Curtis; **Choreography:** Gladys Archbutt; **Producer:** Gordon Sherry; **Company:** George Albu, Cyril Moe, C. O. B. Rees, P. H. Bellew, C. J. Carruthers, R. R. Pennington, R. W. Le R. de Koven, N. Sears, G. Wynne Davies, R. N. H. Moore Stevens, S. Dove Wilson, S. J. A. Livingstone-Learmouth, A. Pershouse, W. F. Blandy, R. L. Glover, W. S. A. Clough Taylor, R. E. Kenny, V. F. Stiebel, R. B. Murdoch, F. G. Wood-Smith, A. E. Aiken, C. M. Perkins, E. A. Holt, G. L. Alcock, L. G. Brewster, P. D. Allen, A. H. Hill; **Musicians:** J. H. Tylee, R. V. S. D'Arcy Hildyard, M. L. Elizalde, D. D. Walker, M. Allom, H. I. C. Wyllie, R. C. Sissons, S. D'Arcy Hildyard. F. A. Cooper, S. C. Maughan, J. Pardo.

1927   **President:** H. C. Martineau (Trinity); **Vice-President:** L. C. Rowe, (Clare); **Hon. Vice-Presidents:** C. H. Budd, C. W. Long, H. Rottenburg, H. Curtis; **Hon. Secretary:** C. O. B. Rees (St. John's); **Stage Manager:** M. F. V. Phillipps (Caius); **Musical Director:** H. Curtis (Emmanuel); **Hon. Assistant Treasurer:** R. R. Pennington (Magdalene); **Business Manager:** T. Powell (Jesus); **Property Manager:** T. L. Jones (St. John's); **Assistant Stage Manager:** D. F. Martineau (Trinity), A. D. Ross (St. John's).

PLEASE TELL OTHERS   *A revue.* **Authors:** Sandy Rowe, Noel Scott; **Music:** Howard Curtis, H. E. R. Mitchell; **Additional Numbers:** M. F. V. Phillipps, Roy Glover; **Additional Lyrics:** M. F. V. Phillipps, W. E. H. Walker; **Additional Sketch:** H. Rottenburg; **Orchestration:** C. F. Smyly; **Orchestra Director:** Howard Curtis; **Choreography:** Robert Gordon; **Scenery:** Herbert M. Prentice; **Producer:** Herbert M. Prentice; **Company:** D. F. Martineau, O. F. Maclaren, M. D. L. Scott, F. C. Scott, C. P. Maturin, A. W. Schuster, C. Davis, G. Vickers, R. Gillett, P. C. Mills, J. I. Fell-Clark, C. B. Ford, B. de C. Holroyd, Hon. C. S. V. Allsop, S. A. N. Watney, S. T. A. Livingstone-Learmouth, R. R. Pennington, C. O. B. Rees, Victor Stiebel, R. E. Kenny, Sandy Rowe, P. Holmes, J. D'Arcy-Hildyard, M. F. V. Phillipps, H. E. R. Mitchell.

1928   **President:** H. E. R. Mitchell (Trinity); **Vice-President:** D. F. Martineau (Trinity); **Hon. Vice-Presidents:** C. H. Budd, C. W. Long, H. C. Martineau, H. Rottenburg, H. Curtis; **Hon. Secretary:** J. I. Fell Clark (Pembroke); **Hon. Treasurer:** H. F. Shaw (Christ's); **Hon. Assistant Treasurer:** R. G. Gillett (Jesus); **Stage Manager:** D. F. Martineau (Trinity); **Assistant Stage Manager:** P. C. Mills (St. Catharine's); **Musical Director:** H. Curtis (Emmanuel); **Business Manager:** C. J. R. T. D'Arcy Hildyard (Pembroke); **Property Manager:** P. E. W. Gellatly (Pembroke).

THIS WEEK OF PACE   *A revue.* **Sketches:** Noel Scott, Sandy Rowe, H. E. R. Mitchell, Pat Mills, Jack Clark; **Music:** Howard Curtis, H. E. R. Mitchell; **Lyrics:** H. E. R. Mitchell, George Walker; **Orchestration:** C. F. Smyly; **Orchestra Director:** Howard Curtis; **Choreography:** R. Cave Rogers; **Scenery:** Andrews O. Buck; **Producer:** Andrews O. Buck; **Company:** H. E. R. Mitchell, Roy Glover, Denis Martineau, Jack Clark, Bill Gillett, Pat Mills, J. D'Arcy Hildyard, J. O. Whitmee, L. McL. Watson, Eric Brown, Phil Scott, Bob Symon, Walter Blandy, M. G. Nimmo, Maurice Green, Jimmy King, Dan Hubrecht, Cliff Cook, Bertie Harwood, Norman Coates, B. Edwards, G. C. Monkhouse, R. V. Battle, F. B. Childe, L. H. Kittredge, J. Donaldson, L. E. A. Foster, B. Norton.

1929 **President:** J. Fell Clark (Pembroke); **Hon. Vice-Presidents:** Senior Proctor, C. H. Budd, C. W. Long, H. C. Martineau, H. Rottenburg, H. Curtis; **Hon. Secretary:** H. C. F. Harwood (St. John's); **Hon. Treasurer:** H. F. Shaw (Christ's); **Hon. Assistant Treasurer:** C. G. B. Standring Smith (Pembroke); **Stage Manager:** P. E. W. Gellatly (Pembroke); **Musical Director:** H. Curtis (Emmanuel); **Business Manager:** John Mason (Caius); **Property Master:** J. Monks (Fitzwilliam).

THE GENERAL (S)ELECTION *A revue.* **Sketches:** Noel Scott, H. Rottenburg, J. Fell Clark, Rupert Rogers, W. Bolger; **Music:** Howard Curtis, H. E. R. Mitchell; **Lyrics:** J. Fell Clark, Rupert Rogers, Bill Gillett, W. Bolger, George Walker, H. E. Bird; **Orchestration:** C. F. Smyly; **Orchestra Director:** Howard Curtis; **Producer:** Rupert Rogers; **Assistant Producer:** Roland Gillett; **Company:** Bill Gillett, J. Fenwick, Jack Clark, J. M. Mason, I. D. Davidson, W. B. Bolger, J. Fell Clark, H. E. Bird, H. C. F. Harwood, M. Glen, J. Monks, C. H. Goff, J. Standring-Smith, D. F. M. Hubrecht, A. C. Byrom, N. U. Coates, L. H. Kittredge, M. S. Embiricos, M. G. Nimmo, P. K. Spurrier, P. A. M. Hill, A. Mazower, Murray Ainsley, R. D. Bickford, John Churchill, Richard Marker, C. H. C. Pickering, J. Griffiths, K. Thornton, Coley Williams.

1930 **President:** J. C. Byrom (Emmanuel); **Vice-President:** R. T. Mulhall (Trinity); **Hon. Vice-Presidents:** The Senior Proctor, C. H. Budd, J. I. Fell Clark, H. Curtis, C. W. Long, H. C. Martineau, H. Rottenburg; **Hon. Secretary:** T. W. Reese (St. Catharine's); **Hon. Treasurer:** H. F. Shaw (Christ's); **Hon. Assistant Treasurer:** H. Sidenberg (Downing); **Stage Manager:** J. Monks (Fitzwilliam Hall); **Musical Director:** H. Curtis (Emmanuel); **Business Manager:** L. H. Kittredge (Pembroke); **Property Master:** D. F. M. Hubrecht.

SAY WHEN *A mixture in two acts.* **Sketches:** Brian Davies, H. Rottenburg, George Walker, H. Clarke, R. S. Hill, Ronald Brandon, R. Marker; **Lyrics:** R. S. Hill, George Walker, Rupert Rogers; **Music:** Howard Curtis, R. L. Philpott, R. S. Hill; **Orchestra Director:** Howard Curtis; **Choreography:** Dickie Pounds; **Producer:** Ronald Brandon; **Scenery:** I. Sanderson; **Company:** J. C. Byrom, R. H. Kittredge, Hugh Clarke, Ronald Hill, E. Norman Jones, T. A. Martin, F. B. Newbould, Henry Pierce, S. G. Rix-Hill, M. E. I. Searle, J. Fenwick, C. J. M. Van Bergen, B. H. Fawcett, D. M. Henderson, I. P. Sherring, E. G. Villiers, R. J. H. Kaulback, O. R. Bruce-Dick, T. W. Reese, I. Sanderson, Muir Glen, **Musicians:** George Monkhouse, R. M. Glen, P. Simpson, N. Dainty, R. Bickford, G. V. Aldridge, E. Griffiths, R. L. Philpott, R. Marker, T. Eeles, C. Beatty, N. Ryland.

1931 **President:** R. S. Hill (Christ's); **Vice-President:** H. H. Pierce (Clare); **Hon. Vice-Presidents:** The Senior Proctor, C. H. Budd, J. I. Fell Clark, H. Curtis, C. W. Long, H. C. Martineau, H. Rottenburg; **Hon. Secretary:** M. E. I. Searle (Christ's); **Hon. Treasurer:** R. H. Adie (Trinity); **Hon. Assistant Treasurer:** R. W. Bate (Trinity); **Stage Manager:** B. H. Fawcett (Clare); **Musical Director:** R. H. Philpott (Jesus); **Business Manager:** W. M. L. Fiske (Trinity Hall); **Property Master:** J. Fenwick (Emmanuel).

ONCE AGAIN *The 1931 revue.* **Sketches:** Peter Lyon, Henry Pierce, Roland Gillett, G. B. Shields, Ronald Hill, A. E. Bolton, H. Rottenburg; **Lyrics:** Ronald Hill, Roland Gillett; **Music:** R. L. Philpott, Howard Curtis, Ronald Hill; **Orchestrations:** C. F. Smyly, F. C. Becke, R. L. Philpott; **Orchestra Directors:** R. Speer, Howard Curtis; **Choreography:** Sheila Dexter; **Producer:** Roland Gillett; **Company:** R. Dunsford, Ronald Hill, M. E. I. Searle, Peter Lyon, S. E. MacKenzie, G. E. F. Douty, H. N. G. Allen, Wynyard Browne, H. S. Hoff, G. B. Shields, R. Kaulback, D. Dunsford, G. G. Landon, George Russell, Bobby Fisher, Peter Hole, R. J. A. Kaulback, A. E. Boulton, Jit Singh, B. H. Fawcett, Ivan Sanderson, Richard Philpott, D. J. M. Smith, R. W. Greenwich, J. R. Ainsworth, Roy Speer, Nigel Ryland, W. Russell.

1932 **President:** P. E. Lyon (Magdalene); **Secretary:** W. G. C. Farquar (Christ's); **Assistant Treasurer:** R. W. Bate (Trinity); **Stage Manager:** P. Nickols (Trinity Hall); **Musical Director:** R. Pearce (Trinity).

LAUGHING AT LOVE *A new style musical comedy.* **Story:** Peter Lyon: **Dialogue:** John Davenport; **Lyrics:** Holt Marvel, John Davenport, Malcolm Lowry; **Music:** George Posford, Howard Curtis; **Additional Numbers:** Robin Pearce, Malcolm Lowry; **Orchestra Directors:** Howard Curtis, Roy Speer; **Producer:** Roland Gillett; **Company:** Gwen Pauley, Peter Lyon, Newton Branch, Antony Marr, Andrew d'Antal, Wynyard Browne, W. R. Nichols, Constance Shotter, Eric Duncannon, Naomi Waters, H. J. H. Weekes, Peter Nickols, Nigel Fisher, Anna Lee, Alison Langley, M. Heward Bell, Norman Allen, Joan Robinson, Robin Pearce, Margery Morris, Nancy Scott-Morgan, Monica Perry, Percy Charlesworth, W. Fiske, Bob Greenish, Peter Gourlay, Roy Speer, Malcolm Lowry.

1933 President: J. A. Coates (Pembroke); **Vice-President:** A. L. d'Antal (St. John's); **Hon. Vice-Presidents:** The Senior Proctor, C. H. Budd, J. I. Fell Clark, H. Curtis, C. W. London, H. C. Martineau, H. Rottenburg; **Hon. Secretary:** W. R. Nichols (Caius); **Hon. Treasurer:** J. S. Alexander; **Hon. Assistant Treasurer:** J. Chaplin (Magdalene); **Stage Manager:** N. K. Branch (St. John's); **Musical Director:** N. G. K. Burgess (Trinity); **Business Manager:** Lord Killanin (Magdalene); **Property Master:** D. C. Bain (Pembroke).

NO MORE WOMEN!   **Sketches:** John Chaplin, Frederick Brittain, H. Rottenburg, John Coates, Bill Bain, Wynyard Browne, Lord Killanin. **Lyrics:** Nigel Burgess, Robert Hamer, Newton Branch; **Music:** Nigel Burgess, Geoffrey Wright, Jack Barker, John Greening; **Orchestrations:** Chas. H. Meek; **Orchestra Director:** Nigel Burgess; **Choreography:** Hedley Briggs; **Producer:** John Chaplin; **Company:** Mark Armstrong, Rupert Brabner, Newton Branch, Jim Chaplin, Brian Coates, Tony Groves-Raines, Richard Harrold, Tony Howes, Tom Johnson, John Laughlin, Michael Killanin, Harry Lee, Harry Milner, George Tacchi, Burton Chalmers, Bill Nichols, Arthur Boyce, Freddie Brittain, Andrew d'Antal, Richard Graham, Jack Barker, Jimmy Cardno, Bill Bain.

1934 **President:** Lord Killanin (Magdalene); **Vice-President:** Newton Branch (St. John's); **Hon. Vice-Presidents:** C. H. Budd, Frederick Brittain, J. I. Fell-Clark, J. Chaplin, H. Curtis, J. R. Houldsworth, C. W. Long, H. C. Martineau, H. Rottenburg; **Hon. Secretary:** Douglas Riley Smith (Trinity); **Hon. Treasurer:** J. S. Alexander; **Hon. Assistant Treasurer:** H. I. Lee. (Magdalene); **Stage Manager:** Peter Nourse (Fitzwilliam); **Musical Director:** N. G. K. Burgess (Trinity); **Business Manager:** Hon. W. McClintoch Bunbury (Trinity); **Property Master:** H. G. Milner (Magdalene).

SIR OR MADAM   **Book:** Lord Killanin, Charles Langmaid, Harry Lee, E. Roxburgh Smith, David Yates Mason; **Lyrics:** George Anthony, Nigel Burgess, H. M. Penny, David Yates Mason; **Music:** Jack Barker, Nigel Burgess, H. M. Penny, Fredrick Stevens, Geoffrey Wright; **Choreography:** Carrie Graham; **Producers:** C. Dennis Freeman, Lord Killanin; **Company:** Jack Alexander, Jack Barker, Bill Baxter, Brian Bulmer, Humphrey Bourne, Nigel Burgess, Charlie Cassidy, Peter Crane, Pat Church, James Creedy, Frank Cooper, John Drew, Geoffrey Eager, Tony Ellison, Frank Elvins, John Ewing, Bill Gregg, Tony Groves Raines, Anthony Inwards, John Jameson, Michael Killanin, Michael Landon, Hugh Latimer, Harry Lee, Philip Lever, John McConnel, Robin MacDowall, Harry Milner, Gordon Musgrove, Bill Nichols, Peter Nourse, Douglas Riley Smith, Gek Sanders, Basil Smailes, Fredrick Stevens, John Swann, Marcus Watson, Andrew Winser, Geoffrey Wright.

1935 **President:** Harry Lee (Magdalene); **Vice-President:** Lord Killanin (Magdalene); **Hon. Vice-Presidents:** C. H. Budd, Frederick Brittain, J. I. Fell-Clark, J. Chaplin, H. Curtis, C. W. Long, H. C. Martineau, H. Rottenburg; **Hon. Secretary:** Douglas Riley Smith (Trinity); **Hon. Treasurer:** James Cardno (Trinity); **Hon. Assistant Treasurer:** Tony Ellison (Jesus); **Stage Manager:** Peter Nourse (Fitzwilliam); **Business Manager:** A. Pilkington (Pembroke); **Property Master:** Hugh Latimer (Caius).

NUTS IN MAY   **Book:** Harry Fitzgerald, Michael Killanin, James Wort; **Music:** Bill Dodd, Frederick Stevens; **Choreography:** Florence Graham; **Producer:** Philip Godfrey; **Additional Music:** Marcus Watson, Lionel Salter, James Wort, John Hotchkiss; **Additional Words:** K. Eccleshare, Bill Bain, David Croom-Johnson, Tom Girton, Paul Nash, Philip Gee; **Company:** Bill Baxter, Neville Blackburn, Paddy Boden, Arthur Boyce, Tatton Brinton, Peter Crane, Bill Dodd, Tony Ellison, John Ewing, Colin Hardinge, John Hotchkiss, Anthony Inwards, Hugh Latimer, Harry Lee, Robin MacDowall, John McConnel, John MacMullen, Michael Morris, Paul Nash, Ian Nikols, Doug. Riley Smith, Frederick Stevens, Chris Swan, John Walker, Marcus Watson, Andrew Winser, James Wort, Terence Young, James Cardno, Harry Fitzterald, Pat Church.

1936 **President:** Peter Crane (Trinity); **Vice-President:** W. Martin Murphy (St. John's); **Hon. Vice-Presidents:** C. H. Budd, Frederick Brittain, J. I. Fell-Clarke, J. Chaplin, H. Curtis, C. W. Long, H. C. Martineau, H. Rottenburg, G. H. W. Rylands, J. F. Cardno; **Hon. Secretary:** C. A. Winser (St. Catherine's); **Hon. Treasurer:** R. Branston; **Hon. Assistant Treasurer:** A. W. Ellison (Jesus); **Stage Manager:** P. Nourse (Fitzwilliam); **Musical Director:** F. J. Scholl (Christ's); **Business Manager:** C. S. Swan (Christ's).

TURN OVER A NEW LEAF   **Book:** Colin Forster, Patric Dickinson, Arthur Marshall, Bill Murphy, Charles Hughes, Vivian Cox, David Yates-Mason, George Rylands. **Music:** Frank Scholl, A. K. Arnold, Geoffrey Wright, Marcus Watson, Cecil Burns, Michael Hole; **Choreography:** Robert Helpmann (Vic-Wells Ballet); **Orchestrations:** Bill Trethowan; **Producer:** George Rylands; **Assistant Producers:** Peter Crane, Bill Murphy; **Company:** Peter Crane, Bill Murphy, Colin Mann, Robert Graham, Albert Robinson, Michael Douglass, Neville Blackburne, Colin Harding, Paul Kramer, Dick Stewart, Paddy Boden, M. Hilson, Eric Laman, John Wilson, James Creedy, Alistair Johnston, Terence Young, Chris Swan, Tony Ellison, Peter Meyer, Tito Arias, Theo Arias.

1937 **President:** Albert E. P. Robinson (Trinity); **Vice-President:** Chris Swan (Christ's); **Hon. Vice-Presidents:** C. H. Budd, Frederick Brittain, J. I. Fell-Clark, J. Chaplin, H. Curtis, C. W. Long, H. C. Martineau, H. Rottenburg, G. H. W. Rylands, J. F. Cardno, P. S. Crane; **Hon. Secretary:** W. Michael Douglass (Caius); **Hon. Treasurer:** R. Branston; **Hon. Assistant Treasurer:** S. Paul Kramer (Trinity); **Assistant Stage Manager:** J. F. H. Hamilton (Trinity Hall); **Musical Director:** F. J. Scholl (Christ's); **Business Manager:** R. H. Stewart (Trinity); **Property Master:** P. B. Meyer (Trinity Hall).

FULL SWING   **Book:** Arthur Marshall, Peter Duffield, Vivian Cox, Paul Kramer, Colin Forster, Donald Beves, Eric Laman, Rob Milton, Tim Fortescue, Warrington Baxter, Tito Arias; **Music:** Frank Scholl, Alfred Arnold, Geoffrey Kitchin, Stanley Banyard, David Edwards; **Sets:** Rene Misteli; **Choreography:** Robert Helpmann (Vic-Wells Ballet); **Orchestrations:** Frank Scholl, Geoffrey Kitchen, Bill Trethowan; **Producer:** Donald Beves; **Assistant Producer:** Albert Robinson; **Company** Albert Robinson, Chris Swan, Michael Douglass, Paul Kramer, Dick Stewart, Frank Scholl, Peter Meyer, Peter Duffield, Michael Duffield, Michael Pooley, John Munn, M. Hilson, Robert Lewis, John Gordon, Michael Hadow, Tim Fortescue, Vivian Cox, Rob Milton, Eric Laman, Alistair Johnson, Tito Arias, Harmodio Arias, John Kennett, David Edwards, Robert Graham, Peter Wolf, Guy Halahan, Terence Young, S. Heywood-Smith, Peter Nash, Douglas Jones, Robert Ricketts, Clarence Wilkinson, James Hamilton.

1938 **President:** P. B. Meyer (Trinity Hall); **Vice-President:** M. G. G. Duffield (Trinity); **Hon. Vice-Presidents:** D. H. Beves, Frederick Brittain, C. H. Budd, J. F. Cardno, J. Chaplin, H. Curtis, J. I. Fell-Clarke, C. W. Long, H. C. Martineau, H. Rottenburg, G. G. W. Rylands; **Hon. Secretary:** T. V. N. Fortescue (Kings); **Business Manager:** J. C. W. Munn (Caius); **Hon. Treasurer:** S. Riddiough; **Hon. Assistant Treasurer:** R. M. Hadow (King's); **Musical Director:** W. H. Trethowan (Clare); **Stage Manager:** M. Hilson (Trinity Hall).

PURE AND SIMPLE   **Book:** Colin Eccleshare, Patric Dickinson, Arthur Marshall, David Yates Mason, Bob Ricketts; **Music:** Alfred Arnold, Bill Trethowan, Geoffrey Wright. **Sets:** Fernando d'Ornellas, Grahame Drew; **Choreography:** Robert Helpmann; **Orchestrations:** Bill Trethowan; **Producers:** George Rylands, Leonard Thompson; **Company:** Alfred Arnold, Pat Blockley, Meric Dobson, Michael Duffield, Peter Eade, Colin Eccleshare, Frank Falkner, Tim Fortescue, Michael Hadow, Guy Halanan, Peter Johnson, Douglas Jones, Robert Kent, Bill Lloyd-Jones, John McAnally, Peter Meyer, John Munn, Peter Nash, Michael Pooley, Bob Ricketts, Arthur Rose, Ted Rowlands, Ian Scott-Kilvert, Pat Shuldham-Shaw, Bob Tomlinson.

1939 **President:** Sir Robert Ricketts, Bart. (Magdalene); **Vice-President:** T. V. N. Fortescue (King's); **Hon. Vice-Presidents:** D. H. Beves, Frederick Brittain, C. H. Budd, J. F. Cardno, J. Chaplin, P. S. Crane, H. Curtis, J. I. Fell-Clarke, C. W. Long, H. C. Martineau, H. Rottenburg, G. H. W. Rylands; **Hon. Secretary:** Frank Falkner (Corpus Christi); **Business Manager:** J. M. B. Pooley (Trinity); **Hon. Treasurer:** S. Riddiough; **Hon. Assistant Treasurer:** R. Tomlinson (Corpus Christi); **Musical Director:** M. Schofield (Clare); **Stage Manager:** J. M. B. Pooley (Trinity).

THE FOOTLIGHTS REVUE. THE 1939 ALL-MALE REVUE **Book:** Members of the Club; **Music:** Alfred Arnold, Oliver Beckett, David Edwards, Bernard Rose, P. N. Shuldham-Smith, Steven Wilkinson; **Sets:** Grahame Drew; **Choreography:** Robert Helpmann; **Orchestrations:** Bill Trethowan; **Producer:** Donald Beves; **Assistant Producers:** George Rylands, Leonard Thompson; **Company:** George Banner, Denys Barnard, Oliver Beckett, John Bloch, Pat Blockley, David Bloom, Peter Eade, Jimmy Edwards, Frank Falkner, Peter Johnson, Bill Lloyd-Jones, Tony Mellows, Ronald Millar, Peter Rawlinson, Denis Richard, Bob Ricketts, Leslie Sayers, Eddie Stables, Bob Tomlinson, Bill Vincent, Paul Wingate.

1947 **President:** D. C. Orders (Trinity Hall); **Vice-Presidents:** D. H. Beves, F. Brittain, C. H. Budd, J. F. Cardno, P. S. Crane, H. Curtis, J. I. Fell-Clarke, C. W. Long, H. C. Martineau, H. Rottenburg, G. H. W. Rylands; **Secretary:** B. Garside Gradwell (Queens'); **Senior Treasurer:** F. Brittain (Jesus); **Junior Treasurer:** K. H. G. Willis (Jesus); **Musical Director:** P. Tranchell (King's); **Producer:** M. S. Joseph (Jesus).

1947 MAY WEEK REVUE **Words:** Peter Tranchell, Stephen Sutherland, Ken Willis, John Boston, Stephen Joseph, David Eady, Kenneth Poolman, Ian Clements, Ben Gradwell, D'Arcy Orders, Bill Reader; **Music:** Peter Tranchell, Ben Gradwell, James Brown, D'Arcy Orders; **Producer:** Stephen Joseph; **Music Director:** Peter Tranchell; **Company:** David Eady, Kenneth Poolman, D'Arcy Orders, Ken Willis, Bernard Langley, John Boston, George Davis, Tony Galloway, Ben Gradwell, Elster Kay, Ian Clements, Christopher Pike, Maurice Price, Derek Sears, Michael Westmore, Charles Parker; **Pianos:** Peter Tranchell, Richard Baker, James Brown.

1948 **President:** D. C. Orders (Trinity Hall); **Vice-Presidents:** M. S. L. Joseph (Jesus); **Secretary:** B. G. Gradwell (Queens'); **Senior Treasurer:** F. Brittain (Jesus); **Junior Treasurer:** K. H. G. Willis (Jesus); **Musical Director:** P. A. Tranchell (King's); **Stage Manager:** J. W. Sutherland (Queens'); **Business Manager:** M. N. Westmore (St. Catharine's); **Wardrobe Master:** J. A. Morley (St John's).

LA VIE CAMBRIDGIENNE   **Words:** Richard Armitage, Stephen Joseph, David Eady, Kenneth Poolman, Ian Clements, Ben Gradwell, John Morley, Geoffrey Beaumont, Peter Tranchell, Ted Cranshaw, Charles Parker, Michael Westmore, Richard Baker, Adrian Vale, Simon Phipps; **Music:** Peter Tranchell, John Morley, Ben Gradwell, Richard Armitage, Keith Thomas, Charles Parker, Geoffrey Beaumont, Peter Cooper; **Choreography:** Michael Wilson, Harold Perkin, Alexander MacDougall; **Producer:** Stephen Joseph; **Company:** Michael Westmore, John Morley, Kenneth Poolman, David Eady, John Marriott, Ian Lang, D'Arcy Orders, Christopher Pike, Michael O'Donnell, Michael Wilson, Harold Perkin, Ronald Shephard, Maurice Price, John Silverlight, John Shearme, Cyril Hartley, Elster Kay, Charles Parker, Adrian Vale; **Scenery:** Stephen Joseph, Peterjohn Darvall, Gerald Shipman.

1949   **President:** Simon Phipps; **Secretary:** Ken Willis; **Senior Treasurer:** F. Brittain; **Committee Members:** Ted Cranshaw, Bill Mainprice, Michael O'Donnell, Gerald Shipman, Peter Tranchell; **Press:** Peter King; **Stage Manager:** Ted Cranshaw; **Business Manager:** Michael O'Donnell; **Property Master:** George Noordhof.

ALWAYS IN JUNE   **Producer:** Simon Phipps; **Script:** Simon Phipps, Peter Shaffer, Robert Baylis, Victor Menzies, Robin McEwen, Adrian Vale; **Lyrics:** Simon Phipps, Peter Tranchell, Robert Baylis, John Caffyn, Julian More, Ian Robertson; **Music:** Peter Tranchell, Geoffrey Beaumont, Ken Ferris, Thurston Dart; **Décor:** Gerald Shipman, Peterjohn Darvall, Patrick Robertson, Quentin Lawrence; **Company:** Richard Bird, Charles Canner, Michael Davidson, Ken Ferris, Martin Forrest, John Gayer-Anderson, Alistaire Kaye, Mark Kernick, Howard Letty, Stephen Lucas, Victor Menzies, Derek Moore, Julian More, George Noordhof, Simon Phipps, Ken Poolman, Ian Robertson, Desmond Scott, Julian Slade, Frederick Smith, Adrian Vale, Ken Willis.

1950   **President:** Adrian Vale; **Secretary:** Victor Menzies; **Senior Treasurer:** F. Brittain; **Committee:** Desmond Scott, Ken Ferris, Jimmie Batten, Malcolm Burgess, John Hosier; **Press:** Peter Shaffer.

COME WHAT MAY   **Words:** Adrian Vale, Julian More, Anthony Shaffer, Simon Phipps, Victor Menzies, Oliver Pemberton, Julian Slade, John Caffyn, Les Leski, Denys Amos; **Music:** John Hosier, Paddy Dickson, Geoffrey Beaumont, Julian Slade, Ken Ferris, Peter Tranchell; **Musical Director:** John Hosier; **Dances:** Tony Reid; **Décor:** Malcolm Burgess, Peterjohn Darvall, Colin Brown; **Producer:** Adrian Vale; **Company:** Denys Amos, Jimmie Batten, Malcolm Burgess, Leslie Clarke, Ken Ferris, Guy Hitchings, Peter Jeffrey, Ian Kellie, Malcolm Kernick, Howard Letty, Stephen Lucas, Neill McGregor-Wood, Victor Menzies, Ben Meredith, Michael Miller, Julian More, Simon Phipps, Graham Reid, Tony Reid, Dennis Russel, Desmond Scott, Frederic Smith, Robin Tuck, Adrian Vale, Colin Webb, Peter Williams, Jack Carruthers-Smith.

1951   **President:** Ian Kellie; **Vice-President:** Julian Slade; **Secretary:** Peter Jeffrey; **Senior Treasurer:** Dr F. Brittain; **Junior Treasurer:** John Maltby; **Musical Director:** Ken Ferris; **Stage Manager:** Angus Thomas; **Business Manager:** Richard Mayne; **Décor:** Malcolm Burgess; **Press:** Warden Miller; **Revue Secretary:** Julian More.

A FLASH IN THE CAM   **Words:** Mike Hall, Peter Firth, Michael Young, Ian Kellie, Peter Jeffrey, Michael Miller, Julian More, Robin Tuck, Malcolm Burgess, Christopher Pym, David Davis, Mike Hall, Brian Rees; **Lyrics:** Ian Kellie, Andrew Davidson, Geoffrey Beaumont, Julian More, John Caffyn, Julian Slade, Barney Miller, Peter Tranchell, Brian Rees, Alastair Sampson, Christopher Pym; **Music:** Andrew Davidson, Geoffrey Beaumont, Ken Ferris, Julian Slade, Barney Miller, Alastair Maclean, Brian Rees, Alastair Sampson; **Music Arranged:** Ken Ferris, Andrew Davidson; **Settings:** Malcolm Burgess; **Devised and Produced:** Ian Kellie; **Company:** Mike Hall, Peter Firth, Mark Kernick, Michael Young, Michael Miller, Julian More, Robert Busvine, David Allan, Peter Matthews, Angus Thomas, Cyril Horsford, Jimmy Cellan-Jones, Harry Streets, Peter Jeffrey, Ian Kellie, Ken Ferris, Joseph Bain, Donald Rudd, Robin Tuck, Barney Miller, Christopher Pym, John Bartlett, Dennis Russell, Brian Cannon.

1952   **President:** Andrew Davison; **Vice-President:** Robin Tuck; **Secretary:** David Morgan Rees; **Senior Treasurer:** Dr F. Brittain; **Junior Treasurer:** Peter Firth; **Musical Director:** Ken Ferris; **Stage Manager:** Dick Robertson; **Business Manager:** Michael Young; **Press:** Barney Miller; **Production Secretary:** Kennedy Thom.

TIP AND RUN   **Words:** Robin Tuck, Alastair Sampson, Colin Pearson, Roderick Cook, Kenneth Alexander, David Morgan Rees, Michael Young, Peter Townsend, Laurence Fleming; **Lyrics:** Andrew Davidson, Kennedy Thom, Colin Pearson, Peter Firth, Leslie Bricusse, Kenneth Alexander, Laurence Fleming, Christopher Pym, Robin Tuck, John Caffyn, Donald Rudd, Geoffrey Beaumont, Michael Young; **Music:** Andrew Davidson, Kenneth Alexander, Peter Firth, Leslie Bricusse, Geoffrey Beaumont, Raymond Leppard, Ken Ferris, Harold Cannon, Denis Rothwell, Brian Rees; **Décor:** Malcolm Burgess; **Music Arrangers:** Ken Ferris, Andrew Davidson; **Devised and Produced:** Andrew Davidson; **Company:** Robin Tuck, Kenneth Alexander, Barney Miller, Michael Young, David Nott, Leslie Bricusse, David Morse, Peter Townsend, Kennedy Thom, David Morgan Rees, Gavin Blakeney, Neville Hudson, Laurence Fleming, Dennis Millmore, Peter Stephens, Ken Ferris, Peter Firth.

1953 **President:** Peter Firth; **Vice-President:** Kennedy Thom; **Secretary:** Leslie Bricusse; **Senior Treasurer:** Dr F. Brittain; **Junior Treasurer:** Peter Stephens; **Musical Director:** Robin Beaumont; **Stage Manager:** Dick Robertson; **Business Manager:** Colin Pearson; **Press:** Peter Townsend; **Production Secretary:** Dermot Hoare; **Property Master:** Geoffrey Brown.

CABBAGES AND KINGS   **Sketches:** Frederic Raphael, Tony Becher, Peter Townsend, Colin Pearson, Leslie Bricusse, Neville Hudson, Geoffrey Brown, Dermot Hoare, Leslie Williamson, Peter Stephens, Dickie Glyn Jones; **Lyrics:** Colin Pearson, Peter Firth, Leslie Bricusse, Peter Stephens, Kennedy Thom, Malcolm Burgess, Leslie Williamson, Robin Bazeley-White; **Music:** Robin Beaumont, Robin Bazeley-White, Peter Firth, Peter Tranchell, Roger Lavelle, Rory McEwen; **Décor:** Malcolm Burgess; **Music Arranger:** Robin Beaumont; **Producer:** Peter Firth. **Company:** Bernard Barr, Robin Bazeley-White, Tony Becher, Leslie Bricusse, Geoffrey Brown, David Conyers, Peter Firth, Dermot Hoare, David Jenkins, Gerald Manners, Rory McEwen, Dennis Millmore, Frederic Raphael, Gerard Roessink, Peter Stephens, Kennedy Thom, Peter Townsend.

1954 **President:** Leslie Bricusse; **Vice-President:** David Conyers; **Secretary:** Peter Stephens; **Musical Director:** Neil Sutherland; **Senior Treasurer:** Dr F. Brittain; **Junior Treasurer:** Sebastian Dalrymple; **Business Manager:** Tony Becher; **Press:** Frederic Raphael; **Stage Manager:** Dick Robertson; **Production Secretary:** Brian Marber; **Property Master:** Trevor Williams; **Advertising:** John Anstis.

OUT OF THE BLUE   **Sketches:** Robin Bazeley-White, Frederic Raphael, Leslie Bricusse, Tony Becher, Jonathan Miller, Brian Marber, Geoffrey Brown, John Quashie-Idun, Neil Sutherland, Tony Wescott, Leslie Williamson; **Lyrics:** Leslie Bricusse, Simon Phipps, Gordon Pask, Maurice Holt, Tony Becher, Julian More, Colin Pearson, Geoffrey Beaumont, Harry Porter; **Music:** Neil Sutherland, Simon Phipps, John Anstis, Leslie Bricusse, Robin Beaumont, Maurice Holt, David McCarthy, Geoffrey Beaumont; **Décor:** Malcolm Burgess; **Music Arranger:** Neil Sutherland; **Devised and Produced:** Leslie Bricusse; **Company:** Bernard Barr, John Preston Bell, John Pardoe, Trevor Williams, Dermot Hoare, Brian Marber, David Conyers, Robin Bazeley-White, Frederic Raphael, Jonathan Miller, Willy Eustace, Peter Stephens, John Quashie-Idun, Leslie Bricusse.

1955   **President:** Brian Marber; **Vice-President:** Trevor Williams; **Secretary:** Roddy McKelvie; **Musical Director:** Alan Vening; **Senior Treasurer:** Dr. F. Brittain; **Junior Treasurer:** David Cregan; **Décor:** Dr. Malcolm Burgess; **Business Manager:** Maurice Holt; **Press:** Bob Heller; **Stage Manager:** Graeme MacDonald; **Assistant Stage Manager:** Dick Robertson; **Production Secretary:** Tim Berington; **Revue Business Manager:** Clive Eckert.

BETWEEN THE LINES   **Sketches:** Simon Phipps, Arthur Marshall, Jonathan Miller, Bob Heller, John Pardoe, Peter Vincent, Ted Taylor, Leslie Bricusse, Tony Becher, Frederic Raphael; **Lyrics:** Gordon Pask, Neil Wilkie, Maurice Holt, David Cregan, Frederic Raphael, Tony Becher, David Gribble, Rory McEwen, Julian Jebb, Keith Pound; **Music:** Alan Vening, Rory McEwen, David Wykes, Tony Westcott, Frederic Leslie, Noel McKee, Alan Pattillo, David Gribble, Maurice Holt, John Anstis, Joe Lyde; **Décor:** Joan Jefferson Farjeon; **Music Arranged:** Alan Vening; **Producer:** Brian Marber; **Company:** Jonathan Miller, Allan Mitchell, John Ticehurst, Trevor Williams, Willie Eustace, Brian Welsh, Peter Woodthorpe, Tim Berington, John Pardoe, Roddy McKelvie, Tony Westcott, Ted Taylor, Julian Jebb, Brian Marber, Rory McEwen.

1956   **President:** Tim Berington; **Hon. Vice-President:** Dr. F. Brittain; **Vice-President:** Willie Eustace; **Club and Production Secretary:** Allan Mitchell; **Musical Director:** Alan Vening; **Senior Treasurer:** Rev. Simon Phipps; **Junior Treasurer:** Clive Eckert; **Décor:** Dr. Malcolm Burgess; **Registrar:** Brian Welsh; **Press:** David Gribble; **Stage Manager:** Graeme MacDonald; **Assistant Manager:** Dick Robertson; **Revue Business Manager:** David Bastin; **Production Assistant:** John Keogh.

ANYTHING MAY . . .   **Lyrics:** David Gribble, Peter Vincent, Michael Frayn, Geoffrey Strachan, Andrew Sinclair, Tim Berington, Dick Gilling, John Pardoe, Bamber Gascoigne, Brian Welsh, John Villiers, Mick Melluish; **Music:** Alan Vening, David Wykes, Denis Rothwell, John Beale, Keith Statham, John Anstis, David Gribble; **Scenery:** Joan Jefferson Farjeon; **Music Arranged:** Alan Vening; **Producer:** Hugh Southern; **Company:** John Rees-Osborne, Dennis O'Meagher, John Keogh, Kit Ackroyd, Peter Woods, Nick Raffle, Brian Welsh, Tim Berington, Allan Mitchell, Willie Eustace, Dan Massey, Robert Wellings, John Villiers.

1957   **President:** Allan Mitchell (Fitzwilliam); **Vice President:** Graeme McDonald (Jesus); **Secretary:** Kit Ackroyd (Magdalene); **Senior Treasurer:** Simon Phipps (Trinity); **Junior Treasurer:** David Bastin (Pembroke); **Musical Director:** Keith Statham (Magdalene); **Committee:** Ben Nash (King's), John Villiers (King's), Peter Vincent (Corpus).

ZOUNDS   **Script:** Michael Frayn, John Edwards; **Music:** Keith Statham; **Additional Music:** Colin Purbrook, Christopher Sarson; **Producer:** Graeme McDonald; **Design:** Ben Nash; **Company:** Kit Ackroyd, Michael Collings, Ann Jones, Dorothy Mulcahy, Bob Wellings, John Edwards, Joe Melia, John Villiers, Allan Mitchell, Michael Frayn.

1958   **President:** Peter Stroud; **Vice-President:** John Villiers; **Secretary:** Michael Collings; **Senior Treasurer:** Rev. Simon Phipps; **Junior Treasurer:** Malcolm Davidson; **Registrar:** Bamber Gascoigne; **Musical Director:** Christopher Sarson; **Master of Cabaret:** John Drummond; **Press:** Robert Hort.

SPRINGS TO MIND   **Sketches:** Adrian Slade, Martin Monico, Bob Sale, John Aarons, David Nobbs, Bamber Gascoigne, John Drummond, Michael Wood, Peter Tranchell, Geoffrey Strachan, David Monico, Charles Goodhart, David Gillmore; **Music:** Christopher Sarson, Keith Statham, Patrick Gowers, Bob Sale; **Design:** Ewan MacLeod, Gerald Coral, David Buck, Wilfred Shawcross, Malcolm Burgess, James Meller, Kamal Mangaladas; **Musical Director:** Christopher Sarson; **Director:** Robert Hort; **Company:** Timothy Birdsall, Michael Collings, Fred Emery, David Johson, Joe Melia, David Monico, Geoff Pattie, Adrian Slade, Bill Wallis.

1959   **President:** Adrian Slade (Trinity); **Vice-President:** James Cornford (Trinity); **Secretary:** David Monico (Corpus); **Senior Treasurer:** Rev. Simon Barrington-Ward (Magdalene); **Junior Treasurer:** David Howell (King's); **Registrar:** David Johnson (St. John's); **Musical Director:** Michael Bowtell (Jesus); **Press:** Clive Swift (Caius).

THE LAST LAUGH   **Script Committee:** John Bird, Peter Cook, James Cornford, David Monico, Martin Monico, Geoff Pattie, Adrian Slade; **Additional Material:** Timothy Birdsall, Anthony Firth, E. Duncansson, Geoff Wilson, John Read, Jackie Thompson; **Music:** Patrick Gowers; **Additional Music:** Jackie Thompson; **Music Director:** Patrick Gowers; **Sets Devised:** John Bird; **Sets Designed:** Timothy Birdsall; **Producer:** John Bird; **Company:** Peter Bellwood, Timothy Birdsall, Peter Cook, David Johnson, Ray Mitchell, David Monico, Geoff Pattie, Adrian Slade, Eleanor Bron.

1960 **President:** Peter Cook (Pembroke); **Vice-President;** Michael Bowtell (Jesus); **Secretary:** Ray Mitchell (Selwyn); **Senior Treasurer:** Rev. Simon Barrington-Ward (Magdalene); **Junior Treasurer:** Nick Luard (Magdalene); **Registrar:** David Frost (Caius); **Musical Director:** Jackie Thompson (Trinity); **Press:** Peter Bellwood (St. Catharine's).

POP GOES MRS JESSOP **Script Committee:** John Wood, Peter Cook, Colin Bell, David Frost, Peter Bellwood; **Music:** Patrick Gowers; **Additional Music:** Hugh Macdonald; **Choreography:** Colin Bell; **Musical Director:** Patrick Gowers; **Director:** John Wood; **Company:** Peter Bellwood, Mike Burrell, Peter Cook, David Frost, Desmond Jones, Tony Murray, Hugh Walters, Giles Slaughter, Patanne Fairfoot, Liz Proud.

1961 **President:** Peter Bellwood (St. Catharine's); **Vice-President:** John Wood (King's); **Secretary:** David Frost (Caius); **Senior Treasurer:** Rev. The Hon. Hugh Dickinson (Trinity); **Junior Treasurer:** Peter Raby (Magdalene); **Registrar:** Ray Mitchell (Selwyn); **Musical Director:** Hugh Macdonald (Pembroke); **Press:** Desmond Jones (Christ's).

I THOUGHT I SAW IT MOVE **Script Committee:** David Frost, Peter Bellwood, John Wood, Desmond Jones, David Reid; **Music:** Hugh Macdonald; **Decor:** Ann Jasper; **Choreography:** Bill Drysdale; **Additional Material:** Robert Atkins, Paxton, Drysdale, John Cleese, Alan Hutchison, Scott, Firth, Bussmann, Altman, Smith, Hill, Alan George; **Director:** David Reid; **Company:** Humphrey Barclay, Desmond Jones, Peter Bellwood, Tony Murray, Mike Burrell, Hugh Walters, David Frost, John Wood, Patricia Ashworth, Marion McNaughton.

1962 **President:** Robert Atkins (Corpus); **Vice-President and Musical Director:** Hugh Macdonald (Pembroke); **Secretary:** Humphrey Barclay (Trinity); **Senior Treasurer:** H. C. Porter (Selwyn); **Junior Treasurer:** Tim Brooke-Taylor (Pembroke); **Business Manager:** Chris Stuart-Clark (Pembroke); **Registrar:** John Cleese (Downing); **Member Without Portfolio:** Graham Chapman (Emmanuel).

DOUBLE TAKE **Script Committee:** Robert Atkins, John Cleese, Humphrey Barclay, Tony Hendra, Tim Brooke-Taylor, Anthony Buffery, Ian Lang, Graham Chapman, Hugh Macdonald, Trevor Nunn; **Music:** Hugh Macdonald; **Producer:** Trevor Nunn; **Additional Material:** Bill Oddie, John Cassels, Lewis, Alan George, Nigel Brown, Cliff, Chris Stuart-Clark, Mayes; **Designer:** Ann Jasper; **Company:** Robert Atkins, Miriam Margolyes, Tim Brooke-Taylor, Nigel Brown, Humphrey Barclay, Graham Chapman, Tony Hendra, John Cleese, Alan George.

1963 **President:** Tim Brooke-Taylor; **Committee:** Hugh Macdonald, Humphrey Barclay, Chris Stuart-Clark, Dr H. C. Porter, John Cleese, Nick Ullett, David Gooderson, Jeremy Heal, Graeme Garden; **Business Manager:** Chris Stuart-Clark; **Stage Manager:** Tim Fell.

A CLUMP OF PLINTHS   **Script:** John Cleese, David Hatch, Chris Stuart-Clark, Bill Oddie, Tony Buffery, Tim Brooke-Taylor, Graeme Garden, John McEwen, Jeremy Heal, Hugh Macdonald; **Music:** Hugh Macdonald, Bill Oddie; **Musical Director:** Hugh Macdonald; **Producer:** Humphrey Barclay; **Company:** Chris Stuart-Clark, Jo Kendall, Anthony W. H. Buffery, Bill Oddie, David Hatch, John Cleese, Tim Brooke-Taylor; **Band:** Hugh Macdonald, Fred Yeadon, Martin Kemp, Jonathan Lynn, Chris Hilton.

1964 **President:** Graeme Garden; **Vice-President:** David Gooderson; **Secretary:** John Cassels; **Senior Treasurer:** Dr. H. C. Porter; **Business Manager:** Jeremy Heal; **Junior Treasurer:** Mervyn Riches; **Major Domo:** Jim Beach; **Victualler:** Eric Idle; **Committee Member:** Anthony Buffery; **Co-opted for Revue:** Mark Lushington.

STUFF WHAT DREAMS ARE MADE OF   **Script:** Eric Idle, Graeme Garden, Flick Hough, John Cameron, Mark Lushington, Andrew Mayer, Jim Beach, Brian Gascoigne, Jeremy Heal, Anthony Buffery, Robert Cushman, Sue Heber-Percy, Lewis, Jonathan Lynn, Richard Eyre, Osmotherly, Jones, Johnson; **Music:** Brian Gascoigne, John Cameron, Jim Beach, Anthony Buffery, Bill Oddie; **Musical Director:** Brian Gascoigne; **Producer:** Mark Lushington; **Company:** Graeme Garden, John Cameron, David Gooderson, Jonathan Lynn, Guy Slater, Mark Lushington, Flick Hough, Sue Heber Percy.

1965 **President:** Eric Idle; **Vice-President and Musical Director:** John Cameron; **Secretary:** Chris Hyde; **Senior Treasurer:** Dr H. C. Porter; **Junior Treasurer:** Clem Vallance; **Business Manager:** Mervyn Riches; **Major Domo:** Brian Sommers; **Recorder:** Robin Nelson; **Victualler:** Andy Mayer; **Revue Director:** John Hope-Mason; **Committee Member:** Carey Harrison.

MY GIRL HERBERT   **Script:** Graeme Garden, Anthony Buffery, John Cameron, Eric Idle, Clive James, Sheila Buhr, Andrew Mayer, M. Z. Lewin, Robin Nelson, David Gillies, Mike Rose; **Music Director:** John Cameron; **Producer:** John Hope-Mason; **Company:** Eric Idle, Sheila Buhr, John Cameron, Christie Davies, John Grillo, Germaine Greer, Robin Nelson, Mervyn Riches, Matt Walters.

1966 **President:** Andrew Mayer; **Vice-President:** Robin Nelson; **Secretary:** Mike Lewin; **Senior Treasurer:** Dr H. C. Porter; **Junior Treasurer:** David MacMillan; **Major Domo:** Roger Gartland; **Victualler:** Richard Syms; **Registrar and Cabaret Director:** Clive James; **Committee Members:** Dr A. Buffery, Brian Sommers, Clem Vallance.

THIS WAY OUT; **Company:** Andrew Mayer, Germaine Greer, Richard Syms, Richard Harris, Jane Barry, Richard Crane, Ray Elmitt, Tim Davies, Chris Mohr; **Script:** Richard Crane, Ray Elmitt, Clive James, Eric Idle, Anthony Buffery, Andy Mayer, Short, Chris Allen, Hill, Robin Nelson, Cocking, David Lascelles; **Musical Director:** Ray Elmitt; **Producer:** Richard Syms; **Business Manager:** Mike Lewin.

1967 **President:** Clive James; **Vice-President and Cabaret Director:** Richard Harris; **Secretary:** Peter Cochran; **Senior Treasurer:** Dr H. C. Porter; **Junior Treasurer:** David MacMillan; **Musical Director:** Daryl Runswick; **Major Domo:** Jonathan James-Moore; **Victualler:** Tristram Ricketts; **Registrice:** Germaine Greer; **Committee Members:** Pete Atkin, Tony Buffery.

SUPERNATURAL GAS   **Director:** Clive James; **Musical Director:** David Lund; **Company:** Pete Atkin, Sue Bates, Robert Buckman, Julie Covington, Alan Sizer, Richard Harris, Jonathan James-Moore, Diana Lubbock, Tristram Rickets; **Script:** Pete Atkin, Barry Brown, Tim Butchard, Sherman, Lewis, Lawrence, Robert Buckman, Clive James, David Lund, Ian Taylor, David Turner, Lee, Weston, Kerry Crabbe, Gibson, Richard Harris.

1978 **President:** Jonathan James-Moore; **Vice-President, Musical Director and Cabaret Director:** Pete Atkin; **Secretary:** Tristram Ricketts; **Senior Treasurer:** Dr. H. C. Porter; **Junior Treasurer:** Stephen Wyatt; **Major Domo:** Brett Usher; **Registrice:** Julie Covington; **Victualler:** Barry Brown; **Falconer:** Robert Buckman; **Without Portfolio:** Dr A. Buffery, Clive James, David MacMillan.

TURNS OF THE CENTURY   **Director:** Kerry Crabbe; **Musical Director:** Pete Atkin; **Company:** Pete Atkin, Barry Brown, Robert Buckman, Julie Covington, Russell Davies, Jonathan James-Moore, Maggie Scott, Stephen Wyatt; **Script:** Peter Atkin, Barry Brown, B. Clud, Clive James, Mike Hodges, Robert Buckman, Robert Orledge, Russell Davies, Stephen Wyatt, Christopher Hourmouzios, Will Van Zwanenberg.

1969 **President:** Barry Brown; **Vice-President:** Robert Buckman; **Secretary:** Russell Davies; **Senior Treasurer:** Dr H. C. Porter; **Junior Treasurer:** John Greeen; **Major Domo:** Neil Ross; **Cabaret Director:** David Turner; **Musical Director:** Robert Orledge; **Executive Secretary:** Ian Taylor; **Falconer:** Bill Gutteridge; **Victualler:** Adrian Edwards; **Without Portfolio:** Stephen Wyatt.

FOOLS RUSH IN   **Director:** Clive James; **Cast:** Barry Brown, Robert Buckman, Russell Davies, Adrian Edwards, Bill Gutteridge, Neil Ross, Ian Taylor; **Musical Director:** Robert Orledge; **Script:** Clive James, Robert Orledge, David Turner, Robert Buckman, Russell Davies, Bill Gutteridge, Adrian Edwards, Neil Ross, Ian Taylor, Alan Sizer.

1970 **President:** Adrian Edwards; **Vice-President:** Bill Gutteridge; **Secretary:** John Green; **Senior Treasurer:** Dr H. C. Porter; **Junior Treasurer:** Neil Thomas; **Musical Directors:** Paul Goodwin, Bill Ives; **Victualler:** Richard McKenna; **Decor Master and Costumier:** Mark Wing-Davey; **Major Domo:** Robert Whitehouse; **Without Portfolio:** Stephen Wyatt, John Stevenson; **Our Man in Paris:** Robert Orledge.

THE FOOTLIGHTS COMIC ANNUAL   **Director:** Kerry Crabbe; **Cast:** Adrian Edwards, Bill Gutteridge, Richard MacKenna, Graham Preskett, Maggie Scott, Mark Wing-Davey, Stephen Wyatt; **Script:** Kerry Crabbe, Paul Godwin, Graham Preskett, Richard Mackenna, Perlmutter, Paul Wolfson, Bill Gutteridge, Adrian Edwards, Bill Ives, Fellowes, Mark Wing-Davey, Maher, Steel, Brown; **Directors:** Bill Ives, Graham Preskett.

1971 **President:** Richard MacKenna; **Secretary:** Rob Whitehouse; **Senior Treasurer:** Dr. H. C. Porter; **Junior Treasurer:** Neil Thomas; **Victualler:** Steve Thorn; **Major Domo:** John Parry; **Falconer:** Paul Wolfson; **Without Portfolio:** Adrian Edwards, Bill Allan, Robert Orledge.

GONE WITH THE CLAPPERS   **Producer:** Bert Parnaby; **Musical Director:** Graham Ripley; **Designer:** Tim Foster; **Cast:** Sarah Dunant, John Parry, Steve Thorn, Adrian Edwards, Robert Rowe, Rob Whitehouse, Richard MacKenna, Christine Stopp, Paul Wolfson; **Sketches:** Graham Ripley, Barry Brown, Steve Thorn, P. Tyson, Paul Wolfson, Raymond, John Parry, Robert Orledge, Rob Whitehouse, Alan Drury, Brooke, Robert Parnaby, C. Bailey, Robert Rowe, Adrian Edwards, Clive James, Richard MacKenna, Jill Durne, Wilde, Nicholas Lom, R. Burgess, Sarah Dunant, J. Smith; **Choreography:** Jill Durne.

1972 **President:** Steve Thorn; **Vice-President:** Paul Wolfson; **Secretary:** John Parry; **Senior Treasurer:** H. C. Porter; **Junior Treasurer:** Harold Frayman; **Cabaret Director:** Rob Whitehouse; **Victualler:** Simon Jones.

NORMAN RUINS   **Director:** Barry Brown; **Cast:** Sarah Dunant, Simon Jones, Sue Limb, John Parry, Steve Thorn, Rob Whitehouse, Paul Wolfson; **Musical Director:** Jon Cole; **Sketches:** Barry Brown, John Cameron, Steve Thorn, Paul Wolfson, John Parry, Jon Canter, Simon Jones, Swanson, Jeremy Browne, Donegan, Neil Thomas, Small, Adrian Edwards, Rob Whitehouse, P. Tyson, Cole, Robert Benton, John Green.

1973 **President:** Robert Benton; **Vice-President:** Jeremy Browne; **Secretary:** Jon Canter; **Senior Treasurer:** Dr H. C. Porter; **Junior Treasurer:** John Parry; **Without Portfolio:** Roger Etkind.

EVERY PACKET CARRIES A GOVERNMENT HEALTH WARNING   **Director:** Stephen Wyatt; **Cast:** Mary Allen, Robert Benton, Jeremy Browne, Jonathan Canter, John Lloyd, Griffith Rhys Jones, Frank Ries, Pam Scobie; **Musical Directors:** Nigel Hess, Nic Rowley; **Choreography:** Frank Ries; **Sketches by:** Stephen Wyatt, Jeremy Browne, Nigel Hess, Nic Rowley, John Parry, Jennens, Martin Smith, Will Adams, Alan Drury, Raymond, Simon Jones, Clive Anderson, Griff Rhys Jones, John Lloyd, Jon Canter, Robert Benton, Stead, Simon Levene, Paul Wolfson, Adrian Edwards, Richard Burridge.

1974 **President:** Jon Canter; **Secretary:** Martin Smith; **Senior Treasurer:** Dr H. C. Porter; **Junior Treasurer:** Antony Root; **Committee Members:** Douglas Adams, Will Adams, Clive Anderson, Simon Levene, Griff Rhys Jones, Stephanie Weldon, Eric Waley, Nic Rowley, Nigel Hess, Alex Ingram.

CHOX   **Director:** Robert Benton; **Cast:** Sue Aldred, Clive Anderson, Jon Canter, Jane Ellison, Geoff McGivern, Griff Rhys Jones, Martin Smith, Crispin Thomas; **Music:** Musical Director: Simon Joly; **Sets:** Richard Wilkinson; **Choreography:** Robert Benton; **Sketches:** Robert Benton, Nigel Hess, Simon Joly, Clive Anderson, John Lloyd, Jon Canter, Simon Levene, Griff Rhys Jones, Seigleman, Will Adams, Martin Smith, Douglas Adams.

1975 **President:** Clive Anderson; **Vice-President:** Simon Levene; **Senior Treasurer:** Dr H. C. Porter; **Junior Treasurer:** David Burnett; **Committee Members:** Alex Ingram, Christopher Keightley, Griffith Rhys Jones, John Stroud, Eric Waley.

PARADISE MISLAID   **Director:** John Lloyd; **Designer:** Tanya McCallin; **Musical Director:** Alex Ingram; **Choreography:** Jenny Arnold; **Written by:** Clive Anderson, Simon Levene, Griff Rhys Jones, Chris Keightley, Bob Knowles, John Lloyd; **Additional Material:** Dave Adelman, Rob Wye, John Parry, Adams Smith Adams, Richard Gledhill, Martin Gayford; **Cast:** Clive Anderson, Hilary Cobb, Chris Keightley, Bob Knowles, Simon Levene, Geoff McGivern, Griff Rhys Jones, Jeremy Thomas.

1976 **President:** Chris Keightley; **Vice-President:** Griff Rhys Jones; **Senior Treasurer:** Harry Porter; **Junior Treasurer:** John Stroud; **Secretary:** Jeremy Thomas; **Committee:** Lindsay Bridgewater, Nick Hytner, Charles Shaughnessy, Jimmy Mulville, Nonny Williams, Steve Walker.

A KICK IN THE STALLS   **Director:** Douglas Adams; **Designer:** Peter Hammond; **Written by:** Douglas Adams, Chris Keightley, Rory McGrath, Jimmy Mulville, Michael Landymore, Charlie Shaughnessy; **Additional Material:** Martin Smith, Will Adams, Jon Canter, John Parry, Mike Murray, Oenone Williams, Andy Greenhalgh, Paul Hudson, Geoff Nicholson; **Music:** Lyndsay Bridgewater; **Additional Music:** Douglas Adams; **Choreography:** Jenny Arnold; **Cast:** Andrew Greenhalgh, Penelope Johnson, Michael Landymore, Jimmy Mulville, Michael Murray, Charles Shaughnessy, Jeremy Thomas, Oenone Williams.

1977 **President:** Jimmy Mulville; **Vice-President:** Nick Hytner; **Senior Treasurer:** Harry Porter; **Junior Treasurer:** Tim Yealland; **Secretary:** Charlie Shaughnessy; **Committee:** Rory McGrath, Mike Landymore, Martin Bergman, Robert Bathurst, Carrie Simcocks, Mike Murray, Lindsay Bridgewater, Chris Keightley.

TAG!   **Director and Designer:** Griff Rhys Jones; **Written by:** Martin Bergman, Rory McGrath, Jimmy Mulville, Griff Rhys Jones; **Additional Material:** Charles Bott, Paul Hudson, Pete Smith; **Music:** Peter Fincham; **Cast:** Robert Bathurst, Martin Bergman, Paul Hudson, Rory McGrath, Jimmy Mulville, Carrie Simcocks.

1978 **President:** Martin Bergman; **Vice-President:** Charles Bott; **Secretary:** Robert Bathurst; **Senior Treasurer:** Neil Thomas; **Junior Treasurer:** Luke Hughes; **Archivist:** Dr H. C. Porter; **Falconer:** Rory McGrath; **Clubroom and Nostalgia:** Chris Keightley.

STAGE FRIGHT **Director:** Clive Anderson; **Designer:** Peter Hammond; **Musical Director:** Nick Burstin; **Written by:** Clive Anderson, Martin Bergman, Rory McGrath, Robert Bathurst, Owen Brenman; **Additional Material:** Douglas Adams, Bob Bryan, Sean Cranitch, Tom Lubbock, Jon Canter, Chris Keightley, Nicholas Symons, Anthony Berendt, Andy Ingram, David Jeffcocks, Roger Mills; **Music:** Nick Burstin; **Cast:** Robert Bathurst, Bob Bryan, Richard Harffey, Jan Ravens, Martin Bergman, Sean Cranitch, Sarah Palmer.

1979 **President:** Robert Bathurst; **Vice-President:** Sarah Palmer; **Secretary:** Jan Ravens; **Senior Treasurer:** Neil Thomas; **Junior Treasurer:** Rowena Watson; **Archivist:** Dr H. C. Porter; **Ex-President:** Martin Bergman; **Committee:** Sean Cranitch, Hugh Laurie, Emma Thompson, Simon McBurney, Antony Berendt, Paul Fincham, Belinda Giles, Alison Hattersley, Nick Symons.

NIGHTCAP   **Director:** Martin Bergman; **Designer:** Andy Perrins; **Musical Director:** Paul Fincham; **Cast:** Robert Bathurst, Hugh Laurie, Nick Miles, Martin Bergman, Simon McBurney, Emma Thompson; **Written by:** Martin Bergman, Owen Brenman, Sean Cranitch, Hugh Laurie, Nick Symons; **Additional Material:** Karen Adler, Antony Berendt, John Lloyd, Simon McBurney, George Melly, Roger Mills, Kjartan Poskitt, Emma Thompson, Robert Bathurst, Dave Jeffcock, Tom Lubbock, Rory McGrath, Nick Miles, Jimmy Mulville, Sandy Toksvig, Susan Imfould.

1980 **President:** Jan Ravens; **Vice-President:** Simon McBurney; **Secretary:** Nick Symons; **Senior Treasurer:** Paul Hartle; **Junior Treasurer:** Richard Hytner; **Archivist:** Dr Harry Porter; **Committee:** Anthony Berendt, Steven Edis, Katie Kelly, Hugh Laurie, Paul Shearer, Emma Thompson.

ELECTRIC VOODOO   **Cast:** Anthony Berendt, Sheila Hyde, Anne McLaughlin, Jan Ravens, Nick Symons, Sandi Toksvig; **Music:** Steven Edis; **Script by:** Anthony Berendt, Hugh Laurie, Peter Mudd, Jan Ravens, Nick Symons, Sandi Toksvig; **Additional Material:** Annabel Arden, Christopher Cowell, Sean Cranitch, Stephen Fry, Sheila Hyde, Richard Hytner, Jonathan Kreeger, Simon McBurney, Brian Quinn, Jonathan Rathbone, Dominic Scott-Malden, Martin Smith, Emma Thompson; **Producer:** Crispin Thomas; **Choreography:** Jenny Arnold.

1981   **President:** Hugh Laurie; **Vice-President:** Emma Thompson; **Secretary:** Katie Kelly; **Senior Treasurer:** Paul Hartle; **Junior Treasurer:** Kim Harris; **Falconer:** Paul Shearer; **Archivist:** Dr H. C. Porter; **Committee:** Stephen Fry, Steven Edis, Will Osborne, Greg Brenman, Tony Slattery, Neil Mullarkey, Dave Meek, Paul Simpkin.

THE CELLAR TAPES **Cast:** Penny Dwyer, Stephen Fry, Hugh Laurie, Paul Shearer, Tony Slattery, Emma Thompson; **Written by:** Stephen Fry and Hugh Laurie with Penny Dwyer, Kim Harris, Katie Kelly, Jan Ravens, Paul Shearer, Tony Slattery, Emma Thompson; **Additional Material:** Anthony Berendt, Greg Brenman, Dave Meek, Neil Mullarkey, Greg Snow, Nick Symons, Sandi Toksvig; **Music:** Steven Edis with Hugh Laurie and Tony Slattery; **Director:** Jan Ravens.

1982   **President:** Tony Slattery; **Vice-President:** Will Osborne; **Falconer:** Paul Simpkin; **Archivist:** Dr H. C. Porter; **Junior Treasurer:** Neil Mullarkey; **Senior Treasurer:** Dr Lisa Jardine; **Secretary:** Greg Brenman; **Committee:** Chris England, David Grant, Robert Harley, Dave Meek, Steve Punt, Richard Vranch.

PREMISES, PREMISES . . . **Cast:** Morwenna Banks, Kate Duchene, Robert Harley, Neil Mullarkey, Will Osborne, Tony Slattery; **Written by:** Morwenna Banks, Kate Duchene, Chris England, Robert Harley, Dave Meek, Neil Mullarkey, Will Osborne, Steve Punt, Paul Simpkin, Tony Slattery, Richard Turner; **Music:** Richard Vranch, Tony Slattery, Robert Harley; **Director:** Richard Turner; **Designer:** Kevin McCloud.

1983   **President:** Neil Mullarkey; **Vice-President:** Paul Simpkin; **Secretary:** Dave Meek; **Senior Treasurer:** Dr. Lisa Jardine; **Junior Treasurer:** Robert Harley; **Falconer:** Chris England; **Archivist:** Dr H. C. Porter; **Junior Archivist:** Steve Punt; **Member:** Morwenna Banks.

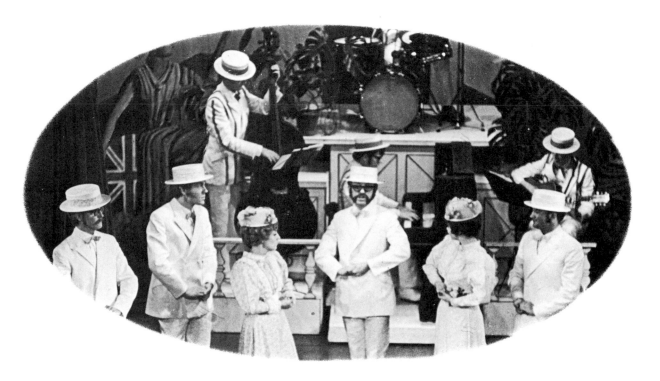

List of Illustrations

The illustrations for this book have been collected and their subjects identified as a result of much patient and generous help from many individuals and organisations. Every effort has been made to describe the subjects and attribute picture sources correctly and trace copyright owners. Apologies are made for any errors or omissions.

Index